The Power of Brand Ownership

How do brands cultivate loyalty and influence consumer purchasing decisions? *The Power of Brand Ownership* explores the complex dynamics between branding and consumer identity within both the physical and digital realms that form our cultural landscape. Miriam J. Johnson uncovers a symbiotic relationship where brands serve not merely as navigational aids in a consumer's journey but also as integral components of self-identity and social projection, and the power that entails. Investigating the nuances of power shifts, brand authenticity, activism, and the gendered nature of consumption, Johnson asserts that brands are both influenced by and influencers of the cultural terrain they inhabit as well as the temporal contexts in which they interact. Theoretical frameworks articulate the fluidity of capital within the consumer–brand nexus whilst insightful case studies illustrate industry examples, revealing the shifting strategies employed by companies to make brands identifiable and desirable in the ever-changing cultural landscape.

MIRIAM J. JOHNSON is a Senior Lecturer in the Oxford International Centre for Publishing at Oxford Brookes University. Her research focusses on marketing, digital humanities, and AI, and her work has appeared in *Logos: Journal of the World Publishing Community*, *Publishing Research Quarterly*, and *The Journal of Social Media for Learning*. She is the author of *Books and Social Media* (Routledge, 2021), and *Social Media Marketing for Book Publishers* (Routledge, 2022) which home in on digital community dynamics.

Addressing the topic of branding from a much-needed fresh angle, *The Power of Brand Ownership* offers a unique and valuable perspective which incorporates cultural landscape, gender, activism, power, authenticity and other relevant topics that have been less frequently represented in this area. Highly thought-provoking content and the use of case studies enhances the book even more.

Professor Joe Bogue & Dr Lana Repar Cork University
Business School, University College Cork

Tackles the complex topic of brand identities in a new way by considering their role in shaping the cultural landscape and, in particular, the role of gender.

Professor Alistair Williams Johnson & Wales University Charlotte

The Power of Brand Ownership

Marketing in the Cultural Landscape

MIRIAM J. JOHNSON
Oxford Brookes University

CAMBRIDGE
UNIVERSITY PRESS

Shaftesbury Road, Cambridge CB2 8EA, United Kingdom

One Liberty Plaza, 20th Floor, New York, NY 10006, USA

477 Williamstown Road, Port Melbourne, VIC 3207, Australia

314–321, 3rd Floor, Plot 3, Splendor Forum, Jasola District Centre,
New Delhi – 110025, India

103 Penang Road, #05–06/07, Visioncrest Commercial, Singapore 238467

Cambridge University Press is part of Cambridge University Press & Assessment,
a department of the University of Cambridge.

We share the University's mission to contribute to society through the pursuit of
education, learning and research at the highest international levels of excellence.

www.cambridge.org
Information on this title: www.cambridge.org/9781009538404

DOI: 10.1017/9781009538350

First published 2025

A catalogue record for this publication is available from the British Library

Library of Congress Cataloging-in-Publication Data
Names: Johnson, Miriam J., author.
Title: The power of brand ownership : marketing in the cultural landscape /
Miriam J. Johnson, Oxford Brookes University.
Description: Cambridge, United Kingdom ; New York, NY : Cambridge
University Press, 2025. | Includes bibliographical references and index.
Identifiers: LCCN 2024020826 | ISBN 9781009538404 (hardback) |
ISBN 9781009538350 (ebook)
Subjects: LCSH: Consumption (Economics) – Social aspects. | Branding
(Marketing) – Social aspects. | Cultural landscapes.
Classification: LCC HC79.C6 J654 2025 | DDC 339.4/7–dc23/eng/20240503
LC record available at https://lccn.loc.gov/2024020826

ISBN 978-1-009-53840-4 Hardback
ISBN 978-1-009-53838-1 Paperback

This book is dedicated to Blythe, who reads everything in record time, edits, feeds back, and makes my writing magically better, all while keeping Dudley on the go. Special mention to Claire who listened to me go on about my concept for the book well before I had written a word and encouraged me to go for it while keeping in mind industry, and for Rosie – who makes me get up and leave the computer at reasonable times.

Contents

Introduction   1

1   What We Mean When We Talk about the
Cultural Landscape   6

2   Using Brands as Landmarks for Mapping the
Cultural Landscape   27

3   Brand Capital, Perspective, and Power   43

4   The Role of Gender   63

   Case Study 1 Gender: Virgin Atlantic and Bud Light   80

5   The Importance of Authenticity   93

6   Brand Activism as a Power Dynamic   110

   Case Study 2 Activism: Kate Spade and Change Please   129

7   Ownership as Power   141

8   The Transience of Power in the Cultural Landscape   157

   Case Study 3 Shifting Power: Skype, Burberry,
and Old Spice   173

9   TL;DR: The Application to Industry   184

Works Cited   197

Index   258

Introduction

The central question, thus becomes, what are the core or master symbols, and how do they articulate with the other symbols constituting the culture under study, integrating them into a coherent system.

> J. G. Feinberg, Schneider's symbolic cultural theory:
> an appraisal, *Current Anthropology*

In a world where physical and digital realms increasingly intersect, the concept of the cultural landscape emerges as a dynamic and multifaceted arena where consumers, brands, and topographies intersect to create meaning and value; it is an overarching term for the liminal space between the physical and digital geographies.

Cultural landscape is a term that is used in the area of media, culture, and communication studies, but it is a term that lacks boundaries and is hard to pin down; which is not unlike the concept that it maps. Historically, cultural landscapes were linked to physical landscapes, studies in cultural heritage, and geographical concepts. As the term has gained a foothold in the humanities and evolved to areas of cultural geographies, the way we understand it must shift to accommodate these changes that now include the human aspect of spaces and how we inhabit them. This can be mapped across the digital sphere, where it plays a key role in the creation of communities in digital hubs and in developing digital suburbs.

Part of the role of brands in this space is how they put down roots here in order to become navigational beacons for consumers as they move through the space and construct their identity. Though there are parts of the cultural landscape that map over the physical landscape, much of the terrain is fluid and dynamic, and evolves as the sociopolitical and economic contexts ebb and flow within a particular area of the landscape. The dynamic movement of the cultural landscape opens up the potential for power and ownership to shift from brands to consumers and communities.

1

The adjustment that happens when power is moved from a brand to consumers and back again is akin to how consumers in the physical world use landmarks to navigate their spaces and move towards or away from a destination. Chapter 2 focusses on the role that brands play as landmarks which, while they do act as navigational beacons and provide pathways to the brand in the form of structural narratives, are more than the brand's physical assets. Brands in the cultural landscape are a symbol of the brand's equity and image that consumers can use as a means of closing the gap between their self-identity and self-projection. These two interrelated concepts of identity are how some consumers see themselves and how they want to be seen by others. Brands in this sense are both cultural and situational identifiers that consumers use to bring together their sense of self-alignment and identity. When brands are able to put down roots and grow as landmarks in the cultural landscape, consumers look to them to navigate the terrain.

This navigation simultaneously happens in digital spaces, which has altered how brands and consumers interact with one another and has brought about two-way communication. It has also highlighted the fact that every consumer has an individual identity and what a brand symbolises for one consumer might not be the same for another. By paying attention to consumer communities when they speak to and of brands, brands can better walk the line between knowing too much about a consumer and knowing enough that the consumer feels a connection with the brand. When brands become landmarks in the cultural landscape they are able to be utilised by both those consumers who love them and those who know of them, but choose to steer clear.

When we talk about how brands and consumers co-create meaning and value in the cultural landscape, this has to do with how capital is formed and exchanged. Chapter 3 highlights the value that combining the perspectives of economic-, consumer-, and society-focussed approaches can bring to the understanding of capital in this space. Drawing on the ideas of Foucault and Bourdieu help to define capital as a concept in the cultural landscape and trace how it shifts as contexts alter. Leveraging different forms of capital enables both consumers and brands to understand and navigate their spaces, while also showing how capital exchange sometimes follows its own route, which is directly related to, but does not determine, power dynamics in the cultural landscape. Power here is not a top-down process. It is disseminated in, and sometimes concealed by, societal norms and the changes within them.

One area where societal norms seem to be challenged is in that of gender. In Chapter 4 the focus is on gender and the role it plays for brands and consumers. The act of consumption is often considered feminine and this can alter how brands develop their structural narratives. Brands seeking to develop themselves as landmarks in the cultural landscape need to be aware that most aspects of the shared landscape are gendered and that gender is related to, but is not the same as, sex. There is an element of performance of gender that is related to the consumer's performance of self. How consumers identify within the framework of gender alters how they relate to a brand, with research finding that consumers tend to be more attracted to brands that best reflect how they see themselves and how they want to be seen. With this in mind, brands can develop their image to more closely align with gendered elements that consumers can pick up on. Doing this has pros and cons. Some consumers will see the gendered nature of a brand and avoid it, but for those consumers who feel that they more closely identify with a brand's gendered elements, they can feel that that brand is a safe space around which they can potentially develop a community.

How consumers and brands relate to gender is linked to the interplay between the power within societal norms and the socio-political and economic contexts within a particular location in the cultural landscape. The performance of gender within the cultural landscape is not dissimilar to the concept of authenticity, which is the topic of Chapter 5. Authenticity is a means of connecting one's inner and outer self, though it has an abundance of nuanced definitions. While being aware of the slipperiness of defining authenticity, we can better define this by relating authenticity to the consistency of internal and external expressions, and looking at how being authentic relates to an external referent and how well authenticity conforms to categorical norms. Grappling with authenticity is increasingly important for both brands and consumers as the changes across the cultural landscape move at pace. Alongside this we begin to see aspects of authenticity that are taken for granted. For example, in behind-the-scenes imagery and content where there is a level of intimacy and perceived authenticity between consumers and brands, and the spaces they inhabit become the norm, consumers seek something *more* authentic. As this chapter traces the movement towards the edges of authenticity it highlights the value that consumers put on the concept, while also seeking more reassurances from brands and others in the cultural landscape to both normalise the edges and bring consumers a sense of belonging.

Chapter 6 considers brand activism, which often goes hand in hand with authenticity. As more and more brands sell the same sorts of products or services at roughly the same prices, consumers are seeking ways to differentiate between them. Brand activism is a progression of corporate social responsibility that hones the concept of 'doing good' to focus in on key platforms. In the era of the public, in which we currently find ourselves, consumers expect more from their brands than for them to have an environmental impact statement; aspects that are widely considered good are often now simply expected of a brand. What consumers, led by Millennials and Gen Z, now expect is for brands to take a stand on social and political topics. Furthermore, they do not give much leeway for brands to straddle the line. This chapter hones in on what brand activism means in the current cultural landscape, its relationship to authenticity, and the pros and cons of capitalism and activism being bedfellows. It also touches on the balance that must be maintained by brands who also want to reach consumers who do not agree with their activist positions, and gives some examples on what happens when it all goes wrong and brands begin to lose a sense of ownership.

This loss of ownership and the transient movement of power are the subjects of Chapters 7 and 8. The ownership of items, content, and so on is directly linked to the ways that consumers are able to navigate their alignment of self-identity and self-projection in the cultural landscape. Every time that a consumer comes into contact with a brand – whether that is by purchasing a branded product, joining a branded community, or simply seeing another consumer associated with the brand – the perception of the brand develops further. Not only does the consumer have a role in ownership of a brand, those who work for and around a brand also have a key say in how that brand image is created and portrayed based on the employee and brand knowledge/power relationship. Ownership, then, is not simply physical possession; it is a state of mind that enables consumers to utilise the brand's structural narratives to navigate the cultural landscape. With this in mind, we can begin to split the concepts of ownership and control. As the brand puts down roots in the cultural landscape and builds a base that can begin to serve as a landmark, consumers become co-creators in that space. This can take a myriad of formats, such as consumers specifically developing community groups, helping to clear paths for the brand's narrative structures, or highlighting the brand to other consumers. The brand no longer has complete control over their brand image and they must work with the consumers as power ebbs and flows.

Much like the streams of socio-political or economic contexts are ever changing as they move across the cultural landscape, so too do the power dynamics between the landscape, the consumers, and the brands alter. Chapter 8 digs into the ways that these power dynamics shift and the role that the exchange of capital plays as a catalyst. While consumers can become co-owners of a brand and help develop the brand's narrative structures, this can also go the other way, with consumers using their ownership of the brand and the power that amasses in brand communities to obscure the pathways leading others to the brand. This can happen in both physical and digital spaces; brands can be cut off or boosted as power shifts between them and the spaces they inhabit.

While it may be tempting to see this shift in power dynamics as a negative aspect of the relationships in the cultural landscape, this is not the case. Shifts in power can lead to positive changes for both brands and consumers. The final chapter in this book covers the application to industry in a too long; didn't read (TL;DR) format. If time is short, read this book from the back starting with Chapter 9, then read the other chapters to get in-depth considerations of each of the topics.

In addition to the main chapters of this book case studies are interspersed to highlight the ways the theoretical concepts are playing out in real time. These include Case Study 1, which considers how Virgin Atlantic and Anheuser-Busch's Bud Light engage with gendered aspects of their brand and marketing. A key element of this case study is the ways that these two brands embody authenticity, or not, and how consumers have reacted. Case Study 2 deals with a topic that skirted around the edges of the Virgin Atlantic and Bud Light advertisements: brand activism. By digging into both Kate Spade and Change Please, this case study shows how brands are able to engage with authentic activism and use partnerships to extend their reach while staying true to their values. The final case study, Case Study 3, follows the deep dive into power and its transience in the cultural landscape. With that in mind, it covers Skype, Burberry, and Old Spice and their capabilities to navigate the changes that come with shifts in power in different contexts.

1 | *What We Mean When We Talk about the Cultural Landscape*

One of the most significant moments in the study of landscapes was the 'cultural turn' in geography of the 1970s and 1980s, which highlighted the roles of language, meaning and representation in the construction of social realities.

M. Atha et al., *The Routledge Companion to Landscape Studies*

Once used as a term linked to cultural heritage based in physical landscapes, over time the phrase 'cultural landscape' has moved beyond the recognition of geographical and archaeological modalities to take on a 'cultural turn' (O'Keeffe, 2007, p. 3). This has enabled the phrase to be 'conceived of as an emblematic site of representation, a locus of both power and resistance' (Moore, 2007, p. x). Researchers of heritage, history, and landscapes have moved into adopting a more humanities-based understanding of the interactions of landscapes and the peoples and societies that inhabit them. They often go beyond the understanding of the landscape as an entity that exists outside the realm of society and look to the development (and sometimes loss) of collected memories that develop around a physical space. These social formations and institutions are fluid, context-bound, move across cultures, and transverse historical periods (O'Keeffe, 2007, p. 8).

This era of landscape culturalism in which we find ourselves must take into account the growth and development of digital landscapes that overlie physical landscapes and are inherently intertwined with cultural, and individual, identity. We must also consider the memories that are embedded within landscapes and the different institutions, organisations, power dynamics, and identity performances at play. With this in mind, a natural step is in moving to better understand how companies, organisations, and products – all considered here under the umbrella of 'brands' – interact with the landscape, each other, and consumers (as individuals). In order to do so, this chapter first explores the changing ways we consider the cultural landscape and the evolution of consumer culture. It goes on to show how elements such as identity and brands are overlaid on a complex duality of physical and digital spaces in order to develop a theoretical mapping of the cultural landscape. Once the cartography of this space is outlined, we then consider how consumers read the map of the cultural landscape and learn how to move around it, the role of technology, and finally, the growth of the digital suburbs and how these elements extend, and potentially warp, the cultural landscape.

Co-opting the Cultural Landscape

To better break down the different layers of the cultural landscape as a basis for exploring the concepts of branding and power, we first consider the history of the term 'landscape', which dates back to thirteenth-century Dutch and relates to a land region that has been reclaimed or remade (Antrop, 2020, p. 1). With its introduction into English, we see the term being defined more widely, with aspects of art, metaphor, development, and more being ascribed to it, and with definitions altering based on the stance and agenda of those who are defining the term. Glossing over a long and rich history of the intertwined relationship between 'landscape', its myriad of definitions, and the study of geography and architecture enables us to arrive in a fuzzy area where the term has a 'multiplicity of disciplinary interpretations' (Atha et al., 2020, p. xxi), where landscapes after the mid 1980s can be seen as having both natural and cultural layers, which are further complicated by the digital.

In his work on the emergence of a cultural landscape, Taylor (2012, p. 23) notes that '[t]he assumption that is often made that "cultural landscape" is only to do with agricultural settings is misplaced: it is concerned with all human places and the process of making them and inhabiting them'. In the early to mid 1900s, Sauer (1969, p. 343) defined the cultural landscape as being a space that is 'fashioned from the natural landscape by a cultural group. Culture is the agent, the natural area is the medium, the cultural landscape is the result.' It is the place where humanity has impacted the natural environment (Jones, 2003). The shift to incorporate the human element of making and doing into landscape studies was enhanced in the early 1990s when the term 'cultural landscape' was further validated by its inclusion as a conservation category by the United Nations Educational, Scientific and Cultural Organization's (UNESCO's) World Heritage Committee. This inclusion enabled the examination of heritage based on both its locational significance and its intangible cultural aspects (Taylor & Xu, 2020, p. 314).

While the use of the term by UNESCO seems to be a means by which the term can be cemented into the lexicon of studies of the places that humanity and landscapes come together, instead it is often seen as a 'chaotic concept' (Sayer, 1992), whose definition is messy, hard to pin down, and 'forever being re-organized. [Different understandings of the term …] encroach upon one another, absorb one another, expand, contract, multiply, disappear' (Jackson, 1971, p. 188). In his work on defining the cultural landscape, Jones (2003) identifies no less than twelve working definitions by scholars and in administration that cross areas such heritage, conservation, physical geography, and agriculture. Likewise, Rowntree (1996) concludes that the use of the term 'cultural landscape' will continue, not because of its precision in identifying a specific concept, but due to its widespread use as relating to a variety of interactions between landscapes, societies, and the cultural meanings that different groups attach to different spaces.

Though some scholars consider culture as part of the landscape and therefore just choose to term all aspects as simply 'landscape',[1] there is also an adjacent area of research into cultural geographies that has 'long argued the importance of cultural artifacts of many kinds in mediating human experiences of place, space and landscape' (Rose, 2016, p. 334). These artefacts can be brands, products, or even pop culture (Hastie & Saunders, 2023). Here the term 'culture' is applied to indicate the ephemeral aspects of the landscape that are both physical (with real estate and locations that map onto brands) and intangible or cognitive (the digital and theoretical locations that a brand occupies for a consumer), linked to what Hodge and Hallgrimsdottir (2019, p. 11) call 'culturescapes', which 'are a kind of "ephemeral geography"'.

For this book, the cultural landscape is a space that is malleable in that the way organisations, societies, and individuals view it alters depending on their identity, on temporality, and on the

---

[1] For more information on the dropping of 'culture' from 'cultural landscape', begin with Jones, 2003 and Rowntree, 1996.

possession and movement of capital as a means of shifting power. While it has physical dimensions, it is more of a perspective on a series of overlapping topographies than a space that can be physically inhabited. With this in mind, we can begin to consider how each location, landmark, and individual views the cultural landscape and how they exist and move within it.

One of the ways that the cultural landscape is embodied is in how power moves within and across it. The cultural landscape goes beyond reflecting the relationships of power within the community that inhabits it to actually being a means and space in which that power can manifest (Rowntree & Conkey, 1980), inferring 'cultural context, human action and activity and also change over time' (Taylor, 2012, p. 22). Depending on the point in history from which we consider the cultural landscape, we will see aspects of it that have been preserved and imbued with symbolic significance by a group or society (Rowntree & Conkey, 1980). In the world of legacy brands such as Coca-Cola, Disney, Justin Boots, and so on, these brands have staked out a space and existence over a span of time long enough that they become embedded into the fabric of the cultural landscape. They are examples of the human application of culture to a physical landscape. For instance, Justin Boots make footwear for horse riders, yes. But what they really do is embody the concept of what it is to be a cowboy, an 'icon of western culture' (Justin Boots, 2023). Their placement within the cultural landscape and their value as an 'icon' enables Justin Boots to maintain their position on the map through several layers of topographical interpretation.

This placement gives the brand staying power within the landscape to become a landmark or anchor – a place that consumers all see within their cultural landscape that is steady and can be used as a navigational beacon.[2] Part of a brand's drive to becoming a landmark is related to ownership of space. For Justin Boots, it's boots, but it's also a narrative about the legacy of the West, the hard and honest work of a cowboy, and the ideals the cowboy symbolises; where these 'intangibles, such as social identity [in this case, as a cowboy, or at the least as someone who identifies with the ideals of freedom the cowboy represents], are ... realized by the landscape' (Rowntree & Conkey, 1980, p. 474).

---

[2] The concept of brands as landmarks in the consumer's cultural landscape is covered in depth in Chapter 2.

These intangible assets that Justin Boots and other brands hold are forms of cultural capital that consumers seek out to best reflect both who they are (self-identity) and who they want to be seen to be (self-projection).[3] By staking out their location in the cultural landscape, these brands are able to wield the power of ownership to engage with consumers. The cultural capital that brands hold is deeply rooted in the space they occupy in the landscape and how they are viewed by consumers. This is connected to the cultural recollections of accrued capital, where 'memory is collective, plural and yet also individual' (Robertson & Hall, 2007, p. 21) and is thus activated by the 'memory' of landmarks – brands – that draw on this recollection of symbolism and prompt a consumer to act accordingly.

With this in mind, brands can take advantage of the uneven population and topography of the cultural landscape as an opportunity to take pieces of land and develop them in a way that will turn small ideas, or 'whys' (Sinek, 2011), into cultural landmarks. Along with this development to remake the natural landscape into something that better suits a community's, or brand's, needs comes the potential for influence and power. However, while remaking a cultural landscape to suit the needs of a brand might enable the latter to be the largest landmark within the area (be it clothes, shoes, cars, etc.), if this development is done with short-term gain in mind, it can overlook the potential longer-term ramifications, as well as refusing to acknowledge the brand's 'immense power as an agent of change' (Salter, 1971, Introduction) and the responsibility that entails.

Historically the ownership of land 'creates power and influence' (Munton, 2009, p. S55) and much of that power was (and still is) held in the hands of a select group of landowners, which creates a hierarchy that decides how land can be used and by whom. Notably, the ownership of a particular piece of real estate doesn't necessarily mean that neighbours will all be competitors or compatriots; these elements shift depending on the wider culture of a temporal period. For instance, if we consider mainstream clothing retailers, such as Zara, Urban Outfitters, H&M, UNIQLO, and so on, as holding landmark spaces as high-street/mainstream brands, they often physically exist in similar locations (such as Oxford Street, London), in clusters,

---

[3] An in-depth look at how the movement of cultural capital relates to identity and branding is provided in Chapter 3.

as neighbours. These brands also exist as holding an intangible space within the cultural landscape as 'more than just a clothing brand. But a way of thinking. A steady consciousness of constant change, diversity, and the challenging of conventions' (UNIQLO, 2023) – a sentiment that is often replicated across similar clothing brands. By working together as landowning brands in the cultural landscape, these brands are able to wield large amounts of power that goes beyond what they produce and sell. They are able to dictate what style is and how much clothing should cost for consumers within different locations in the cultural landscape.

The intangible aspects of a brand's power in the cultural landscape are less concerned with what product a brand is selling and instead are more closely linked with the ideals and mission of a brand. A consumer does not go across London to shop at the flagship Urban Outfitters because they want a specific top; they are going because that store is a landmark for a specific type of cultural capital that is manifest in the clothes the brand sell and in the consumers that are drawn to the brand. They go to Urban Outfitters because the brand is curated 'with an eye towards creativity and cultural understanding' (UO, 2023) and that speaks directly to how the consumer sees themselves and wants to be seen by others. The ability for a brand to enable a consumer to bring into alignment their self-identity and self projection in a way that fulfils them is a powerful thing; it can generate a variety of feelings for a brand such as love, commitment, attachment, and trust.[4]

Brands that are grouped together based on either the tangible products or intangible aspects of cultural capital can develop clusters of landmarks that exude magnetic power over those who want to be associated with the brand and its ideals. A consumer may not be able to afford a multi-thousand-pound designer bag, but going to a designer brand's location, such as London's Bond Street, The Village

---

[4] The following citations are a small entry point into areas of study with rich histories and robust publication lists and so this list is not comprehensive. For more information on brand love see Albert et al., 2008; Palusuk et al., 2019; Ahuvia et al. 2020; and Iqbal et al., 2022. For brand commitment see Osuna Ramírez et al., 2017; Singh et al, 2022; and Khodabandeh & Lindh, 2021. For brand attachment see Shimul, 2022; and Huaman-Ramirez & Merunka, 2019. For brand trust see Delgado-Ballester & Manuera-Alemán, 2005; Delgado-Ballester et al., 2003; and Dam, 2020.

at Westfield London, Rodeo Drive in Beverly Hills, Triangle d'Or in Paris, or the Via dei Condotti in Rome, brings with it a sense of aspiration or belonging to a particular community who holds similar values. With brands able to mould a sense of community identity that consumers seek out and buy into (both with tangible products and with the intangible sense of belonging), they can use the power of that loyalty to shift the cultural landscape itself and develop more robust structural narratives that lead to the brand.

However, different topographies will have different allowances for power, capital, and rules for how a brand or individual can hold power or divest from it based on the interplay between their self-identity and self-projection. The acquisition and divesting of power, as power is entangled with brands and cultural capital, are in themselves a means of moving across the cultural landscape, and they speak directly to how consumers have evolved to both buy into, and take possession of, the power of brands in the cultural landscape.

The Evolution of Consumer Culture

The history of branding and marketing, and their relationships to the consumer, is long and has been well researched;[5] therefore in order to establish the consumer's relationship to the cultural landscape we begin with a more modern conceptual starting point where 'culture pervades consumption and marketing phenomenon' (Visconti et al., 2020, p. 2) and where brands and consumers work together to develop meaning. Neither is the idea of the co-creation of value and cultural meaning new. Sellers, vendors, companies, brands, and individuals have always sold more than simply products; they sell symbols that a consumer can use to help them understand their self-identity, how they want to project themselves to others, and where they are situated within the cultural landscape (Levy, 1959).

Marketing and advertising, in this model of meaning and co-creation of value, are the 'conduit[s] through which meanings are constantly transferred from the culturally constituted world to the consumer goods' (McCracken, 2005, p. 164). The model has moved from producer-centred brand consciousness (Davies & Elliott, 2006),

---

[5] For example, see the Routledge studies in the history of marketing series; Tadajewski & Jones, 2008; Jones, 2017; and Room, 1998.

where advertising was being pushed onto consumers for awareness of products that exist in a world of less competition, to a world where the value of the product for the consumer must go beyond its 'utilitarian character and commercial value' (McCracken, 1986, p. 71). In doing so, the changing ways that we consider brands are more tied into the culture from which the brand originates and within which it is purchased or consumed.

Though it is not necessarily true that 'to be a consumer today means happiness' (Benn, 2004, p. 110), consumption is a way in which individuals develop community and are able to identify and interact with one another within the cultural landscape. Though the increase of choices for the consumer has been found to be initially confusing (Davies & Elliott, 2006), consumers are able to utilise brand landmarks in order to better understand where they (as consumers) exist in the cultural landscape and where they need to move in order to better align their self-identity with their self-projection. This movement across the cultural landscape is facilitated by brands positioning themselves in spaces that they can claim and put down roots, and potentially draw consumers to them.

The subsequent movement of consumers through the cultural landscape, via the exchange of capital, is a performance of self that brands can tap into as symbolic purveyors of culture through the positioning of their products. As performances that are physically/digitally and temporally bound, tied to symbolic representation, where a consumer is 'guided and restricted by tradition, rules and repetition' (Verhoeven, 2011, p. 118), rituals are a part of consumer culture.[6] They play a key role in the cultural landscape as a performance of self, in drawing in an audience and in staking out space in the cultural landscape. Take, for instance, a consumer who, every Friday afternoon after work, goes into her favourite wine café, makes small talk with the barista, buys a glass of the café's most expensive wine, sits in the window seat, pulls out her laptop, her notebook, and her pen, and then sits down to write at least 500 words of her novel. This ritualistic behaviour consists of a series of repeated, consecutive events

---

[6] Rituals and ritualistic behaviour are rich areas of study and though not foci of this chapter, it is worth considering various aspects of these in relation to religion (see Rappaport, 1999; Insoll, 2011; and Hollenback, 2016) and society (Rao, 2006; Gusfield & Michalowicz, 1984).

(going to the café, sitting in the same space, writing the same amount of words), a script that is followed (in the small talk with the barista), the purchase and use of artefacts (buying of the wine), and has the potential to have an audience (sitting in the window – the performance of 'being a writer' in a public space) (Rook, 1985).

While different groups in a wider community may come together to participate in a ritual, the understanding of what that ritual means, and who actually controls the ritual, 'can shift in response to outside events of long-term contextual changes' (Busteed, 2007, p. 75) and are linked to the power embedded in the ownership and use of space marked out in the cultural landscape. In order to understand how these shifts in experience and understanding happen, and the elements of power that are exchanged during them, we must look to the ephemeral aspects of an urban space (Atha, 2020) and the 'rituals of inhabitation' of such spaces (Smith, 2010, p. 46). Though each consumer constructs and views their cultural landscape in different ways (Moore, 2007), the rituals they take part in allow them to imitate others and develop social cohesion (Whitehouse, 2021).

The ritualisation of consumer culture also crosses over into, and straddles, the digital realm, where, for instance, Gen Z will use social media to show they have ordered a book, upload unboxing videos of the physical item, tag the content with hashtags to insert it into a conversation,[7] and then actively post that they are signing off to read offline. They then step away from social media to give themselves space to focus on one media format that is purposefully not digital (Duffy, 2023). Even the aspects of digital detoxing and disconnecting can become performative rituals and are growing more prevalent as more people move online (Stäheli & Stoltenberg, 2022). Once the offline reading has been completed, these consumers will then reconnect online and may be inclined to post reviews or engage in further discourse around the book.

Both the ritualistic unplugging from and plugging into digital settings takes place in the consumer's cultural landscape, where the book is used as a cultural marker 'to convey their sense of who they are, who they want to be – or not be, what is important to them, and how they relate to others' (Visconti et al., 2020, p. 2). This draws on

---

[7] The purposeful and active use of hashtags enables people to feel connected as part of a community and facilitate discussions (Dobrin, 2020).

how a consumer experiences a landscape and is linked to how they construct their identity via mapping key aspects of their journey between self-identity and self-projection and what this means for their own interpretations of a wider cultural landscape.

Mapping the Consumer to the Cultural Landscape

A key aspect of the consumer's cultural landscape is that it can be understood as a map that can be used for 'wayfinding and navigation' (Duxbury et al., 2015, p. 1); a means of how a consumer views the physical and intangible space they inhabit and makes a plan to traverse that space, using the map as a guide. The consumer's route and how long it will take them to reach their goal is contingent on how they self-identify and self-project. Depending on how they see themselves and how they want to be seen, their paths will alter as they move towards and away from different brand landmarks that they feel best symbolise the complex relationship between their self-identity and self-projection in relationship to the exchange of capital.

The way that consumers do this is linked to cultural mapping, which is a new way 'of describing, accounting for, and coming to terms with the cultural resources of communities and spaces … that can serve as a point of entry into theoretical debates about the nature of spatial knowledge and spatial representation' (Druxbury et al., 2015, p. 2). Much of the consumer's cultural landscape is a juxtaposition of brand landmarks that help the consumer develop their identity by moving towards them, some of which become familiar enough that the consumer does not notice them in their daily life and movements. For instance, if a consumer wants to be a foodie, they will often seek to move towards brands that are landmarks in the cultural landscape, such as Noma, Alchemist, The Chairman,[8] and so on, and in their travels (which is also imbued with how they shape the ways that they see themselves and how they want to be seen by others), they may not notice the smaller cultural locations they see all the time, such as fast food, street-food vendors, local cafés, and so on.

Just because the consumer might not allow for the brands they see all the time to become landmarks in their cultural landscape in the

---

[8] These three restaurants are listed in the top fifty restaurants in the world in 50 Best's The World's 50 Best Restaurant list, awarded June 2023.

same 'beacon-like' way that an aspirational brand might, it does not mean that these smaller, local, everyman brands have no place in the landscape or are of any less value to an individual consumer or the community in which the brand is located. The familiarity that a consumer can have for brands that they see and interact with all the time can imbue a sense of comfort, home, and well-traversed structural narratives. Likewise, these brands are often pillars of their local areas, with space staked out within the landscape that is directly tied to the way the brands interact with the local communities around them. They can delineate neighbourhoods, provide structure and shelter to a landscape, and allow consumers to get their bearings within a cultural space, and with this comes power.

There is power in map-making and how landscapes and cultures are defined. Harley (1989) makes this a focal point of his work on the power and knowledge of maps, where he draws on Foucault and Derrida to note that mapping is about creating rather than revealing knowledge. Much like in the technical work of cartography, where one can change the borders and terrain of a place by altering its rendering on a map, the cultural landscape can also be altered and remade depending on who is viewing the landscape, what shared landmarks there are, and what the mapmakers themselves want to communicate. The cultural mapping of a landscape is arguably more complicated than the physical mapping as one must take into account the subjective decisions by those who have the power to 'officially' create the map (cultural organisations such as museums, galleries, festivals; cultural bodies such as UNESCO or National Endowment for the Arts; etc.), the work of brands to build landmarks that are culturally relevant and stable across different views of the map, the inclusion of digital culture and landmarks and how these move into the physical space, as well as the myriad of ways that consumers move through the fluid landscape by exchanging forms of capital to better align their self-identity and self-projection.

With this complexity come aspects of a power dynamic that is balanced among cultural organisations, brands, platforms, and consumers. There is a give and take that changes the shape of the cultural landscape for some consumers, while for others it might remain unaltered. This can lead to an uneven development of space, which can be seen as an opportunity for brands and communities to claim ownership (Robinson & Hall, 2007, p. 28). This ebb and flow of power across the landscape is manifest in cultural capital being held and changing hands,[9] where much of the bulk of the power is held by the consumers, as power comes from below and is projected upwards; '[m]aps are thus the product of privileged and formalized knowledges and they also produce knowledge about the world' (Kitchin & Dodge, 2007, p. 332). The power dynamics the role of mapping the cultural landscape entail are, much like the wider role of cartography and cultural mapping, temporal in nature and dependent on their location in the discourse and the point in time at which they are considered, and are inseparable from the knowledge and personal identity of a consumer or brand.

With this in mind, we can see some resistance to power in and across the cultural landscape with the role of counter-mapping, which is an approach to viewing maps in a way that 'unsettles and unpacks the spatial assumptions upon which maps are crafted' (Boatcă, 2021, p. 245) and critiques maps as 'self-evident representations' (Wainwright & Bryan, 2009, p. 154). This can be seen when groups seek to change the status quo, whether that be by brands aligning themselves with particular causes (Patagonia and the environment, Ben & Jerry's and political issues), or by individual consumers or communities, who leverage their space in the cultural landscape to flock to brands and causes that spur a shift in the power dynamics by altering who has the power to develop the cultural map, and stake out space within it. This is linked to brand activism and cancel culture and there are many examples where communal participation has destroyed the landscape (Roe, 2020, p. 408). This speaks to how maps are 'always remade every time they are engaged with; mapping is a process of constant reterritorialization. As such, maps are transitory and fleeting, being contingent, relational and context-dependent. Maps are practices – they are always mapping' (Kitchin & Dodge, 2007, p. 335).

How Consumers Read the Cultural Landscape

'Maps chart the journeys we have taken and symbolize places along the routes that we traverse' (Woodward, 2002, p. 65) and, as such, they need to be read via symbolic systems based on a reader's position in the landscape and how they plan their journey. In understanding

---

[9] This is covered in detail in Chapter 3.

how a consumer chooses to move across their cultural landscape, we must first try to identify the consumer and the groups to which they belong. Much like a marketer will identify the target market in order to better focus their structural narratives, via advertisements and marketing strategies to reach consumers, locating the consumer in their cultural landscape requires the brands to understand that a consumer can start anywhere and end up anywhere else (Geertz, 1973). This is not to say that brands will be unable to follow the roads that a consumer follows from point A to B, but it does mean that they must start from their own landscape and from there look outward concentrically.

Because 'communities invest in landscape formation, and ... they locate their identities in landscapes' (O'Keeffe, 2007, p. 9), the communities around a brand are a good place to develop an understanding of how consumers read their cultural maps. Landscapes and cultural forms can be read as texts (Cosgrove & Jackson, 1987; Geertz, 1973) and even those who are illiterate are able to share in the community and find their way from point A to B by following along with others and by moving towards the brand landmarks that enable consumers to know where they are within the landscape. Texts are spaces that encourage a consumer to take them apart and redevelop in a way that works for them (Duncan & Duncan, 1988) and they need not do this in a linear fashion. For instance, consumers can go straight for a particular niche brand within an area of interest, such as buying a Brompton folding cycle for their commute; however, they can also go from brand (Dahon) to brand (B'Twin) in a non-linear fashion before they land on one that suits them and their individual needs and identity (Brompton). Since the consumer's cultural landscape is open to traverse in the ways that suit a particular consumer best, consumers can jump from brand to brand, decide to abandon a path altogether, or decide to stop and start at an entirely different point (such as deciding that instead of using a folding bike, they should use a scooter or get a cab, etc.).

Consumers and brands will interpret the texts of a landscape in different ways, regardless of the brands' intentions or the consumers' interpretation; therefore, '[l]andscape texts bear their own inherent meaning potential' (Bellentani, 2016, p. 79), which exist outwith those who occupy or traverse these. The existence of a cultural landscape beyond the limits of textual boundaries brings into focus the places where landscapes can be read beyond textual analysis based on developed maps, as practices where things in the landscape are related to one another through 'various spaces through a continuous and largely involuntary process of encounter' (Thrift, 2007, p. 8). Interpreting spaces that brands occupy (and the spaces they do not) within cultural landscape as spaces where shared meaning is made by the brand and consumers, is tied to how identity, capital, and value are created and exchanged within these locations. Where '[m]aps represent another way of attempting to pin down identity, to structure what matters by picking out the key places, the main links and attempting to secure them' within the cultural landscape as landmarks on the map (Woodward, 2002, p. 68).

The clustering of landmark brands in the consumer's cultural landscape are akin to areas of a city's map that are given over to particular types of zoning, officially or unofficially: one area is where the bookstores are located, another might be the place to go for a night of good cocktails and music, another might be a grouping of sports facilities such as a stadiums – examples of this clustering crops up in American cities such as Philadelphia where the stadiums housing the city's National Basketball Association (NBA) and National Hockey League (NHL) teams (76ers and Flyers), MLB (Phillies), and NFL (Eagles) teams are all within a mile of each other. This is repeated in Detroit, Houston, Cleveland, and so on. Another example of this is are cities' financial districts – the City of London, La Défense in Paris, Pudong in Shanghai, and the Central Business District in Sydney, among many others. Even in university towns across the USA, fraternities and sororities are often grouped together in similar parts of the town/across campuses. This clustering creates a sense of identity of a space, a space within the landscape where a consumer knows where to go to obtain certain things.

The physical manifestation of space and brands can be replicated across the cultural landscape – when a consumer wants to feel at home in a suit and tie and be surrounded by money and business they move towards spending time in the financial districts; if they are keen on high-end watches they go to Geneva's Rue du Rhône. The development of a collective identity of space that is both plural and individual can solidify within a collective memory of space and is activated by the 'notion of "landmarks". These ... engender recollections and act as prompts for actions' (Robertson & Hall, 2007, p. 21).

Moving beyond the aforementioned reading of a landscape as text, here landmark brands serve as cultural anchors that both draw consumers into their space and incite them to act. The actions that brands ask consumers to undertake will alter depending on the goals of the brand, its personality, equity, and relationship to the consumers. Consumers, for their part, will respond to brands differently if they are part of a busy community in a space held by the brand, or if they are on their own and considering how they want to engage with the brand and how it relates to their overarching identity. As the symbols that embed brands within the cultural landscape can be deceptive and transient depending on their relative positioning they are hard to pin down and must be understood as an interpretation of space at a particular point in time (Burch, 2015).

Participation can be 'an unstable process' (Roe, 2020, p. 412) in communities, consumption, and in developing a reliable cultural map that can be used, or indeed reused, by an individual consumer or wider cultural group. This instability of participation is why the 80/20 rule is prevalent in business and marketing. The fluctuation is made by 80 per cent of consumers in moving to and from a brand within the landscape who are less stable in their loyalty to a brand than those 20 per cent of consumers who utilise the brand as part of their own identity. For the 80 per cent, the brand may be just one stop on their journey as, through the exchange of capital, they are able to traverse the cultural landscape.

Much of the work on the cultural landscape is theoretical in concept and deals with things unseen and transitory, so, in order to ground the term within tangible actions that are of value to both the consumer and a brand, we have attached to it the physical nature of a geographical landscape. Many of the terms used here are borrowed from the areas of cartography, geography, and cultural studies, and this is not accidental. By taking these related concepts and applying them to the ways that brands and consumers interact, we are able to better understand the relationships between brands and consumers, brands' cultural and theoretical lands, and how consumers utilise brands to manoeuvre in time and space. In its most simplistic iteration the cultural landscape can be conceived of as a primary map of a physical space with a variety of ephemeral layers sitting atop. What these different layers consist of will alter for each reader of the map, regardless of whether they are a consumer, group, brand, organisation, government, and so on. Though all maps will have a base landscape layer – it may have hills and a river, for instance – the individualised topography of that map indicates how the consumer will identify where they exist within the landscape and how they move around it, both in the physical and digital worlds.

The Impact of Technology and the Growth of Digital Suburbs

The development and spread of the internet has continued, with over 64 per cent of the world's population connected (We Are Social, 2023a). The potential connectivity provided by access to the internet has constructed spaces where the geography of the cultural landscape has been mapped across a digital realm into a 'third space that simultaneously straddles and obscures the physically territoriality of the border, while enhancing their cultural demarcations' (Hodge & Hallgrimsdottir, 2019, p. 2). This has had two outcomes: it facilitates the development of communities both within major digital hubs and in newly created digital suburbs, and brings to the cultural landscape digital topographical elements.[10]

The communities developed in digital settings are characterised by 'personal intimacy, moral commitment and social cohesion' (Dodge & Kitchin, 2003, p. 35), and the growth of communities of like-minded people in digital settings has enabled conversations to happen as if we are all neighbours in a 'global village' (McLuhan, 1962). In this conception, popularised by McLuhan, consumers are all close enough to one another in digital settings for miles and borders to be erased, as we can engage with each other as simply as if we were doing so in the physical world. This development of digital communities is complicated by the digital divide, which can be defined as 'a division between people who have access and use of digital media and those who do not' (Van Dijk, 2020, p. 1). Not only is access to digital spaces gatekept by governments, companies, and individuals – enlisting aspects of embedded offline power dynamics – there is not necessarily an equality of access with regard to how consumers are able to use the technology. Not all consumers

---

[10] For more information on digital geographies, see Ash et al., 2018, and McLean, 2020.

have the knowledge to access digital communities, nor might they have time to do so, or the capital to purchase tools to do so (computers, tablets, smartphones, etc.).

The value of starting with the concept of the global village is in the ability to map it in ways that provide tangible understanding of an ephemeral setting. By considering the role of community-building and consumer identity online we are able to explore how 'people live in an experimental continuum, running from the materiality of geographic space through to the virtuality of cyberspace' (Dodge & Kitchin, 2001, p. 32) and apply some parameters and identifiable landmarks. In doing so, we first must zoom out from the village metaphor and instead consider the whole of the digital landscape, which consists of cities, towns, villages, and rural spaces. While the concepts of these terms can mostly align with the habitation and development of digital spaces, wherein cities are spaces that are busy and have many inhabitants and spaces of work – spaces such as popular social media platforms – and rural areas are more niche spaces, such as communities built around a love of barefoot running shoes, they do not always align. Much like in a physical city there can be urban deserts where communities are sparse within a busy cityscape.

In this same vein, digital suburbs have grown to envelop the outskirts of cities and towns. Most physical suburbs are filled with like-minded people who often have similar lifestyles and homes and sign up to abide by the rules and regulations of a local homeowners' association – they form a community. These consumers have found a 'city' that they enjoy being in, such as a large online forum such as Reddit, and they have sought out a suburb adjacent to it where they feel they fit. While platforms such as Reddit or Facebook can be seen as large cities, the suburbs around them are less busy, harder to reach, less prone sense of pattern and loyalty. Cities, on the other hand, are crowded, full of different conversations and areas that are easily connected.

Brands, in this digital map, want people to move to suburbs where they have a presence. Once the consumer has decided that the digital space they want to be is in a community where they feel comfortable around a topic or brand, they move into an area of brand loyalty. The brand must therefore maintain a presence in the consumer's neighbourhood, but can work to maintain goodwill and focus their wider marketing efforts elsewhere in the heart of the bustling cities. Once a suburb community around a brand has grown it becomes a space that is identifiable to those outside the community as a location they can visit, shop around, and decide if they want to become a part of it longer term. Once the brand has a pipeline from city marketing to suburb brand community they have begun to embed themselves into the cultural landscape as a landmark for consumers to move towards as they work to define their identity.

Suburbs can be sprawling and are not isolated from other suburbs or access to cities, towns, or other rural areas. Consumers are not tied to a space and can move to develop relationships in other communities in other towns and cities across the global digital landscape wherein brands have put down roots. The ease of movement is facilitated by consumers' use of the internet, and is subject to how they see themselves and how they want to be seen. The continual development and changes of the digital cities and suburbs are also subject to the different topographical elements that affect the cultural landscape more widely.

The instantaneous connection digital media provides enables culture to form and change more quickly within the digital landscape than in the physical world. Consumers are able to hop a fence and jump from their suburb into the heart of another city and back again in moments. Consumers and brands have learned how to navigate these changing spaces as they have become more digitally connected. However, it does mean that brands need to be more aware of the pace of movement and understand how it interacts with the temporal nature of the way consumers continually interpret where they are in the cultural landscape at any given point. One of the key ways that consumers do this is by engaging with brands and products that symbolise their identity as part of a particular community or not. A consumer who is into counterculture might inhabit digital spaces that revolve around aspects of subverting the status quo; they may do this in spaces that aren't part of mainstream digital locations (such as Facebook, X, or other large social platforms). This consumer might engage with brands that help them to identify and project their connection to this ideal, such as wearing Doc Martens. Consumption, in this sense, allows for a consumer to gain access to a suburb or city where they feel most at home near the brand landmarks with which they choose to identify, the exchange of capital helps them to move to, and take up residence, in that space.

Business Scenario: Yoga with Adriene

In 2012 yoga instructor, actor, and entrepreneur Adriene Mishler began sharing her videos of different yoga routines on YouTube. With names such as 'Yoga for back pain', 'Morning Yoga – Yoga to start your day', 'Yoga for tired feet', her videos fit into what one might expect from a yoga instructor. She also provides videos that are more esoteric, with titles including: 'Yoga for creativity', 'Yoga for gratitude', and 'Yoga for insecurity', among others. With this simple format, Mishler has grown her YouTube following to 12.5 million subscribers and offers 736 videos.[11] She's had over a billion views of her content and the majority of it is free.[12] As a brand that shares yoga with the masses, Adriene is aware that she is able to go straight into people's homes, and that is 'their most vulnerable place' (Mishler quoted in Bramley, 2018).

Her understanding of the growth of the digital suburbs has enabled Mishler to expand her brand in the cultural landscape in ways that other brands cannot. Though her physical studio is in Texas, she runs two app-based services. Her Kula by Yoga with Adriene is a free community-based app that helps the brand reach its goal of 'making real connections with people' (Bowman, n.d.). In order to develop narrative structures that enabled the highest number of consumers to move towards the brand, Yoga with Adriene opted to keep YouTube as Mishler's main digital access point, but to also move away from the other major social platforms in order to develop a space that felt more open to consumers. Her two apps are the basis of that movement into the digital suburbs: meeting people where they are and in ways which they can access the platforms. Kula by Yoga with Adriene has well over 200,000 members who communicate directly with each other.

This free app and the free videos on YouTube give consumers the choice of staying with the free community around the brand or downloading the subscription app: Find What Feels Good. This paid-for app is a 'personal yoga studio' at $129.99 per year. It provides a more exclusive community, premium courses, and exclusive video content from the brand. While Mishler continues to create her free YouTube content, this is a specific choice that allows for ease of entry into the brand; consumers who subscribe are part of the

---

[11] As of February 2024.   [12] As reported by Social Blade in February 2024.

co-creation process in that they are told that, by contributing as a member, they are helping to keep the YouTube channel alive.

Yoga with Adriene is a business case that highlights the value of choosing one digital city (YouTube) and from there moving into the digital suburbs via apps that enable consumers to both develop their own 'safe' community spaces, to help support the brand, and to get valuable content streamed directly to their local spaces in the cultural landscape. Here, 'above all, Mishler offers privacy; specifically the freedom to suck at yoga without judgement' (Young, 2020). The narrative structures of free content and yoga for everyone have enabled the brand to move outward and grow.

Conclusion

The cultural landscape is a complex and ever-shifting space where brand and consumers come together to make meaning, exchange value, and construct identity. It encompasses both material and symbolic dimensions across physical and digital realms, where the ephemeral processes of encounter and interpretation underlie shared spaces. The cultural landscape becomes a map for performing and contesting identity through ritualised actions that are always temporally situated. Its topography consists of not just physically located brands and consumers, but also imagined landmarks, such as legacy brands, which anchor collective memories and prompt a consumer's movements between self-identity and self-projection.

Within this fluid terrain, capital circulates in economic, social, cultural, and symbolic forms. Brands and consumers continuously renegotiate power and prestige through owning or accessing these forms of capital and the spaces they inscribe. Mapping and reading the cultural landscape involves constant struggle over what matters, which symbols take root, and who controls the dominant narratives. From early notions of creating value through meaning transferral, marketing has evolved into a more collaborative construction of culture. Through rituals of habitation and wayfinding guided by landmark brands, individuals locate themselves in relation to shared theoretical suburban communities and cityscapes. This conceptual cartography illuminates how elusive notions of identity, community, and capital interact through tangible and intangible spaces. There is a constant redrawing of the cultural landscape to both bind and unbind shared meaning.

Key Points

- The term 'cultural landscape' has evolved from its original connection to physical and geographical landscapes to encompass a broader understanding. This includes the roles of language, meaning, and representation in constructing realities, and it recognises cultural landscapes as loci of power influenced by the interactions of consumers, brands, and shifting socio-political contexts.
- Consumers use brands as landmarks for navigation within the cultural landscape. The role of cultural mapping is a method for understanding spatial knowledge and the subjective nature of map-building and place-making, based on individual experiences and the interplay between a consumer's self-identity and self-projection.
- The impact of digital technology on the cultural landscape is significant, creating digital neighbourhoods and suburbs where consumers engage with brands and each other.

2 | *Using Brands as Landmarks for Mapping the Cultural Landscape*

[T]he role of brands as guarantor of quality may be diminishing. This, coupled with disintermediation, creates a threat for brands that needs to be addressed.

K. Gielens and J. B. E. Steenkamp, Branding in the era of digital (dis) intermediation, *International Journal of Research in Marketing*

There is a long history of branding that predates the modern usage, but what we consider '[m]odern branding and the use of individual brand names has its origin in the nineteenth century' (Room, 1998, p. 14) with the Industrial Revolution and the need for a means to identify an item by a particular manufacturer using a simple, memorable format. This sense of identification is still the case today, where a brand's visual identity is often a first harbinger of product, quality, or status. However, the roles of brands and branding have altered dramatically with the development and growth of the internet and ubiquitous mobile devices that allow the consumer wide access to content, communities, and products, and they have multiplied in complexity.

In past decades an organisation worked to create a strong brand identity by consistently pushing a brand image and managing the 'relevant touch points' with consumers (Aaker & Joachimsthaler, 2000; Keller & Lehmann, 2003; Lobschat et al., 2013). The way that these brands must reach consumers has altered. Word of mouth (WOM), brand advocacy, information, affiliation, identity, and utility (Trudeau & Shobeiri, 2016) are now key aspects in how a brand must situate itself in the consumer landscape. Therefore, understanding the role of brand equity is a source of competitive advantage – especially in areas where the 'main benefit is intangible and consumers perceive high risk' (Christodoulides et al., 2006, p. 800). Where a brand exists in the consumer landscape relates directly to the wider cultural panorama and where/how a consumer sees themselves. The role of the brand is to develop and utilise the signs and symbols at their disposal to establish a relationship with the consumer, while keeping in mind that not all signs and symbols are interpreted in the same way by all consumers; nor do all consumers choose to interact with all brands.

Business Scenario: Tiffany & Co.'s Landmark at Fifth Avenue and *Breakfast at Tiffany's*

Founded in 1837, Tiffany & Co. evolved to become a purveyor of luxury accessories with a focus on jewellery. From their first mail-order catalogue, the Blue Book Collection, Tiffany's & Co. was set up to introduce a growing American market to luxury goods and jewels brought in from Europe. Over the decades it grew to become synonymous with American luxury and the global brand value has grown from $4.127 billion in 2010 to $7.931 billion in 2023 (Interbrand, 2023). When consumers think of Tiffany & Co., they think of the store experience, the brand in popular culture, and the trademarked tone of the iconic blue box.

The blue box 'instantly became a symbol of exclusivity, sophistication, and elegance' (Kaur, 2016). The colour, the box, and the brand have become symbolic of cultural and economic capital that the brand has understood and utilised to develop structural narratives that consumers can use to draw close to the brand and develop communities. One of the ways that Tiffany & Co. has done this is by allowing films to be shot at their iconic New York City location. Most recognisably, perhaps, is the 1961 film *Breakfast at Tiffany's*; followed later by *Sleepless in Seattle* (1993) and *Sweet Home Alabama* (2002). Additionally, the recognisable Tiffany & Co. items and branding play a role in several other films such as *Legally Blonde* (2001) and *The Great Gatsby* (2013), and in other forms of popular media. By tapping into the cultural capital of media personalities, Tiffany & Co. continually ensures that consumers across the cultural landscape see the brand as a landmark that represents not only a physical location (such as New York City or Mayfair, London) but a sense of identity. By being able to see Tiffany & Co. from a variety of spaces and contexts within the cultural landscape, consumers can use the brand as a landmark for navigating their sense of self-identity and self-projection, and they are able to follow the brand's narrative structures in order to understand where they stand in relation to others.

What Tiffany & Co. understands particularly well in their role as a landmark brand in the cultural landscape is how to stay rooted in their location, where they are recognisable from a variety of positions, and also how to open up narrative structures that enable new consumers to move towards them. They do this by engaging with other brands, such as Beyoncé, where Tiffany & Co. is the official jeweller of Beyoncé's Renaissance World Tour – a tour that boosted the American economy by $4.5 billion, 'about as much as the 2008 Olympics did for Beijing' (Wortham, 2023).

Tiffany & Co. stays authentic to its brand image while also enabling consumers to feel they have part ownership over the brand. One example of this is the sense of experience the company offers consumers who are able to physically visit their store, called The Landmark, at 57th Street and Fifth Avenue in New York City. Likewise, if consumers are in New York and want to have the Tiffany & Co. experience, they can book a table at the Blue Box Café, a dining experience in Tiffany & Co.'s landmark store (with a Michelin-starred chef at the helm) that draws closer links between the elegance and sophistication of the brand and popular culture. At the Blue Box Café, consumers can enjoy their own breakfast at Tiffany's, even if they cannot afford a piece of jewellery. In the digital space, Tiffany & Co. have engaged directly with consumers via microsites (such as the now-defunct whatmakeslovetrue.com) and by showcasing their approach to brand activism, which appeals to modern consumers.[1]

Symbols, Signs, and Situational Identifiers

Noted by Percy as far back as 2003, the American Marketing Association definition of a brand (which remains mostly unaltered) 'reminds us of the reasons for a brand' (Percy, 2003, p. 12) but gives no real indication of what a brand is or what is meant by the term 'brand'. A brand will have certain visual, aural, or physical indicators that relay information about a product or service to a consumer, but it is much more than a reference for said products. A brand incorporates intangible properties and assets such as 'identity, associations, and personality' (Mercer, 2010, p. 18) and, as such, brands have the power to change shape, alter their identifying marks without losing

---

[1] For more info on the role of brand activism, see Chapter 6.

their essence, and shift tone to speak to different audiences. This relates directly to the roles of the signs and symbols of the brand and their signification to a particular receiving group.

Something can be symbolic when it 'implies something more than its obvious and immediate meaning. It has a wider "unconscious" aspect that is never precisely defined or fully explained' (Jung, 1964 pp. 20–21). In the case of modern branding we can consider the brand of Coca-Cola as symbolic. For instance, in 2021 a stock analysis profile indicated that Coca-Cola had $18.682 billion in property, plant, and equipment costs at the end of that year (Coca-Cola Co. (NYSE:KO), 2021). However, Forbes (2022) indicates that their overall brand value in 2022 is $64.4 billion, Interbrand (2021) values the brand at $57,488 billion, and the Brand Finance (2022) Global 500 report values Coca-Cola's brand at $35,379 billion. The discrepancy here lies in the intangible assets of the brand's value, with nearly $19 billion of the value being physical in nature, the other $16,697–45,718 billion being the symbolic nature of what the brand represents. As noted by Drescher (1992), all of the physical assets of Coca-Cola could go up in flames overnight and there isn't a bank that wouldn't loan Coca-Cola the funds for rebuilding.

While Coca-Cola is an obvious example of a brand whose value is much more than their tangible assets, we can also apply this to less traditional forms of branding, such as the branding of an influencer or content creator, where the symbolic nature of their brand indicates that they are a key gateway to an area of interest. Fashion bloggers, for example, often show up to fashion week events in New York, London, and so on in their best clothing, 'peacocking' for photographers. They may not have tickets for any of the exclusive shows or events, but they come to these events nonetheless for the exposure (Duffy, 2017) and to use the content they create to both share their perceived insider status with their followers and to grow their audience. This perceived status represents the symbolic nature of an influencer who speaks for a much wider, sometimes intangible and inaccessible, concept. In the case of the fashion influencer, they represent a human aspect of the massive industry of fashion and design.

The symbolic nature of branding and brand-building is closely related to that of the signs that brands use to indicate 'a way of denoting that an object is what it is and then becomes a form of naming something' (Batsos & Levy, 2012, p. 349), a 'conventional naming of things and functions' (Meltzer, 1997, p. 175). Whereas a 'sign is always less than the concept it represents … a symbol always stands for something more than its obvious and immediate meaning' (Jung, 1964, p. 55). In this consideration, a sign can become a symbol, much as a Bic simply means 'a pen' in some locations and, in the Southern States of the USA, a Coke means any soft drink, not just the branded item.

Signs, however, are more than simply indications of what something is or what it may stand for. 'Meaningful, semiotic signs are exchanged among consumers and brand owners as a form of social currency' (Lawes, 2019, p. 252). These signs can link to larger, symbolic forms and institutions and can draw lines and parallels to abstract concepts such as joy, happiness, and worth. Renn, referencing Schultz, considers these links to be appresentation, wherein a 'representational relation between intentional objects and signs in terms of immediate coupling which excludes the need of active inference' (Renn, 2006, p. 9). For instance, a cross and a steeple on a building will likely lead one to identify that building as a Christian church without a conscious effort to do so. This does not mean that all signs and symbols are appresentational, and we see in brand-building that developing this unconscious tie between a brand and its intended meaning is something brands continually work to develop and engrain in the cultural consciousness.

Understanding the value a brand has relates to how 'signs and symbols are meaningfully connected to society, culture, and ideology' (Lawes, 2019, p. 252). This is due to the fact that signs and symbols not only become currencies used in everyday life (Meltzer, 1997), they become situational identifiers. When a brand has reached the point of becoming a situational identifier it can move onto becoming a brand icon; such icons have 'extraordinary value because they carry a heavy symbolic load for their most enthusiastic consumers' and have 'such compelling myths that they have become cultural icons' (Holt, 2004, pp. 2, 5).

It is much too simplistic to consider that by 'cultural icon' or 'situational identifier' we mean that a consumer can see a particularly branded store, advertisement, webpage, social media vibe, and so on and know where they are in a physical or digital space. This is certainly true in some situations, such as in Clanton, Alabama, where the large peach-shaped water tower highlights to those passing that they are entering the area known as Peach Central, a concept central to Clanton's branding as a town. The Rodeo Drive sign in Beverly Hills, California, means that the consumer is about to hit one of the exclusive shopping streets in the country, while the layout of a tweet/post, even taken as a screenshot, indicates that the content comes from that social platform.[2] Signs and symbols as situational identifiers in the physical sense are the most obvious iteration of branding a space. However, equally, or perhaps more, important are the cultural, social, emotional, and ideological indications of brands as they situate a consumer.

This 'consumer culture' is well researched (Featherstone, 1990; Kozinets, 2001; Sassatelli, 2007) and conceptualises an 'interconnected system of commercially produced images, texts and overlapping objects that groups use … to make collective sense of their environments and to orient their members' experiences and lives' (Arnould & Thompson, 2005, p. 869). Modern consumer culture is more sensitive to the roles of differing cultures, in both macro and micro instances, the crossover of multinational brands, and the ways a consumer or group of consumers interpret the signs and symbols produced and shared by the brand. By placing culture at the centre of understanding the consumer we can better understand how brands fit within that fabric, become a part of the cultural landscape, and develop narrative structures that lead back to themselves.

If we take, for example, the Ford Mustang's place in the cultural landscape of America, the muscle car, first built in 1964, is often called an 'icon in American culture' (Scott, 2004) and is linked to the concept of freedom, as in a *New York Times* article where Ford's President of Global Markets said that the 'Mustang means freedom. It means taking a road trip in a convertible down the West Coast. That's what people all over the world imagine America to be' (Farley quoted in Stewart, 2018). Farley goes on to call the mustang a '"mind-set" vehicle' (Stewart, 2018), which links to the social and emotional signifiers of the car in the wider consumer culture, where it has become an 'international pop icon' (Herincx, 2016). Tapping into this appeal to an ideology and emotional attachment

---

[2] Sometimes platforms can be confused with others due to the cannibalisation of features. This is evident in how Instagram works to bring onboard TikTok-like features and how Truth Social looks and feels much like Twitter.

to the American way of life and the 'freedom' that represents has helped to make the Ford Mustang the world's best-selling sports car (Ford, 2021). Not only has the Mustang done consistently well in the USA, it has exported its ideology of freedom, power, and community (Gay, 2022) to international markets where it is much more expensive (£47,000+ compared to the USA's $27,470+)[3] and competes with cars in a more luxurious bracket such as Porsche's Cayman (£47,000) and Boxster (£49,700).[4]

The idea of the Mustang sociologically and culturally situates the consumer in the mindset of freedom, fast cars, and open roads, while also conveying to others in the consumer culture that those who drive the Mustang in the UK are economically capable of doing so and that they value the concepts the Mustang embodies, including those potentially positive and negative stereotypes. Seeing a Mustang in a city such as London or Birmingham might also indicate that the driver is using the car as a status symbol and not for the value it has on the open roads, much like the appearance of 'Chelsea tractors' in cities become status symbols beyond their original, and perhaps most valuable, use.

Aligning oneself with a branded item, whether a car, handbag, book, piece of tech, or a social platform has to do with the consumer developing an understanding of themselves in relation to a brand in a landscape that is an individually curated, wider cultural panorama. Brands can help consumers identify, locate, and potentially engage with a community that 'stems from mutual brand usage and is usually linked to specific behaviours or experiences that are perceived as unique or special' (Schögel et al. quoted in Zinnbauer & Honer, 2011, p. 52). This allows consumers within a wider cultural panorama to find like-minded communities and develop a sense of affinity within these, therefore creating social value, including belongingness (Trudeau & Shobeiri, 2016, p. 98). Part of the value of brands in situating consumers within a community, whether digitally or physically – by being surrounded by people wearing Wrangler jeans and Justin boots – is to facilitate social engagement, which 'has been

---

[3] The amount of £47,000 is equivalent to $52,404, based on the exchange rate on 3 October 2022, though it must be noted that early October 2022 saw a market crash for the British pound and this rate might not be generally representative.

[4] Prices of all cars mentioned here are direct from the company website in the country where the price is quoted.

found to be strongly linked to enhanced feelings of belonging, especially in consumption contexts [at a rodeo, western store, or horse show in the case of Wrangler and Justin] where engagement generates social benefits' (Bowden & Mirzaei, 2021 p. 1420).

However, when considering how a brand wields their power within these landscapes it is important to note that not all consumers interpret the signs and symbols in homogenous, or expected, ways.

The Problems with Signs and Symbols

Not all signs and symbols are 'created in the mind of the speaker' (Meltzer, 1997, p. 175) and are often received from society rather than pushed into it. And the ways that signs and symbols can be interpreted will vary based on the consumer's own individual and cultural aspects. This relates to the way that an individual consumer first identifies a brand, or often a brand mark, and then to how that brand is interpreted in the mind of that consumer in that particular space and time (Renn, 2006). These can be considered separate actions: the identification of a brand (seeing a Cambridge University Press logo on a spine), followed by linking that brand image to a set of interpretations (the book must be rigorously peer-reviewed and therefore trustworthy, as it's published by CUP). The main consideration for brands is to help consumers form the link from the recognition of a brand to the preferred brand interpretation. This is harder than it seems as each individual consumer has their own interpretations of signs and symbols in relation to the wider socio-political and economic cultural landscape in which they exist.

For example, not all consumers will look at AT&T in the USA as simply one of the largest and most comprehensive providers of 5G tech, fibre broadband, and a vast cellular network. It is all of those things, but post the overturning of *Roe* v. *Wade*,[5] it is also a brand that has, for some of areas of consumer culture, a stigma attached to it for financially supporting anti-abortion politicians in all thirteen states with trigger laws – to the tune of 'nearly $1.2 million' (Giadiano et al., 2022).

---

[5] The Supreme Court of the USA overturned the national legalisation of abortion in America on 24 June 2022, effectively kicking the decision on abortion back to individual states and triggering a variety of abortion bans (trigger laws) that came into effect immediately.

This is not far removed from the consideration of the statue of Fearless Girl (2017), which I often mention when teaching marketing classes. On the surface, the bronze statue of the small girl defiantly facing down the bull of Wall Street brings to mind feminism, strength, and determination in the face of adversity. However, when unpacking the issues behind the statue, its purity as a symbol of female strength dwindles. Fearless Girl was, and remains, little more than a marketing mechanism for State Street Global Advisors (SSGA), which coincided with their move to push the companies they invest in into having more women on their boards. This is not altruistic. There is a positive accounting return for those organisations with female board representation (Post & Byron, 2014). In fact, when placed in situ facing Charging Bull the artist herself claimed that the statue was 'strong but not belligerent … She is proud but not confrontational' (Visbal, quoted in Pinto, 2017). However, in more recent years there have been trademarking issues and lawsuits over reproductions of the statue (which the artist is selling non-fungible tokens (NFTs) of Fearless Girl to fund) and Visbal has said of Fearless Girl that 'She legally stands for equality, equal pay, supporting women in leadership positions, the empowerment of women, education of women, education for the prevention of prejudice, and the general well-being of women' (Visbal, quoted in Palumbo, 2022).

Regardless of the final outcome of the lawsuit between Visbal and SSGA, the statue itself, which felt like a fresh look at feminism and equality, now has an air of 'false feminism' (Bellafante, 2017), though it is still used for feminist-linked, promotional purposes.[6]

Depending on a consumer's position within the socio-economic and cultural landscape, their interpretation of AT&T, SSGA, Visbal, and Fearless Girl as branded entities will differ. This is the case for all brands, from personal branding to the branding of a multinational corporation. And in order to understand the relationship of signs and symbols as brands to a consumer's interpretation of those signs and symbols we must better discern how consumers utilises brands as a means to situate themselves. The signs exchanged between brand

---

[6] These promotions sometimes come from the community, as when someone placed a lace collar on her within 24 hours of Supreme Court Justice Ruth Bader Ginsburg dying. Likewise, in 2021, SSGA installed a shattered glass ceiling around Fearless Girl, which currently faces the New York Stock Exchange (NYSE) while the city plans for a permanent home.

owners and consumers are known as 'social currency' and make up 'one of a brand's most important strengths' (Zinnbauer & Honer, 2011, p. 50). Much like different nations have different monetary currencies, the currency that is in use in a particular consumer's cultural landscape can serve as a means of grounding the consumer.

To this end, if we take Schutz's work on appresentation and further concept of transcendence and link these directly to the realm of consumer culture, his use of signs and symbols as a means of first making sense of what is within a person's individual cultural landscape, then being able to have an understanding of a consumer's cultural landscape – though a brand cannot directly step into their shoes – we can begin to see how symbols come to exist in a shared cultural landscape through a variety of prisms such as political ideology (left and right), brand value (Gucci is high, Old Navy/Primark is low, for example), and even musical genres, and so on (Dreher, 2003).

Branding in a Digital World

'A "brand" is a universal concept regardless of setting' (Meyers & Gertsman, 2001, p. 800), but the way a consumer's cultural landscape has shifted to include digital spaces and communities has altered how brands must fit into those spaces and how the consumers interact with brands in such settings. 'The internet has upended how consumers engage with brands' (Edelman, 2010, p. 2). This is due to the increasingly social and connected nature of a consumer's life, brought on by access to the internet and mobile devices and a sense of the world becoming more of a global village (McLuhan, 1962). The internet has allowed geographical and temporal boundaries to blur and the growth of communities of like-minded individuals to flourish. Consumers still want the same quality of product or service as before, but the structural narratives and touchpoints (as advertisements and marketing tools) have altered, as have spaces in which these consumers are more 'open to influence' (Edelman, 2010, p. 2), with brands that simply replicate their offline equity in a digital space often seen as lacking or stale (Meyers & Gertsman, 2001).

The growth of online brand communities (OBCs), which 'are online forums dedicated to a specific brand, where consumers gather, exchange information and socialise' (Meek et al. 2019 p. 426), play a role in the consumer's cultural landscape by allowing the consumer to digitally situate themselves within a community. By actively entering into and engaging in these communities, consumers are able to situate themselves in relation to the brands and other consumers and will likely share particular values and appreciations related to the brand, as '[m]any consumers purchase brands they perceive as self-representative' (Meek et al., 2019 p. 426). And, as such, 'self-brand connections are, therefore, critical to engagement ... when it creates value for them' (Bowden & Mirzaei, 2021, p. 1417), where the more a consumer identifies with a brand, the more likely they are to engage and advocate for that brand (Moliner et al., 2018) and 'develop a sense of affinity with other users of the brand' (Zinnbauer & Honer, 2011, p. 52).

This is not to say that brand communities need to be literal forums such as Reddit or Mumsnet; while there certainly are subreddits and threads dedicated to all aspects of branding and consumer culture, brand communities should be considered a much wider and looser connection of digital ties across platforms and media. Brand communities can be cultivated, such as those 'walled gardens' on Facebook, Twitter/X Circles, WhatsApp groups, metaverse communities, and so on, or they can loosely exist as a series of connections and shared comments, likes, threads, and more on platforms such as Twitter/X, TikTok, Facebook, and so on. It should be noted that digital communities can arise anywhere and these platforms are simply a selection. Platforms can be divided into categories related to the ties created within them, such as weak ties on Twitter/X and strong ties on Facebook or more walled communities (Valenzuela & Zúñiga, 2018). It is just as likely that like-minded consumers will gravitate to the comments sections on their favourite, or most hated, news platform, articles, and podcasts – communities can even form in reviews of products on Amazon pages and Goodreads. Likewise, fandoms can grow on platforms like AO3, Medium, Wattpad, and other digital locations where consumer engagement exists and where that engagement can be 'defined as the emotional bond established between the consumer and the brand' (Moliner et al., 2018, p. 387).

This emotional bond with a brand can be mediated through the connections with other consumers in those digital communities where '[c]onsumer engagement is a composite of interactive, experiential and social dimensions' (Moliner et al., 2018, p. 389). The sense of belonging that collective and reciprocal communications foster in a consumer's cultural landscape can result in positive brand connections and loyalty among those consumers (Loureiro et al., 2017). However, not all OBCs are the same, nor are they the same across platforms. For instance, in my previous work on books and social media reader/author communities, it became clear that gender has a key role in how these communities interact in online settings (Johnson, 2021), a topic that is returned to in Chapter 4.

As such, brands must remain vigilant of the make-up of their communities, keeping in mind their brand equity, values, and the way consumers use the various digital platforms in different ways to different ends. 'The goal [... should be] to more directly enhance the customer journey, adapt to changes in customer behaviours and differentiate the brand experience' (Gielens & Steenkamp, 2019, p. 368). And, in this capacity, '[i]t is the ongoing creation of user-generated content that sustains the life of an OBC' (Meek et al., 2019, p. 426).

Another key role of the brand within a digital environment is to mediate these communities, both as spaces for growing brand affinity via shared narratives (Fowelstone, 2013; Fowelstone et al., 2015) and by developing brand recognition and brand communities as landmarks for consumers. Developing these spaces as recognisable and trustworthy embeds the brand within the consumer's cultural landscape.[7] Therefore, the consumer can situate themselves in relation to other consumers (both in and outwith brand communities) and to the brand itself, and can know where they stand culturally. The ability for a consumer to understand where they currently are and where they want to be, based on their self-identity and self-projection,[8] enables them to utilise brands as landmarks to manoeuvre through the cultural map.

---

[7] The consideration of trustworthiness in digital markets goes as far back as 2000 with quotes such as 'price does not rule the web; trust does' (Reichheld & Schelfter, 2000, p. 107) and the belief that trust will be the difference in a web retailer succeeding or failing (Urban et al., 2000). For more research on brand trust in online settings see Benedicktus et al. 2010; Aribarg & Schwartz, 2020; Bleier & Palmatier, 2019; and Schmidt & Iyer, 2015; among many others.

[8] Though the concept of 'identity' is complex and multifaceted, self-identity as used here refers to how a consumer views themselves as a unique individual within a particular cultural landscape and consists of an amalgamation of markets such as gender, race, sexuality, age, education, personal life history, and more (Davison, 2012). For more research see Papacharissi, 2010;

Brands as Beacons, Not Creeps

When a brand positions itself within a cultural landscape it is important for that brand to serve as a beacon to consumers so that they can find their way to the brand and the communities that come to life around it and navigate their own self-identity. One thing the brand does not want to do, and which happens more as '[m]obile devices play an increasingly intimate role in everyday life' (Shklovski et al. 2014, p. 2347), is to be labelled as creepy. Creepiness often relates to targeted behaviour, where a consumer's internet use is tracked and ads are tailored for them, and retargeting, where a consumer is shown ads for a product they have already purchased (Barnard, 2014). However, by the end of 2024, cookies,[9] which are used to monitor browsing history, will be removed from Google Chrome, which is one of the most used internet browsers and holds over 50 per cent market share in the USA (Vailshery, 2022). This follows companies like Apple Inc. and Mozilla, which no longer support third-party cookies on their browsers.

While there are arguments that the 'death of the cookie' will be potentially bad for the digital advertising market, privacy concerns in recent years have given rise to browsers that make a feature of not tracking users (DuckDuckGo), as well as General Data Protection Regulation in Europe and similar regulations dotted across America and other locations. Other suggestions for cookie replacement, such as zero-party data, rely on the consumer answering some questions (perhaps for access, or a discount), are arguably more accurate (self-reporting issues aside), and makes the consumer feel that this transactional exchange of capital is worthwhile and not exploitative.

With the demise of the cookie and, perhaps, users volunteering more information about themselves to get access to a platform, brands may be less likely to have that creepiness factor, which can

---

Elwell, 2014; and Sheth & Solomon, 2014; among others. Self-presentation differs somewhat from self-identity in that it draws on Goffman's theories of self-presentation as intentional and tangible (Goffman, 1990); in the modern age that sense of controlling 'information to influence the impressions formed by an audience about the self' (Schlenker and Wowra, 2003, p. 871) suits the mediated nature of online communities where users can create profiles of who they want to be instead of who they are.

[9] The year 2024 is the current end date of cookies; however, it must be noted that this date has been pushed back a number of times from 2022.

'denote an emotional response to a sense of wrongness that is difficult to clearly articulate' (Shklovski et al. 2014, p. 2347) or happen when 'tailored communications, designed to be relevant to the consumer, take relevance a step too far, crossing the line into invasiveness' (Barnard, 2014, p. 6). This is especially true when consumers consider their devices as extensions of themselves and social platforms as 'personal space among publics' (Sung & Kim, 2014, p. 236). And, in contrast to those brand communities mentioned, those consumers who feel digital spaces are more personal have the most negative attitude towards brands that show up in those spaces (Sung & Kim, 2014).

As such, brands that repeatedly push themselves into the consumer's cultural landscape risk losing the consumer, as the brand becomes less of a landmark used by the consumer to demarcate where they are situated in the cultural landscape – potentially encouraging them to develop a brand affinity – and more of an advertisement channel that loses relevance in its pervasiveness. Part of knowing how to develop relationships with consumers is to understand who the consumer is and how they approach digital exposure to brands, such as engaging with the fact that 99 per cent of Gen Z choose to 'skip' ads and 63 per cent use blockers to avoid ads altogether (O'Brien, 2022).

This is not to say that brands should stay off of social platforms where a sense of personal space is the highest, but that they should be aware that perceived continual intrusion into a consumer's personal space may not only lead to advertising saturation,[10] it could have consequences for a consumer's self-identity (Shklovski et al., 2014) as they construct new social realities in everyday interactions (Madianou & Miller, 2013). This remains the case even if those consumers are not those entering into practices 'involving participation in the production of content' (Leban et al., 2020, p. 515), also known as 'lurking'; something the majority of digital consumers do (Barnes, 2018; Benevenuto et al., 2009; Van Dijk, 2009). Lurking can be considered a form of engagement and 'refers to the behaviours of viewing messages or member contributions but not posting anything' (Barnes, 2018, p. 6). Lurkers can be 'engaged listeners'

---

[10] Paouleanou (2020) found that the more saturated with ads a social platform is, the more likely it is that users will avoid that platform.

(Barnes, 2016) and 'develop and affective relationship with both the website and the other commentators' (Barnes, 2018, p. 7).

As consumers begin to care more about intangible experiences offered by brands as a means to 'transform their personal identities' (Seo and Buchanan-Oliver quoted in Leban et al., 2020, p. 515), brands are better able to understand lurking as consumption. The value of lurking, for a consumer, is that they can utilise the space where brands exist for 'compassing', a practice that Leban et al. (2020, p. 517) define as allowing 'a user to navigate the space they are in, and thus, to get a sense of their environment'. Lurkers in the digital consumer's cultural landscape often take steps to review content, expand stories, search digital platforms (social and otherwise), and save content to share privately (Audy Martínek et al., 2022, p. 23). Simply because consumers who lurk in online spaces do not visibly engage with content does not mean that they will not become some of the most loyal brand consumers (Kefi & Maar, 2018). What matters most is the perceived choice to engage.

Conclusion

Whether the most vocal brand advocate in a brand community or a lurker, consumer-engagement styles relate back to a sense of self and the freedom to engage with brands in a way of one's choosing. Brands, their signs and symbols, the equity they represent, all must work to serve the consumer to help them situate themselves within both their own and the wider cultural landscape and consumer economy. The use of appresentation by a consumer to unconsciously interpret the signs a brand is communicating goes hand in hand with the ability for a consumer to recognise that they and other consumers can share signs, even though they do not see them identically. This ability to transcend the differentiations in a brand's signs and symbols enables communities to develop around brands. In the modern age many of these communities exist in digital spaces. The lack of physical boundaries and time in digital communities enables consumer groups that share a cultural landscape to evolve a communal sense of identity in relation to the brand. This, in turn, enables consumers to engage within their cultural landscape and use these brands as landmarks to navigate where they, as a consumer, stand in relation to the brands, other consumers, and themselves as they are and where they aspire to be in their journey of identity.

Key Points

- Brands are more than their physical assets; they carry symbolic value and have the power to shift identities and resonate with different consumers.
- Brands are cultural and situational identifiers. Successful brands act as contextual identifiers within the cultural landscape, sometimes becoming cultural icons. They can signal a consumer's location within a cultural, social, or geographic context.
- Not all signs and symbols are interpreted in the same way by every consumer; they are contextual. Sometimes individual relationships with the brand mean more to a community of consumers than society's understanding of the same brand.
- The growth of online communities has shifted how consumers relate to brands. Consumers often move towards brands they feel are representative of themselves, and they engage in digital communities to share information and form bonds with like-minded individuals.
- Brands must balance visibility with privacy concerns in digital spaces. They need to avoid being perceived as invasive and instead serve as beacons for consumers to navigate their cultural landscape without undermining consumers' sense of personal space and identity.

3 | *Brand Capital, Perspective, and Power*

By teaching us the meaning of goods as well as their use, advertising helps create intelligibility; it helps make the categories of culture stable and visible.

Douglas and Isherwood, quoted in J. F. Sherry,
Advertising as a cultural system, Marketing and *Semiotics*:
New *Directions* in the *Study* of *Signs* for *Sale*

Business Scenario: Fitzcarraldo Editions

In 2023, a small, independent publisher of contemporary fiction and long-form essays was once again the publisher of a winner of the Nobel Prize in Literature. Once again, as this was the fourth time they had been the British publisher of a winner. This was quite the feat for a small publisher that was only founded in 2014. Being the 'English language imprint of choice for Nobel laureates' (Marshall, 2022), allows Fitzcarraldo Editions to print and sell many more books than they normally would, with tens of thousands of copies needed when the Nobel Prize is announced. With every literary prize winner Fitzcarraldo Editions publishes, the more the media pays attention, because '[p]rizes possess media power [... and] media power of prizes is an asset, a form of capital' (Driscoll, 2013, p. 106).

Fitzcarraldo Editions gains economic capital from publishing Nobel Prize laureates, which it can then exchange for higher levels of cultural capital in signing on more potential prize winners. Likewise, the brand itself has capital bestowed on it by in the form of institutional capital of the Nobel Prizes. This, in turn, trickles down to the consumer, who exchanges their economical capital for the cultural capital that owning and being seen to own a Nobel Prize-winning work of literature bestows on them. This is tied closely to the consumer's sense of self-identity and self-projection in the cultural landscape, where knowing that the iconic blue-and-white covers of a

Fitzcarraldo Edition symbolises a particular type of book, reader, and relationship to cultural capital allows the consumer to use this information to better navigate the cultural landscape.

The role of brands has begun to shift to become more than a selling point. Brands are both a sign and a symbol of what they sell and stand for, and of their personality or ethos. Brands now must exist across multiple media localities and, as such, they must navigate the same cultural landscape as a consumer, while taking into account how the consumer perceives brands as landmarks for navigating their alignment of self-identity and self-projection. When considering the role of brands and branding across different forms of media, it is of value to consider the cultural, economic, and media context in which these brands are developed and continue, or cease, to exist. While these three contexts can fold into one another, in that a brand with high cultural capital may command the attention of media platforms, which can lead to a rise in economic capital, pulling them apart allows for a better understanding of what is meant by capital, how perspective plays a role, and what the interplay means in the power dynamics of a brand.

The Role of Perspective in the Consumer Environment

In the current highly connected media environment, information is available in overabundance and is readily accessible to most consumers. Branding in this connected world must take on new roles. While there are a myriad of approaches through which the role of branding can be conceptualised, the breakdown that Swaminathan et al. (2020) use is valuable for discerning the connection between the consumer, capital, and power. These perspectives are firm, consumer, and society, and they are worth defining:

- The firm perspective comprises both strategic and financial approaches to brands and 'views brands as assets and examines the various functions and roles that brands serve for firms, both strategically and financially'.
- The consumer perspective 'views brands as signals (economic approach) and mental knowledge cues (psychological approach)'.
- The society perspective 'presents brands in societal and cultural contexts affecting individual consumers both directly and indirectly through social forces, structures, and institutions' (Swaminathan et al., 2020, p. 4).

These perspectives work well in conjunction with a social constructionist approach,[1] which links closely to the societal perspective and relates to defining the 'corporate brand through the social interaction between the company and its environment' (Galvin, 2020, p. 13), arguing that 'individuals subjectively form realities based on social and experiential constructions' (Helal et al., 2018).

It may be tempting to consider brands in the consumer's cultural landscape from a singular perspective, often that of the brand at a corporate level (Balmer & Gray, 2003; Balmer & Greyser, 2003; Kernstock & Brexendorf, 2009), or that of the consumer (Dwivedi & McDonald, 2020; Gómez-Suárez et al., 2017; Keller, 2003) or of society (O'Guinn et al., 2018; Swaminathan et al., 2020). However, it is most valuable when perspectives can be combined, since few brands are purely financial, consumer-driven, or society-informed. Because the question of the relative positioning of both brand and consumer in the wider cultural landscape comes into play when we consider who has the authority to speak within this particular discourse, we must also recognise that in all cases the way companies, brands, and consumers perceive themselves and others are 'human constructions; that is, they are all inventions of the human mind and hence subject to human error' (Guba & Lincoln, 1994, p. 108). Simply because the fallibility of human construction of a cultural landscape and self-identity is a possibility, it does not follow that we cannot consider the interplay between the brand and the consumer and the latter's authority to speak from their individual position within the landscape.

If we take into account Foucault's archaeological tool for questioning, where a speaker is positioned within the wider discourse, in this case branding, this enables us to dismiss a linear account of brand-building in which a company creates a brand and uses it to sell to a consumer, who then joins a brand community to become an ambassador of the brand itself. Instead, the perspective to be used in evaluating a brand should take into account the place from which the speaker comes (Foucault, 2002). Knowledge of the speaker's perspective allows the subject to speak from within a particular body of knowledge (Topp, 2000) and allows those listening to

---

[1] For more research on the social constructionist approach to marketing, see Aggerholm et al., 2011.

understand what field the speakers are situated in (finance, marketing, social media, strategy), what organisations or companies they may have an affinity with, and, simply, who they are and what gives them the power to speak (Topp, 2000). All of this enables the consumer to better understand where they are in relation to brands in the cultural landscape.

If a consumer comes across a content creator's post on a social platform such as Instagram, TikTok, Facebook, and so on, and the post is selling a book, telling other consumers to go and purchase that product, or even simply providing honest reviews, the consumer needs to know where that content creator is situated in that wider body of knowledge. Who gives them the authority to speak on behalf of the book or author they post about? The hashtag #ad enables the consumer to understand that this book may not be one the content creator would have freely chosen to share with their audience, and speaks to what relationship the content creator has to the publisher, the book, and their audience. Requirements from ASA (the UK-based Advertising Standards Agency) to make ads identifiable as such are key to enabling the consumer to know who has given the content creator the authority to speak.[2] The consumer can then consider whether they find the content creator a trustworthy source of information, based on where the content creator exists within the consumer's cultural landscape in relation to the consumer's identity.

Likewise, in an offline space the consumer will come across brands and branded advertisements, in response to which the consumer must determine where the authorisation for those ads to exist originates. This authorisation is the result of a complex body of research by the corporation that owns the brand, including the content of the advertisement (image choice, placement, design, wording, call to action, etc.), where the ad is shared, who the target audience is, and what the desired outcome is for the brand. An ad for designer handbags on Two Towers West, in London (often known as the billboards on the Hammersmith Flyover), for example, will have a complex stance within the discourse. Some of the complexity of the advertisement will be digested without thought (appresentation[3]) while other

---

[2] It must be acknowledged that questions have been raised as to how much ASA accurately reflects 'community standards' in their country of practice (Jones, 2003).
[3] See Chapter 1.

aspects must be considered in relation to all the cultural markers of the advertisement, what the ad is trying to do, and, perhaps, physically in relation to the consumer.

It must be noted that not everyone in the cultural landscape is a consumer for all brands and products; however, these brands continue to exist within the cultural landscape in which particular consumers manoeuvre. The consumer's cultural landscape can become an overwhelming interplay of culture and brands, and brands that sell culture, making it more difficult for the consumer to identify where they are in relation to where they want to be. It is important to question who has the authority to speak for a brand that a consumer does not want to engage with and to which they may in fact develop 'negative emotional reactions' (Redondo & Aznar, 2018, p. 10) when forced to engage. The value for the brand is more about staking out a space in the cultural landscape rather than identifying with every consumer who passes by.

The Brands That Are Not There

In this case, it is valid to also consider which brands are not within a specific location in the cultural landscape and why. Much like the example of the designer handbag ad, the complicated interplay between brand equity, who a brand is targeting, and why, plays into which brands have the ability to exist in particular locations within the consumer's cultural landscape and which do not. The location of the fictional designer handbag ad tells us that the audience is likely to be majority ABC1,[4] and the ad targets the 'top value business audience flying into Heathrow' (*Marketing Week*, 2017), so is '[t]wice as likely to be viewed by high-profile, high earning females compared to the UK average' (*Marketing Week*, 2017). This enables the consumer to know where they stand culturally in relation to the brand, and this knowledge is reaffirmed with potentially more branded advertisements for the designer handbag in the lounges at Heathrow, facilitating the use of brands as landmarks for the consumer to move around the cultural landscape.

---

[4] ABC1 is related to social grade categories where A, B, and C1 are often grouped together to include those who have intermediary to higher managerial roles or professional occupations. They are often called the 'middle class'.

What is not advertised in high-end sites like the Two Towers West, London, or in the pages of *Vogue*, also tells the consumer something about where that brand situates itself culturally. Why a brand appears in one place and not another develops the brand equity and relationships with the consumer, even if that relationship is defined by a brand's absence. A consumer from rural Italy who aspires to be a tennis player can manoeuvre themselves in the cultural landscape away from their lack of tennis-related brands, to find themselves surrounded by them digitally and physically if they attend a match or tournament. In this simplified example, the consumer is using the lack of brands to enable them to move towards an environment where they self-identify as a tennis player.

It would be remiss to consider the consumer's cultural landscape as an idyllic map of brands' narrative structures that lead the consumer directly to become their best self or the self they want to be. Instead, we must consider the lack of brands in the cultural landscape beyond how brands, or the lack thereof, are used as landmarks to help guide a consumer and look to those brands that are actively blocked by the consumer. In the digital sense, ad-blockers that simply 'prevent the display of any advertising content that matches an entry in the backlists maintained by the ad-blocking companies/ user communities' (Redondo & Aznar, 2018, p. 2) are utilised by consumers who do not want to pay the tax for going online and having free access to content-providing websites (Despotakis et al., 2021). In the second tax quarter (Q2) of 2023, there were 912 million ad-block users worldwide (Statista, 2023) across mobile and desktop devices, a number that has grown since 2018 (Stallone et al., 2021), as '80% of ... users are tracked by at least one tracking service within a second after starting web browsing' (Mughees et al., 2017, p. 4). Those consumers who employ ad-blockers are trying to avoid the intrusiveness and negative emotional reaction that these ads might engender, resulting in the consumer being annoyed by the ads (Stallone et al., 2021) and decreased platform engagement over time (Stourn & Bax, 2017).

While five of the world's largest tech companies owned more than 53 per cent of all global ad revenues in 2021 (Fischer, 2022),[5] there are relatively few digital places that are entirely ad-free. Those

[5] Google, Meta, Alibaba, ByteDance, and Amazon (according to GroupM).

that are, are often positioned as exclusively ad-free, such as social network Ello, built as a 'creators network' that had major media buzz when launched in 2014, but has mostly turned into an artist network rather than a general user's social platform. There are also major platforms such as *Forbes*, *The Independent*, and *WIRED*, among others, that have systems in place to block consumers using ad-blockers from accessing their site, giving the consumer the choice of leaving the site, turning off their ad-blocker, or seeking workarounds.

The 'arms race between ad-blockers and anti ad-blockers is a relatively recent phenomena' (Mughees et al., 2017, p. 4) where some argue that ad-blockers actually benefit the brands themselves by filtering out ad-sensitive consumers from sites. In allowing consumers to filter out annoying ads, blockers can help regulate the advertising industry via whitelists for ads and more efficient markets with better content quality on sites (Despotakis et al., 2021 p. 31). However, other research has shown that ad-blockers reduce consumers' online spending (Todri, 2022). This also relates to ad quality, as the platforms do not often directly control what ads are sold into ad space and the value of that ad space goes up when we consider access via a mobile device, where ads may be harder to see, take up too much of the screen, or be too obtrusive, potentially driving away users (Goldfarb & Tucker, 2011; Stourm & Bax, 2017).

This lack of ad space, and use of ad-blockers and anti-ad-blockers, creates a unique tension between the consumer and the brands, where the consumer wants white space in their cultural landscape and brands are pushing into available spaces via programmatic advertising,[6] amongst other means. The value of the white space around a consumer is in giving them the arena in which they can visualise where they exist in relation to brands, and how it interplays with their self-identity. Blocking out brands from encroaching on their immediate, digital space is a move indicative of a consumer who values the ability to survey their cultural landscape and make active choices. In fact, studies have found that those consumers who use

---

[6] For more information on programmatic advertising see Hasri et al., 2022; Barrett, 2022; Häglund & Björklund, 2022; Alaimo & Kallinikos, 2018. And, for concerns related to programmatic advertising, see Palos-Sanchez et al., 2019 and Samuel et al., 2021.

ad-blocking technology 'rely more heavily on their own past experiences with the brands', which could make 'markets more concentrated' (Todri, 2022, p. 5). While the use of ad-blockers may not encourage consumers to try new brands, it does provide them with the space to seek out brands they know in spaces of authority they trust (the brand's website, for instance), where they can fully understand the position from which the brand speaks.

Knowing where a speaker is positioned within the discourse allows the consumer to apprehend a brand's perspective and how that perspective is presented as a form of capital within the cultural landscape. If 'brand equity resides in the mind of the consumer' (Swaminathan et al., 2020, p. 6) and the 'soft' areas of branding, such as the emotions a consumer feels for a brand, and as the consumer is part of a wider societal structure, we can begin to see the relationships between the consumers, the brands, and the cultural institutions in which they were developed. This links directly to the value that individual consumers, wider society, and brands place on different forms of capital within the cultural landscape.

Capital as a Concept

The cultural approach popularised by Bourdieu (1986, 1993, 1996) across his work concerns the ebb and flow of power between different elements of capital and their relationship to culture. Using Bourdieu's theories of cultural capital, habitus, and the cultural field – or the consumer's cultural landscape – as they relate to the ways brands use the media landscape to change one type of capital into another facilitates an exploration of how brands try to connect potential consumers to a product (Mourits, 2021, p. 360). 'Bourdieu's concepts allow for a critical analysis of the process whereby actors deploy and legitimise their stocks of economic, social and cultural resources (capital), while being both influenced by, and simultaneously influencing, an arena's (field) socially shared norms, dispositions and behaviours (habitus)' (Reynolds et al, 2022, p. 2). Bourdieu's theories are particularly valuable in the sense that we can utilise them to consider the relationships between the products, the brands, and the consumer in terms of their historical development, class, and objective position within the field, in this case the consumer's cultural landscape (Johnson, 1993).

Consumers themselves are products of the wider, '"relatively stable cognitive networks" that are to some degree shared by a social group with similar experiences', and derive cultural meaning from how they interpret their experiences; this 'inform[s their] actions in the world' (Fournier & Alvarez, 2019, p. 519). Culture defined as a shared network of similar experiences could, perhaps, be better understood as 'culture becomes purely mental' (D'Andrade, 2001, p. 243), where 'shared objects and the perceptual features of these objects constitute the basic building blocks of culture' (D'Andrade, 2001, p. 246). These cultural building blocks do not just come into existence on the basis of shared mental awareness and interpretations of them, but because 'individuals and institutions produce shared conventionalized manifestations that make them part of everyday social life and experience' (Fournier & Alvarez, 2019, p. 520). This is evident in the links between brands and the consumers in the landscape, and informs the habitus of a consumer.

The Habitus of Branding

'Habitus can be understood to be a series of dispositions, which influences a person's expectations of social life' (Huang, 2019, p. 48) and consists of the 'tastes and distastes, sympathies and aversions, fantasies and phobias which, more than declared opinions, forge the unconscious unity of a class' (Bourdieu, 1996, p, 77). The dispositions within the habitus are developed and continued within a particular field and do not necessarily carry the same significance or meaning in differing fields.[7] For instance, a person who is considered well read in one country may not have the same standing in another country. And, though consumers and brands move across these different fields in the cultural landscape, they 'tend to incorporate into their habitus the values and imperatives of those fields' (Webb et al., 2002, p. 37).

The particular habitus with which we are concerned – that of the brand in the consumer's cultural landscape – can be broken down into two areas: the habitus of the brand and that of the consumer,

---

[7] It is worth noting that not all scholars agree with Bourdieu's concept of habitus. For critiques of this theory see Archer, 2010, 2012; Jenkins, 1982; and Alexander, 1995.

both of which are informed by their history, how they interpret that history within themselves, and the context in which they exist (Schirato & Roberts, 2018). The concept of habitus, generally, is not linear. It shows that 'what might otherwise appear to be disparate categories of social phenomena … are interrelated and tangled' (Ignatow & Robinson, 2017, p. 951). Here, the habitus of the brand and the consumer's cultural landscape relate to the social formations as spaces that can be occupied by any player within the habitus, 'based on the distribution of capital' (Grillo, 2018, p. 418). The networks of multiple discourses, positions, and consumers in the cultural landscape rely on their 'distinctive properties by which [… they] can be situated relative to other positions' (Bourdieu, 1993, p. 30). Even brands in a dominant position rely on the specific conditions enabling them to occupy a location within the landscape in order to maintain that position (Bourdieu, 1993). Brands that come to exist as symbolic objects that represent the equity of a brand must be recognised as such by others in the shared cultural landscape.[8] This allows the brand to manifest itself as having the power to remain in that particular position.

Capital in the Consumer's Cultural Landscape

Much as Bourdieu's (1993, p. 39) concept of the 'autonomous sector of the field of cultural production' relies on a form of cultural production aimed at the audience of other producers, so too the high-end luxury brands in the consumer's cultural landscape are subservient to maintaining a hierarchy of value where they are at the top. Brands are reliant on consumers recognising their brand equity as it is linked to the autonomous principle of their brand and valuing the exclusivity inherent in the expected degree of economic independence the brand conveys in having (often expensive) products that exclude a large portion of the wider consumer base. What allows the brand to stake out its position as an autonomous

---

[8] Brand equity can be defined as brand strength, which consists of the 'brand associations held by customers', and brand value, which comprises the 'gains that accrue when brand strength is leveraged to obtain superior current and future profits' (Lasser et al., 1995, p. 11). More recent explorations of brand equity can be found in Shariq, 2018; Parris & Guzmán, 2022; Veselinova & Samonikov, 2020; and Vukasović, 2022; among others.

producer is the interplay between different forms of capital in the consumer's cultural landscape.

Capital 'refers to stocks of internalised ability and aptitude as well as externalised resources which are scarce and socially valued' (Ignatow & Robinson, 2017, p. 952). The forms of capital valuable to understanding the relationships between the consumer and the brand in the cultural landscape are economic, social, cultural, and symbolic.[9] Different forms of capital can be exchanged to gain access to other forms; for example, economic capital can be exchanged for social capital in the form of a rare guitar or collector's edition of a book. Likewise, economic capital can be exchanged for cultural capital in the form of higher education, which can be exchanged for social capital through sharing learned knowledge at a book group or open lecture.

Economic capital can be broadly defined as being in possession of economic means that can be converted into money (Calderón Gómez, 2021, p. 2537), which 'provides the conditions for freedom from economic necessity' (Bourdieu, 1993, p. 68). Brands that hold economic capital that give them the autonomy to develop high-end, exclusive goods or services can seek to develop relationships with consumers that possess high levels of economic capital and are willing to exchange it for the social or cultural capital the brand offers. Conversely, brands that have high levels of economic capital are also able to wield that capital in order to reach those consumers with less economic capital on a mass scale, as we see with mass-market paperbacks, soft drinks, and, to an extent, clothing, and so on. The lines of economic capital are not clear-cut, especially as they relate to issues of class and habitus where '[t]he hierarchy of the class fractions as regards possession of economic capital … is already less visible when, as here, one is only dealing with indices of consumption' (Bourdieu, 1996, p. 116).

Consumers who hold economic capital have the 'basis of self-assurance' (Bourdieu, 1993, p. 68), which frees them to consider obtaining and showcasing other forms of capital, some of which serves the purpose of allowing their self-identity to match their self-projection in the cultural landscape; for example, wearing head-to-toe Giorgio Armani as means of inducing others to see them as they

---

[9] Symbolic capital in relation the branding was discussed in Chapter 1.

see themselves: people with money and taste. However, the '[a]utonomy based on consecration or prestige is purely symbolic and may or may not imply possession of increased economic capital' of the brand or the consumer (Johnson, 1993, p. 6). In fact, 'the structure of the distribution of economic capital is symmetrical and opposite to that of cultural capital' (Bourdieu, 1996, p. 120) and though the economic is always present, it does not always present itself as such and can manifest itself in access and inclusion (Bourdieu, 2021).

Access to certain spaces in the cultural landscape and inclusion into particular groups are directly related to social capital, which is the 'production and maintenance of social connections and networks' (Schirato & Roberts, 2018, p. 185). It is these groups, or social networks, that imbue the consumer with the 'backing of the collectively owned capital' of the group (Bourdieu, 1986, p. 246). For brands, this can be how they are positioned in the market compared to similar brands, such as collective, sometimes loosely defined, groups like the automotive industry, the tech industry, social media networks, and so on. For the consumer it can be inherently connected to their economic capital, where they are part of a class of consumers that has expendable income and can buy its way into a social group, or it can relate to groups the consumer chooses to join, such as brand advocacy groups or other communities online or offline, which enable consumers to feel part of something larger than themselves.

Social capital can develop in many formats and '[m]any communities are rich in one form of social capital but poor in others' (Chetty et al., 2022, p. 120). Thus, 'capital manifests itself in noneconomic ways' (Yüsek, 2018, p. 1092) that are enhanced and extended by the size of a consumer's social connections and the total capital that these social connections provide. Consumers do not move through their cultural landscape on their own. Their landscapes converge with and diverge from other consumers' cultural landscapes, in which much of the underlying architecture and topography may remain the same (for example, the same top ten songs play on the radio), but each consumer exists in their own individual landscape with pathways, brands, and capital that are valid for them (although the same top ten songs recur, for one consumer song 1 is worth engaging with, whereas for another consumer those worthwhile are songs 2 and 8). The social capital that a consumer has in their networks will influence what products and brands they interact with in their landscape.

Although social capital can shift into other forms of capital as the consumer moves about their networks and cultural landscape in their day-to-day lives, 'social capital is also enhanced and reproduced in a digitally mediated world' (Calderón Gómez, 2021, p. 2546), much like economic capital can be wielded in digital settings with the purchasing and ownership of items such as digital music, non-fungible tokens (NFTs), land in the metaverse or on websites, and, at the factory level, the ownership of digital corporations that make further economic capital by trading in social capital. Social media platforms are examples of digital spaces where capital can be exchanged.

Social capital in the digital realm is reliant on the affordances of the consumer to have the economic capital to pay for access to digital settings, including the technology to access the internet, the skills to utilise the technology, the ability to seek out the communities and information that the consumer wants to locate, and the ability to evaluate what they find and to implement any actions resultant of their digital access (Van Dijk, 2005). But not all consumers have equality of access to these digital spaces and the capital they can potentially provide.[10] 'Widespread digitalization of products and their easy dissemination through social media [and other digital formats such as ebooks or NFTs] fundamentally change how people construct and reveal their sense of self online' (Fournier & Alvarez, 2019, p. 526). This is linked to Bourdieu's concepts of 'playing seriously' and 'the taste for the necessary', where those in possession of higher social capital are able to better able to decode cultural aspects with 'the internal logic of works that aesthetic enjoyment presupposes' (Bourdieu, 1996, p. 2). In digital settings, those with more plentiful capital adopt playful means of moving about their cultural landscape that can grow a consumer's capital over time. These are the consumers who have the time, money, and know-how to access cultural landscapes in a digital setting and can choose to interact with platforms and brands. In contrast, those with less capital tend to utilise digital settings as a means to an end, such as locating information or purchasing a product online; it has been found they do not

---

[10] For more research on access and use of digital technology and potential shortcomings, see van Deursen & Helsper, 2015; Witte & Mannon, 2010; Thomas & Wyatt, 2002; Jenkins et al., 2006; and Henwood & Wyatt, 2019.

gain as much from their cultural landscapes (Ignatow & Robinson, 2017; Robinson, 2009). The latter group is potentially engaging in the cultural landscape in order to 'constitute[e] and represent ... themselves as culturally competent members of our information-age society' (Ignatow & Robinson, 2017).

Though we discuss the forms of capital identified by Bourdieu in terms that suggest that capital has hard forms and shape, in actuality it is fluid between its forms and economic capital can become social capital and/or cultural capital. 'For Bourdieu, this interconvertibility principle ensures a better understanding of the ongoing competition among individuals for valued resources and positions in societies via capital' (Yüsek, 2018, p. 1090). Much like the possession of economic or social capital, cultural capital is not necessarily equitably distributed in the cultural landscape. In fact, embodied aspects of cultural capital from previous generations 'functions as a sort of advance ... [and] enables a newcomer to start acquiring the basic elements of the legitimate culture, from the beginning' (Bourdieu, 1996, pp. 70–71). These are the consumers who come from a family with some standing and appreciation of culture and where, perhaps, higher education and a well-paying job are expectations instead of dreams. Brands that possess embodied capital are those that have a long history in the cultural landscape and are recognised as established and trustworthy. These are the Fords, Coca-Colas, Cambridge University Presses, and IBMs of the consumers' landscape. While these are only a few examples of brands that consistently provide a product or service year on year, brands can develop embodied capital over time as they grow into their position in the cultural landscape and become an architectural feature for those consumers who use the brand as a landmark for identifying where they are and where they want to go within the space.

The role of embodied cultural capital is closely related to objectified cultural capital, where both are tied to a consumer's background, though objectified cultural capital denotes capital that is 'transmitted "materially" both in the form of economic capital [money] and in the form of symbolic capital [ownership or inheritance of a particular collection of books, paintings, or a car]' (Mahbub & Shoily, 2016, p. 3). Embodied and objectified cultural capital are often linked to institutionalised capital, which Bourdieu sets apart as a form of capital likely bestowed by an institution, such as a medical or higher education degree, which 'confers entirely original properties on the cultural capital which it is presumed to guarantee' (Bourdieu, 1986, p. 240).

The Role of the Field

One underlying aspect of cultural capital is that it remains impossible to quantify with an absolute value: 'It only possesses value in exchange and the exchange is a social struggle as much as a struggle of cultural value judgment' (Robbins, 2005, p. 23). Within the cultural field there is a 'dynamics of capital' (Huang, 2019, p. 46) that relates to how we understand the value of capital and the shifting power dynamics of possessing capital. Consumers, brands, economic concerns, creativity, innovation, and cultural aspects do not 'act in a vacuum, but rather in concrete social situations governed by a set of objective social relations' (Johnson, 1993, p. 6). These are the fields that exist in the consumer's cultural landscape as a 'structure of objective relationships permitting the accounting of the concrete form of the interactions' (Bourdieu, 1985, p. 18). For players in the cultural landscape, the structure of relationships indicate that the value that one consumer is willing to place upon a product, brand, location, and so on may not be identical to the value another consumer or brand places upon the same object or idea. There are a range of 'mediating agencies involved in shaping tastes' (Bennett, 2010, p. 107), which vie for power in the cultural landscape, where '"[f]ields" are the building blocks of the social world within which we inhabit' (Mahbub & Shoily, 2016, p. 4).

'Cultural fields are only stable up to a certain point' (Schirato & Roberts, 2018, p. 162); they may change slowly over time and then suddenly, as they interact with other fields externally and as the internal elements of the field alter the conception of capital and power. The shifting commodification of different forms of capital within the consumer's cultural landscape is 'central to an understanding of the dynamics of cultural fields at both the internal and external levels' (Schirato & Roberts, 2018, p. 175); advertising in these fields is 'system of discerning or discovering meaning [... which] socialize[s] individuals into a culture of consumption' (Sherry, 1987, p. 445). It is this dynamic in which consumers find themselves as they move through the cultural landscape. The power that brands have to position themselves as landmarks for the consumer to situate themselves is a powerful indication of the amount of capital a brand possesses.

Where Power Sneaks In

When a cultural landscape 'acts as both a model *of* and a model *for* reality' (Sherry, 1987, p. 447) the topography of the landscape affects the landscape itself and the consumer within it. Brands that exist in that landscape have a role in reflecting and reshaping reality. Both consumers and brands in the cultural landscape produce and utilise cultural goods as a means to highlight the symbolic value associated with themselves. This symbolic value, in turn, enables those brands and consumers to recognise others who also belong to the same group of producers and consumers – thereby serving as landmarks within the wider landscape. In the exchange between production, consumption, and symbolic recognition resides the question of who wields the power in the cultural landscape.

The role of power is 'diffuse and often concealed in broadly accepted, and often unquestioned, ways of seeing and describing the world' (Johnson, 1993, p. 2). This seems obvious when we consider how brands have their brand equity and place in the market. Often consumers do not question why a brand is well respected and well used, such as Nike. Likewise, they regularly associate luxury brands with wealth, status, and quality without questioning whether or not those associations are likely to be true, since 'powerful actors [such as brands or influential individuals] can (and do) uphold one subcultural habitus over others' (Rubtsova & Dowd, 2004, p. 30).

Though Bourdieu 'conceptualizes capital in all forms of power, whether they are material, cultural, social, or symbolic' (Swartz quoted in Yüsek, 2018, p. 1091), it is useful to consider the power dynamics held within different forms of capital to be those of an extension of the 'logic of economic analysis' (Yüsek, 2018, p. 1092) in which we can consider the value of exchange. In the consumer's cultural landscape the value of a luxury item is linked to the ability of certain consumers to exchange one form of capital (economic in the case of a luxury item) for other forms of capital that the item embodies, such as the social and cultural capital of ownership that a luxury item symbolises in the landscape. Furthermore, it is the identification of capital in the cultural landscape that enables the consumer to know where they are in relation to said capital. This relationship is directly tied to their self-identity and self-projection: a consumer sometimes purchases a luxury brand item in order to be seen to have that item (social and cultural capital). This moves the consumer's self-identity and self-projection closer into alignment, such that others understand that for the consumer to possess the luxury item it can be presumed they have certain levels of social, cultural, and economic capital; though not every consumer moves across the cultural landscape to purchase a particular brand.

There is an exchange of power in the move towards a particular brand, even if the consumer does not purchase an item. By being in the vicinity of a brand in their cultural landscape, the consumer is able to appropriate aspects of the capital of the brand. One does not have to be wealthy to feel wealth-adjacent by window-shopping at Tiffany's or going into Harrods to have a browse; though it is worth noting that a level of economic and social privilege may be assumed in a consumer's being able to get to a physical Tiffany's location or in considering going inside Harrods.

In the exchange of power and capital, there is also a change in the self-identity and self-projection of the consumer. As a consumer moves through the cultural landscape, they are developing their identity as they are and as they wish to be perceived. Consumers can gain power in the exchange of capital; the accumulation of certain forms of capital will enhance their self-identity or alter how they wish to present themselves. The goalposts of self-identity and self-projection in the cultural landscape are often moving: when one level of capital is achieved, the consumer can use that as a base to develop their identity and projection further, because the exercise of capital and power 'requires legitimisation' (Yüsek, 2018, p. 1093) – as does a consumer's sense of self-identity and self-projection.

There is a cost to the transformation of capital, but transformation is 'needed to produce the type of power effective in the field in question' (Bourdieu, 1986, p. 252). When we look more closely at the power dynamics at play in the consumer's cultural landscape there might be temptations to conflate aspects of Bourdieu's fields and Foucault's use of discourse. However, we must keep in mind that Foucault concerns himself with the regularities that allow statements and objects to come into existence, and he considers this within a 'slice of history' (Foucault, 2002, p. 211), which can be taken as separate from the linear aspects of habitus and field that are tied to context and historical trajectory. While there is some scope for considering where those who bring statements into existence are located within the wider discourse, it is harder to map Foucault's consideration of discourse onto Bourdieu's fields, as Foucault does not leave room for the consumer's struggle for capital (in all its forms) to be understood fully.

Foucault does indicate that the layers of a discourse do not exist in isolation and must be related to other layers, practices, and so on (Foucault, 2002), and his consideration that 'power is tolerable only on the condition that it masks a substantial part of itself' (Foucault, 1978, p. 86) is valuable as a lens through which to view the power dynamics of capital in the wider cultural landscape. Power in the consumer's cultural landscape cannot 'operate without the delineation of subject positions' (Widder, 2004, p. 423), which allows some actors in the landscape to possess forms of power, in this case capital, that can be used over or against others within that landscape. However, not all power is forcefully wielded and power can be defined in these spaces as 'the capacity to influence other individuals' states' (Ten Brinke & Keltner, 2022, p. 1), a consideration that draws in aspects of status and class and their relationship to the possession of different forms of capital.[11]

What this indicates is that '[p]ower comes from below; ... there is no binary and all-encompassing opposition between rulers [brands] and ruled [consumers] at the root of power relations' (Foucault, 1978, p. 94): within the consumer's cultural landscape the power that is wielded with the exchange of forms of capital is imbued with the capacity to influence that possession of capital and, therefore, power. Because power is malleable and does not come 'from the top down' (Foucault, 1978, p. 94), the wielding of such power ebbs and flows between players in the cultural landscape. Who has the power within this space, between brands and consumers, alters according to the positions of the consumers, brands, and the topography of culture, including the mass connectivity of digital technology, which gives performative platforms to all those who own, or seek to own, capital in the cultural landscape.

---

[11] For more reading on class, status, and power relations see: Sørensen, 2019; Anderson et al., 2015; Mahalingham, 2003; and Aronowitz, 2003.

Conclusion

In exploring the interplay between perspective, capital, and power in the cultural branding landscape, several key themes emerge. Firstly, adopting multifaceted perspectives enables richer analysis of brand positioning and consumer relationships. Viewing brands through the lenses of firm strategy, consumer psychology, and sociocultural forces reveals nuances invisible from a single vantage point. Integrating these viewpoints highlights the complex calculus by which brands accrue value.

Secondly, capital operates as a crucial form of leverage within branding landscapes. Economic capital provides material resources, while social and cultural capital confer the intangible advantages of status, belonging, and distinction. The interconvertibility of capital types allows brands and consumers alike to strategically exchange one for another as they navigate the terrain. Possession of capital thus constitutes an influential asset. However, capital distribution follows its own logic, not necessarily aligning with merit or fairness. Consumers with higher levels of economic, social, or cultural capital possess ingrained advantages for accumulating additional capital. Yet capital alone does not determine power dynamics. This leads to the third theme around brands and consumers continually vying to stake claims of legitimacy. Advertising, as cultural interpreter, plays a key role in mediating this struggle.

Power manifests through diffuse channels, not just top-down authority. Consumers retain agency to bestow or withhold symbolic value. When brands lose cache as landmarks in the cultural geography, consumers reorient their own positioning accordingly. Still, those wielding capital tend to occupy privileged positions in shaping social reality. Hierarchies emerge but remain open to resistance and renegotiation.

Key Points

- To fully understand the role of brands and their complex relationships with consumers within the cultural landscape, we must consider varying perspectives that take into account the economic, the consumer, and the societal.
- Capital is a multifaceted asset that can be economic, social, cultural, or symbolic. Brands and consumers use different forms of capital

to navigate the cultural landscape, with capital acting as leverage that can be strategically converted and exchanged.

- Power in the cultural landscape is not a top-down process but is diffuse and often concealed within societal norms. Consumers have agency in the cultural landscape and can influence brand equity through their social and cultural capital.
- Advertising is an intermediary that both reflects and shapes cultural values.
- The cultural landscape is dynamic, shaped by the accumulation and exchange of capital, and is subject to constant renegotiation of power. Brands and consumers continuously work to assert their value and influence the cultural space.

4 | *The Role of Gender*

Marketing has always been about consumption; gender has always been about difference.

J. Kacen, Girrrl Power and Boyyy Nature: The Past, Present and Paradisal Future of Consumer Gender Identity, *Marketing Intelligence & Planning.*

At its heart, marketing is about consumption, the consumer, and moving a consumer to engage with a brand, product, or service in some measurable way. And, '[f]or most of marketing's modern history, women have been seen as consumers and consumption as a feminine activity, while men have been seen as producers ... and production as a masculine activity' (Kacen, 2000, p. 347). However, in the current age where the consumer's cultural landscape exists by combining the physical and the digital, the role of women as consumers and producers has altered.

The gendered nature of the consumer's cultural landscape has been researched in a variety of ways, including how men and women approach shopping differently (Dennis et al., 2018; Dholakia, 1999), their enjoyment of shopping as an activity (Brosdahl & Carpenter, 2011; Kotzé et al., 2012), how they shop online (Ellis et al., 2012; Passyn et al., 2011; Pradhana & Sastiono, 2019), how they assess online shopping risk (Garbarino & Strahilevitz, 2004), impulse buying (Atulkar & Kesari, 2018; Coley & Burgess, 2003; Ozdemir & Akcay, 2019), and what they buy (Karpinska-Krakowiak, 2021; Pinna, 2020). While all these aspects are valuable in developing an understanding of the gendered nature of the consumer's cultural landscape, here the focus is on the gendered aspects of brand equity and brand affinity in correlation with how brands are utilised by the consumer as landmarks for navigating through the cultural landscape. This navigation takes into account the consumer's self-identity and self-projection as these relate to their position and movement in the landscape, which in itself is a gendered consideration.

Everything Is Gendered

In order to fully explore the role gender plays in the consumer's navigation of their cultural landscape, the first thing to consider is the role of gender more widely, as everything is gendered in some format, and to realise that gender may differ from sex but they are interrelated. Historically, sex and gender first were used separately in the 1950s and 1960s in specialist literature on intersex and trans patients (Koh, 2012; Moi, 1999; Schiappa, 2022). Later, in the American Psychiatric Association's *Diagnostic and Statistical Manual of Mental Disorders* (DSM-III) in 1980, 'gender identity disorder' was listed as a 'disparity between anatomical sex and gender identity' (Koh, 2012, p. 673). In the DSM-V in 2013,[1] this disparity was renamed 'gender dysmorphia'.[2] The UK's Office of National Statistics (ONS, 2019) notes that '[s]ex and gender are terms that are often used interchangeably but they are in fact two different concepts'. Sex is often understood as the 'biological aspects of an individual as determined by their anatomy, which is produced by their chromosomes, hormones and their interactions' (ONS, 2019) and is expressed in culture as male and female (Morgenroth & Ryan, 2021). In recent years, this understanding of sex has expanded to include non-binary options or a third gender (Aboim, 2020; Elias & Colvin, 2020; Herdt, 2020), and sex, much like gender, is generally more accepted as having some fluidity, in that the way a consumer perceives their 'bodily sex' is not the only factor shaping the conception of their gender (Tacikowski et al., 2020), which is traditionally culturally expressed as man or woman (Morgenroth & Ryan, 2021).

Indeed, Butler (2008) indicates that sex can be conveyed by gender, but often gender is considered a binary that follows directly from sex. This proves to be problematic as the binary means of defining terms like sex and gender becomes more politicised in the

---

[1] The fifth edition is the most recent full edition, but in 2022 edits were made to the listing (in the DSM-5-TR (text revision)) on 'gender dysphoria' to include more culturally sensitive language around the topic (APA, 2022).

[2] For a more detailed history of the terms 'sex' and 'gender', as used together, see Schiappa, 2022, and Herdt, 2020.

consumer's daily life and influences the cultural landscape (Schiappa, 2022). While gender and sex are closely linked as terms, gender is often considered to be both the 'cultural interpretation of sex ... and gender identity' (Morgenroth & Ryan, 2021, p. 1115). As a term, 'gender combines reference to a social position [... of the individual and a behaviour] classically referred to as "masculinity" and "femininity"' (Harrison & Hood-Williams, 2002, p. 2); terminology that has been used to identify parts of a brand's personality (Alreck et al., 1982; Neale et al., 2016; Spielmann et al., 2021).

When 'gender is neither the causal result of sex nor as seemingly fixed as sex' (Butler, 2008, p. 8), and is instead the cultural meaning that a 'sexed body assumes' (Butler, 2008, p. 9), along the lines of man/woman or masculine/feminine, we can begin to break apart the concepts of sex and gender, with gender, as the cultural embodiment of the performed sex, being the area of interest in understanding the consumer within the cultural landscape and what we can identify in a brand's persona. It is the concept of gender in this landscape that becomes vital in the performance of gender identity as it relates to a consumer's self-identity and self-projection. In contrast, for brands, 'gender identity is a more effective dimension for customer segmentation than biological sex' (Neale et al., 2016, p. 347).

The focus on gender here is not to set aside the importance of sex, nor the intricate interrelation between sex and gender – as 'sex is always also affected by gender' (Morgenroth & Ryan, 2021, p. 1117), but, in the consumer's cultural landscape, the performance of gender identity, whether consciously or not, is part of what allows a consumer to relate to brands within this space and to utilise brands as landmarks to move around the changeable cultural landscape in relation to their self- and projected identities. A consumer's identity is always shifting based on how they perceive themselves and how they want to be seen – 'no category [is] as fundamental to social perception as gender' (Martin & Slepian, 2018, p. 1681) – and brands can play a role in this.

With this in mind, it is valuable to utilise Bem's lenses of gender to better understand how we expect all aspects of society and culture to be gendered. According to Bem, male and female experiences are the default neutral, and this 'androcentrism' leads societies to expand the male/female divide and cause it to be 'superimposed on so many aspects of the social world that a cultural connection is thereby forged between sex and virtually every other aspect of human experience' in a form of 'gender polarization' (Bem, 1993, p. 2). Most societies impose a level of biological essentialism that 'rationalizes gender polarization and male dominance by treating them as the natural consequences of the inherent biological sex differences' (Gaunt, 2006, p. 523).

As Martin and Slepian (2018, p. 1681) note, '[t]he propensity to "gender" – or conceptually divide entities by masculinity versus femininity – is pervasive'. Everything, from people and animals, to buildings, brands, clothes, books, and more 'are seen as gendered based on abstracted conceptual similarity' (Martin & Slepian, 2018, p. 1681). Humanity's readiness to define things as masculine or feminine partly derives from how prepped society is to 'process information on the basis of the sex-linked associations' (Bem, 1981, p. 355), including how one's self-concept, or self-identity, is gendered. Bem indicates that the gendered nature of self-identity comes from how we learn to apply the schematic dichotomy of masculine and feminine traits, as portrayed by the wider culture, to both our own worldview and self-identity.

By taking into account the proclivity for social institutions and organisations to place males and females into 'different and unequal life situations', individuals 'gradually internalize' society's pressure for androcentrism and gender polarisation (Bem, 1993, p. 3). This pressure manifests in the gendering of a consumer's worldview and all aspects within it, including the people, products, and brands they interact with, because '[b]rands are imbued with a gender identity' (Neale et al., 2016 p. 348), which is a distinct dimension of the brand (Levy, 1959).

Gendering of Brands More Widely

The study of the perceived femininity or masculinity of brands has been a part of the research into brand personality for decades. Brand personality, here, is defined as 'a set of human characteristics associated with a brand' (Aaker, 1997, p. 347), which is a construct developed by and within the societies in which brands and consumers interact. Based on our 'propensity to "gender"' (Martin & Slepian, 2018, p. 1681) and how easily consumers are able to think of brands as individuals or celebrities, and/or link brands to themselves, the personalities and gender a consumer associates with brands 'tend to be relatively enduring and distinct' (Aakar, 1997, pp. 347–348).

The way a brand is designed links to how the consumer perceives its gendered nature as part of the brand's personality. Each element of a brand contributes to its impression as masculine, feminine, or neutral, which, in turn, relates to the societal and cultural structures in which the brand exists. The logo of a brand is a key part of its brand identity and 'may induce brand gender associations' (César Machado et al., 2021, p. 153). For instance, Simonson and Schmitt (1997, p. 90) found that in relation to design features of a brand 'straight shapes are often perceived as masculine, sharp, abrupt, and choppy, while curved shapes are perceived as feminine, soft, and continuous'. The shape of a logo can indicate the gendering of a brand, where round is tied to femininity (women) and angular shapes to masculinity (men) (Lieven et al., 2015; Meiting & Hua, 2021; Slepian et al., 2011).

For example, the Barbie logo is pink and white and is either presented as an almost italicised script, or as looping text with soft edges and flourishes to the edge of letters, all of which code female and link the brand to the dolls it produces. Meanwhile, the parent brand, Mattel, is red and white, with strong blocky text and multiple sharp edges to the logo, coding masculine, as many of the brands in their portfolio also do (Flying Aces, GUTS!, Hot Looks, and more).

Font can also be an important part of brand recognition (Henderson et al., 2004; Tantillo et al., 1995; Wendt, 1968; Zaichkowsky, 2010) and can also be gendered for a consumer, where 'slender, round type fonts likely signal brand femininity, whereas heavier (i.e. boldface), angular fonts signal brand masculinity' (Lieven et al., 2015, p. 150). When fonts utilise script, this enhances a consumer's perception of the brand's association with the female gender. Grohmann (2016, p. 407) found that the type of font used 'strengthens the effect of a brand name with the gender associations on consumer response to the brand'. We can see this with book publishers such as Firefly Press, Grub Street, Polygon, and Pushkin Press, which have curved script in their logo, which can, in the consumer's mind, echo femininity. Bold, strong, or blocky logos such as Sandstone Press, Profile Books, Penguin Random House, and Kogan Page use display-type fonts that appear more masculine. More widely, brands such as Dove, Coca-Cola, and Cartier have curved, loping script in their logo, while Nike, FedEx, and Rolex display fonts that appear more masculine.

The font a brand chooses to spell out their logo gives indications of the gendering of the brand, as does the sound of the brand name itself. Brands 'containing front vowels (e.g. i, e) – as opposed to back vowels (e.g. o, u) – were perceived as more feminine' (Lieven et al., 2015, p. 150). Likewise, brand names that contain fricatives, voiceless stops, and voiceless fricatives,[3] all lead the consumer to consider the brand to be more feminine (Klink, 2000) – such as Fair Acres Press, Floral Street, Pixi, and Yves Saint Laurent.

The colours related to a brand also have gendered intonations. Colour is a powerful marketing tool, as '62–90 percent of the assessment [of an item] is based on colors alone' (Singh, 2006, p. 783) and the perceived gender of those colours influences how a consumer responds to the brand (Lieven et al., 2015). The sociocultural connections between darker blue and associated colours (such as the black in Gillette)[4] are seen as masculine and lighter pink as feminine (such as Victorina Press, with their purple-pink logo) as is evident in Western consumers' gendering of the brand (César Machado et al., 2021). A study by Hess and Melnyk (2016) found that including a feminine colour cue (such as pink in the Lyft logo) increased a product's perceived warmth.

Ethical consumers are drawn to the colour and word 'green', which signals that a product or a brand is considered 'ethical' (Sundar & Kellaris, 2015). The halo effect of the colour green brings to the consumer's mind positive connotations (De Bock et al., 2013), which is linked, in ethically branded products, to doing good, or at least not doing harm, environmentally, by supporting free trade or other such actions. Colours such as green 'for environmentally-friendly products decreases perceived masculinity' (Felix et al., 2022, p. 936), and female-identifying consumers tend to be more ethically sensitive (Bray et al., 2011). This femininity, as it is identified in a brand, 'significantly increases ethical intent, whereas masculinity has an opposite effect' (Pinna, 2020, p. 384). The use of green to appeal to female-identifying consumers is linked to the use of organic logo designs featuring commonly experienced objects, which enhances the feminine perception of the brand (César Machado et al., 2021).

---

[3] Fricatives are the f, s, v, and z sounds – whereas voiceless fricatives are f and s. Voiceless stops are p, t, and k (Klink, 2000, pp. 10–11).

[4] From a Western standpoint. For more information on cultural stereotyping of colours see Cunningham & Macrae, 2011.

Though cultural associations mark pink as feminine in ways that are often used to draw attention in the branding of products, this can, perhaps, be seen as post-feminist as female-identifying individuals embrace both the gendered connotation of the colour and a growing awareness of gender inequality and desire for female autonomy. Arguably, in the post-feminist era of the colour pink, it has become closely related to the gay subculture, recontextualising the colour with the gender identity of a masculine image or brand (Koller, 2008).

The nuances of a brand's look, personality, and equity can signal to consumers their gender personality before a customer considers what individual items the brand itself is selling.[5] Sweet Cherry Publishing's bright colours, sweeping logo font, and use of an organic object (the cherries) indicate that the brand is coded feminine before the consumer goes deeper into the website and reads the feminine-coded 'about' page or sees the child-focussed list.[6] Likewise, we can consider the brand Victoria's Secret, a lingerie, womenswear, and beauty products brand that has been ubiquitous with women's underwear since it was purchased by Leslie Wexner and became a cultural landmark in the consumer's cultural landscape. Originally, the brand was developed to create a more comfortable environment for men to buy lingerie for a woman. In 1983, under Wexner, the brand was revamped to become much more like the Victoria's Secret that took over malls and shopping centres in America in the late 1990s and 2000s. The brand name, pre-2009, was written in pink capital glyphs with thin serifs, which indicate the femininity of the brand, while the graphic logo takes the thin serifs of the written logo's 'V' and wraps it in the loops of an 'S' without sharp edges. The current brand font retains

---

[5] The gender of a brand is one of several aspects of the wider brand personality, but it is the one that is most pertinent to understanding how gender identity works in the consumer's cultural landscape. For more information on the dimensions of brand personality see Aaker, 1997; Geuens et al., 2009; Eisend & Stokburger-Sauer, 2013; and for how these brand personality dimensions exist in other cultures see Chu & Sung, 2011; Muniz & Marchetti, 2012; and Mohtar et al., 2019.

[6] As part of the methodology of this chapter, the 'about' pages were scraped from all UK and Irish publishers (486 after cleaning) and the data was run through a script with gender-coded root words from Gaucher et al.'s 2011 study on gendered wording in advertising. This coded each page as 'masculine', 'feminine', or 'neutral'.

the elegant thin lines, but in a black colour to stand out against the feminine, pink colour palate. 'The visible markers of gender – [... are] carefully curated to give off a distinct and coherent message for both the recipient and the producer' (Lawes, 2019, p. 256).

With Victoria's Secret there is a direct link between the gendered brand identity and the products aimed mostly towards female-identifying consumers, and how those two areas connect with the consumers' self-identity and self-projection in a myriad of complex, performative interactions that can lead to an affinity for particular brands. It should, however, be noted that it is not always the case that a brand's visual gender indicators match their marketing. For instance, the Folio Society's colour and sharp angles of the font code masculine, while the swirling logo codes feminine, and the text on their 'about' page codes masculine. Likewise, cleaning brand Mr Muscle codes masculine, though the brand itself is most likely to be purchased and used by females.[7]

An Affinity for Gendered Brands

Though there is a lack of academic research on the topic of brand affinity as a whole, it is a term that is often bandied about by marketers and advertisers. However, research has been done on related areas such as brand love (Bairrada et al., 2019; Batra et al., 2012; Huang, 2019; Palusuk et al., 2019) and brand attachment (Hemsley-Brown, 2023; Japutra et al., 2014; Park et al., 2008). With over 40 million hits on the term 'brand affinity' on Google,[8] it is worth diving into in more detail to understand how this term relates to companies within the consumer's cultural landscape by first defining it. Aaker and Biel (1993, p. 3) consider brand affinity to be a 'type of consumer esteem based on the sentiments of likeability, suitability, and trust', while Horoszko et al. (2018) calls it a 'metaphor for the proximity that a woman can feel toward a brand'.

Affinity is often considered as a liking or sympathy for, or connection to, a particular brand or its message (Levin, 2020) and can be understood as the 'emotional and intangible benefits of a brand'

---

[7] Based on Armstrong's (2018) report on UK's dividing up of housework gender roles and further supported by a wider EU survey of gendered housework in 2018.

[8] Searched 22 December 2022.

(Leone et al., 2006, p. 4). These emotional and intangible benefits that a brand provides a consumer are the authority or reputation of the brand, how close the consumer's self-identity or self-projection is tied to them, and the space the brand takes up as a landmark in the consumer's cultural landscape (Leone et al., 2006).

In this book, affinity with a brand is defined as a means of leveraging a consumer's preferences in order to build a beneficial relationship with them so that the consumer feels a growing attachment to the brand (Musicco, 2021), which can develop in relation to their own gender identity and that of the perceived gender identity of the brand.

The way a consumer makes purchase decisions is gendered and consumers rely on brands and their products to help perform their own gender identity (Lorber, 1994), where the consumer uses brands to 'adorn [... their] gender displays with brands as tangible markers' (Avery, 2012, p. 323). As the consumer utilises brands as landmarks in their cultural landscape to position themselves, they develop an affinity for the brand that is, perhaps unconsciously, gendered. However, as discussed, all brands, products, and most concepts are gendered in some way. In the gendering of a brand, affinity for them can grow into brand pride (Nandy & Sondhi, 2022)[9] and even take on elements of a higher power with the concept of brand sacredness (Wang et al., 2019).[10]

Affinity for a brand, as related to the brand's gender identity, is not universal. Research has found that 'using feminine brands carries a greater stigma for men than using masculine brands does for women', though 'both men and women prefer brands that express their own gender identity' (Avery, 2012, p. 323). Some brands exude femininity through their logos, fonts, colour schemes, marketing, semiotics, and personality, such as Victoria's Secret, Dove, and Cartier, and are more likely to have female-identifying consumers develop an affinity with them; while brands like Harley Davidson, Vacheron Constantin, and Axe body spray are perceived

---

[9] Brand pride is linked to the repeated use of 'me' in relation to the brand along with a feeling of personal connection to the brand and self-congruence (both inward and outward) – these elements, among others, develop into the concept of brand pride (Nandy & Sondhi, 2022).

[10] Brand sacredness is related to a 'transcendent consumer experience, defense of [a] brand, incorporation [of a] brand in [an] extended-self, brand ritualism and brand evangelism' (Wang et al., 2019, p. 733).

as masculine and will draw in male-identifying consumers. In the luxury market, the link between a consumer's purchasing decision and social consequences, in the sense that going against one's gender presentation is not in alignment with social norms, is not straightforward and 'ultimately depends on the consumption habits' of the consumer's peers (Postlewaite, 2011, p. 243).

Not all brands can develop cross-gender brand extensions in the same way,[11] and the degree to which they can develop an affinity across genders is based on the brand's openness, the values they propose, and how those values are shared across genders (Veg-Sala & Roux, 2018). Female-identifying consumers tend to be more accepting of cross-gender extensions of brands wherein a publisher such as Haynes publishes car manuals and also lifestyle books (Jung, 2006), whereas male-identifying consumers may be less likely to accept a publisher such as Haynes including small feminine elements through their move into lifestyle guides.

Likewise, those consumers who adhere more to 'traditional gendered attitudes' (Ulrich, 2013, p. 794) are more unwilling to accept publishers that challenge their notions of gender roles, and some traditionally masculine consumers even find feminine brands somewhat threatening (Ulrich & Tissier-Desbordes, 2018). The backlash to cross-gender brand extensions is seen when consumers consider such a move by brands to be 'gender contamination [which] threatens this shared interpretation of a brand's meaning' (Avery, 2012, p. 324; see also De Alwis and Ramanathan, 2019); this makes it harder for the average consumer to utilise that brand in their cultural landscape as a landmark for moving towards their self-identity and/or self-projection.

Those consumers who have the financial capability to purchase items that they feel best reflects their self-identity and self-projection are more able to step outside the realm of social and gender norms in their cultural landscape in a consequence-free manner (Harrington, 2018), and in their defiance they can, in turn, influence those wider social norms; for example, male-identifying readers purchasing books with pink covers or female shoppers buying men's designer watches. Part of the social influence those consumers with more

---

[11] For more information on cross-gender brand extensions see Frieden, 2013; Veg & Nyeck, 2007; Reghunathan & Joseph, 2017; and Yuen et al., 2019.

purchasing power have is in indicating that some brands can be represented as safe spaces in a consumer landscape.

Gender as a 'Safe Space' in the Consumer Landscape

The gendered way that consumers utilise digitally social spaces is not isolated from the ways that consumers navigate brand as landmarks in their cultural landscapes. As consumers move to accommodate their self-identity and self-projection, they begin to establish which brands are safe spaces with which to align with their identity. Female-identifying consumers are more likely to test unfamiliar brands and try new products (Karpinska-Krakowiak, 2021) and have 'found some dominance within areas of "social media entrepreneurship"' (Tuite, 2021, p. 421). This dominance is related to the cultural values these communities share in ways that brands can exploit to spur word-of-mouth (WOM) communication among like-minded consumers. In the brand community, defined as a 'specialized non-geographically bound community that is based on a structured set of social relations among admires of a brand' (Muniz & O'Guinn, 2001, p. 412), advice may be given based on socially accepted gender roles in digital settings, where men should act and women should talk (Eisenchlas, 2013).

Both online and offline, 'how a woman interacts with products can supersede what she consumes' and it is the 'camaraderie and emotional support that women find by gathering socially' (D'Antonio, 2019, p. 2) that creates a feeling of a safe community in which to locate their identity. When this feeling of safety is wrapped up with a brand, and the products they release, it can give consumers confidence in aligning themselves with that brand. The brand can then act as a landmark of shelter, acceptance, and space from which to speak within their cultural landscape.

Part of the power to speak within the cultural landscape is due to the language patterns accepted as part of the community in which consumers finds themselves as they navigate between wider brand landmarks. Female-gendered language patterns have been found to 'establish a sense of belonging, thus a sense of safety' (Workman, 2014, p. 49). The platforms on which brands advertise to create structural narratives dictate the ways in which consumers will interact with brands and their products. For instance, Bode (2017) found that female-identifying users were less likely to post new content than male-identifying users, but were just as likely to discreetly engage with content by liking and commenting. On platforms with a higher male-to-female ratio, such as Twitter/X, where globally it is 56.4 per cent male (Dixon, 2022), females are less willing to enter into any uncomfortable or conflicting situations, which are more likely to arise among the weaker ties on the platform. However, the gender gap is less prominent on Facebook (Koc-Michalska et al., 2021, p. 207).

While brand communities have found proliferation in digital settings, they overlap, but are not synonymous, with virtual communities (Ouwersloot & Schröder, 2008, p. 572). However, we can use digital settings as a lens to understand how brand communities become safe spaces for consumers based on how consumers approach their brand personality, of which gender is a large part. Female-identifying users are more likely to venture outwith their area of comfort to seek out and engage with brands that do not have prominent locations in the consumer's cultural landscape, such as small, independent brands.

Those brands that are able to go beyond 'drawing on essentialist assumptions of the inherent differences between men and women' (Mullany, 2004, p. 302) and see female-identifying consumers as more than passive receivers of content and communication are those that will be able to embed their brand as landmarks in consumers' cultural landscape and stand out as places to which consumers can look to align their performance of self- and projected identities and find other like-minded consumers.[12]

The Consumer's Performance of a Gendered Self

The concept of the 'performative' was coined by English philosopher J. L. Austin in his lecture series in the 1950s (Loxley, 2007; Pilgrim, 2001). While Austin outlined the performative into a 'theory of "speech acts"' (Loxley, 2007, p. 2), others such as Derrida took this theory further, deconstructed it, and applied it to literary theory. Beyond this, Jackson underscores the process of '*repetition*

---

[12] Passive reception in marketing literature considers a variety of angles such as passive reception and multitasking (Bardhi et al., 2010; Chinchanachokchai et al., 2015) and the passivity of the consuming audience (Puustinen, 2005).

[… which] is not simply a performance *by* a subject but a performance that *constitutes* a subject and *produces* a space of conflicting subjectivities' (Jackson, 2004, p. 675; original emphasis). Butler's consideration of performance is most pertinent in relation to gender identity in that 'not biology, but culture, becomes destiny' (Butler, 2008, p. 11) as we cannot consider our physical bodies outside of the cultural constructs in which they exist. Where '[o]ur identities are not given by nature or simply represented or expressed in culture: instead, culture is the process of identity formation, the way in which bodies and selves in all their differences are produced' (Loxley, 2007, p. 118). As a process of identity formation, the way people internalise and interpret culture through their gender expression is a performance directly related to the interaction between their culture and products, self-identity, and self-projection.

'Gender reality is performative which means, quite simply, that it is real only to the extent that it is performed' (Butler, 1988, p. 527); this concept plays a significant role in how a consumer identifies and situates themselves in the cultural landscape. As Grohmann (2016, p. 403) notes, 'consumers use masculine or feminine brands to reinforce their self-concept [… and] to express their masculinity/femininity'. Much consideration of the performance of self comes from the field of theatre and performance studies, which looks at, among other areas, performance and the audience.[13] While performance can be used to challenge the status quo, it is also often used to uphold the accepted values of the cultural institutions in which it exists (Feinberg, 2020). In the performance of gender we see this manifest in the brands and items a consumer chooses to purchase, or in the brands with which they align themselves. The very nature of purchasing products, or aligning oneself with a brand, is a performative act that is concerned with maintaining a consumer's self-projection to an audience (Goffman, 1990). This forms a consumer identity, which is 'sustainable only to the extent that it can be expressed in practice' (Klein et al., 2007, p. 29).

The performance of a consumer's self-identity and self-projection are intricately related to how they position themselves in their cultural landscape and how they use brands in that space as landmarks

---

[13] For more on theatre and performance studies, see Leach, 2013; Balme, 2008; Bottoms, 2003; and Solga, 2019, for an introduction into some of the key concepts in this area.

to move around, come closer to, or move further away from the alignment of their self-identity and self-projection. This is not to say that all consumers seek to align their self-identity and self-projection, some consumers seek to develop their identity across different personas and can use brands and products to accomplish this. Studies by Mulder and Yaar (2006) and Marshall et al. (2019), and the works published in Deakin University's *Persona Studies* journal, have shown that some people actively seek to distance how they identify themselves from the way they are perceived by others.

With this in mind, the consumer's identity can be defined as any category label that they associate with, which can be chosen by them or bestowed upon them (Reed et al., 2012; Wheeler & Bechler, 2021) This leads to identity-driven performances in relation to publishing brands, which includes:

> increased attention to identity-related stimuli ... a preference for identity-linked brands ... and more positive reactions to advertisements featuring spokespeople who possess the desired identity ... the selection of media catering to the desired identity ... the adoption of behaviors linked to an identity ... and biased attention toward identity-consistent memories. (Reed et al., 2012, p. 310)

There are a large variety of identities with which the consumer can align themselves,[14] and each of these performative identities can be classified in myriad ways depending on the associations linked to those terms. But it is not just cultural and social norms that guide a consumer's self-identity and self-projection in the cultural landscape: identity is also connected to brands that can 'serve as identity-expression vehicles [... and] indicators of life events and relationships' (Wheeler & Bechler, 2021, p. 6). The materialism of obtaining, possessing, and showing off objects as performance indicates that self-identity is related to a consumer's life narrative or goals. Those objects that anchor consumers to an identity can be understood in terms of the gendered self-identity and self-projection of the individual (Silver, 1996). Because once the consumer has adopted an identity (which may or may not relate to, or fulfil, their

---

[14] For an overview of the literature in the area of identity principles see Reed et al., 2012's chart (p. 314), which lists the relevant research into the five key identity principles of salience, association, relevance, verification, and conflict.

self-projection), 'the surrounding environment [where they are within their cultural landscape] and the people and objects [brands] in it are evaluated for their relevance with respect to the identity' (Reed et al., 2012, p. 319).

The performative nature of the consumer's movement towards their self-identity is only able to exist on a stage (the consumer's cultural landscape) where 'everyone performs [... and] everyone spectates' (Feinberg, 2020, p. 334). The consumer's identity performance is 'inherently embodied and contextually dependent [... on and] embedded in physical architecture and reinforced through the audience' (Boyd & Heer, 2006). It is a communication of behaviours that are directly linked to, or in opposition to, social norms. In the consumer's cultural landscape these social norms are tied up in who the consumer think they are and how they want to be seen, using brands, products, objects, and services those brands may represent to embody their identity in an authentic way.

Conclusion

In the consumer's cultural landscape the concept of consuming is often gendered as feminine, and much research has been dedicated to the roles of sex and gender in advertising and consumption spaces. Everything is gendered, from the way consumers identify themselves to the products they purchase and share. Though this gendering is accepted in research, brands must note that gender is different from sex. Drawing on Butler and Bem, among others, we see that there is a social drive for androcentrism and a gender polarisation that is embedded in Western social norms, where consumers are predisposed to the gendering of their worldview and all that resides within it.

Some brands lean into the gendered element of their brand personality and make active choices to design their brand to engage with gendering elements such as design, fonts, and colours that bring aspects of a particular gender to the consumer's mind. This is not done blindly, as consumers tend to relate more closely to brands that reflect their own self- or projected identities. This helps to form a consumer's affinity for a brand, which can be leveraged to develop an attachment and increase loyalty.

An element of the connection between brands and the affinity that a consumer develops is related to how safe they feel with the brand in relation to the gendered aspects of the brand and the products it creates. Part of the power consumers have to speak and present their self- and projected identities within the cultural landscape comes down to the language used by the brands and by other consumers in the brand's community, and how those linguistic elements feed into the sense of refuge (or not) a consumer feels by aligning themselves with them. This feeling of safety also extends to, and is informed by, the platforms that the brand uses to communicate and the unwritten rules of engagement on those platforms.

The consumer can utilise brands as landmarks to understand which spaces are safe for them to perform their chosen self- and projected identities and to form relationships based on these considerations. Ultimately, the consumer enacts a gendered performance of self in their cultural landscape and, in doing so, they can choose to interact with brands that embody different gendered elements within a complex discourse of consumerism, societal norms and expectations, and perceptions.

Key Points

- Traditionally, marketing has viewed women primarily as consumers and men as producers, with consumption seen as a feminine activity and production as masculine. However, with the merging of physical and digital realms, women's roles as both consumers and producers are evolving.
- The terms sex and gender are interrelated but distinct, with sex referring to biological aspects and gender to cultural interpretations and identities. In the cultural landscape there is increasing acceptance of gender fluidity and this performance of gender influences how consumers interact with brands.
- Brands often have gendered identities, which influence consumer perception and attachment. Brands can use elements such as logos, fonts, and so on to communicate and align with cultural definitions of masculinity and femininity.
- Consumers can develop affinities for brands that align with their gender identities, affecting their loyalty and purchasing behaviours. This affinity is informed by the brand's perceived gender identity and can lead to a deeper emotional connection between the consumer and the brand.

- Brands can create 'safe spaces' for consumers by providing a sense of belonging within their cultural landscape. Female-identifying consumers in particular may seek out brands that offer a sense of community and support, which can lead to brand loyalty and advocacy.

Discussion Questions

1. Choose a brand that you use every day. How does the brand's logo shape, colour, fonts, and even the text on their websites and social platforms indicate a gender? How might these elements align or conflict with consumers' different gender identities?
2. In what ways can brands navigate the complex interplay between gender identity and biological sex to effectively segment their market and build brand affinity without reinforcing harmful gender stereotypes? Consider this in relation to multinational and local brands.

Case Study 1

Gender
Virgin Atlantic and Bud Light

Advertising remains 'haunted by the ghosts of *Mad Men*'.
Boulton quoted in L. Gurrieri and F. Finn, Gender transformative advertising pedagogy: promoting gender justice through marketing education, *Journal of Marketing Management*

We're customers too. I know a lot of trans and queer people who love beer.
D. Mulvaney, 'Happy March Madness!!'

In 1979 Goffman published his landmark work *Gender Advertisements*; with this work he sampled hundreds of print-based, photographic ads that indicated that in ads women were mostly portrayed as subordinate to men. Over the next several decades researchers took up his framework 'as a theoretical barometer for detecting, analyzing, and quantifying gender stereotyping in mass media images' (Butkowski, 2020, p. 90), and work on gender-based content analysis and research into gender stereotyping in advertisements has since been abundant (Grau & Zotos, 2018; Neuendorf, 2002). Within this research into gender roles and gender stereotyping in advertising there are two points of view that can dictate how marketing departments seek to employ gender in their ads: mirroring and moulding. From the point of view of mirroring, we can say that advertising is less manipulative and simply mirrors the society in which it exists, even if that mirror also distorts (Pollay, 1986). In contrast, the view that advertisements actively mould society highlights that 'people's perception of social reality is shaped by the media' that they consume (Grau & Zotos, 2018, p. 762).

When the medium in which content is shared is also part of the messaging we have to consider the platforms on which advertisements are shared and the user demographics of those spaces (McLuhan, 2013).

If we consider the mirror vs mould points of view as a continuum instead of existing as entirely separate poles, we can more easily understand how the influence of society and advertisements work in both directions at different points in time, on different platforms, and within different spaces in the cultural landscape.

For instance, research into gendered advertising has found that ads that match a consumer's values are those to which the consumer is more likely to respond favourably (Garaus & Wolfsteiner, 2023). As conceptions of gender alter in society, and as we (in the West) are more likely to consider gender as a fluid concept that can be divorced from sex, the advertising industry has begun to walk the line where the continuum of mirroring and moulding come together. Where this is successful, multinational companies are able to both reflect the changing values of the societies in which they operate and push the boundaries of what that society is willing to accept in their media marketing.

Organisations such as Virgin Atlantic and Anheuser-Busch (specifically looking at the brand Bud Light[1]) are two examples of companies that have been exploring the spaces where mirroring and moulding come together by helping to amplify diverse voices in their promotional materials on a national and international stage. They seem to embrace 'femvertising'[2] in some campaigns as an advertising style that 'accentuates women's talents, spreads pro-woman messages and decimates stereotyping of women' (Varghese & Kumar, 2022, p. 441). The move towards femvertising indicates that brands such as Virgin Atlantic and Bud Light are aware of the role that brand responsibility and alignment to social issues play in how a consumer makes a decision regarding their brand (Champlin et al., 2019). That being said, both Virgin Atlantic and Bud Light have taken further steps in order to go beyond only empowering female-identifying consumers in their marketing. They do so by explicitly engaging with non-binary, gender-fluid, and transgender representations alongside their brand.

---

[1] The parent company is Anheuser-Busch, but the brand that collaborated with influencer Dylan Mulvaney was Bud Light. The rest of this case study will refer to the brand as Bud Light.

[2] For more detailed research on aspects of 'femvertising' see Hainneville & Guèvremont, 2023; Randhawa, 2023; Gabrina & Gayatri, 2023; Sobande, 2019; Sterbenk et al., 2022; and Gwynne, 2022; among many others.

With this in mind, this case study focusses on Virgin Atlantic and Bud Light's advertisements in the 2020s, with a focus on the role that gender plays in particular pieces. Virgin Atlantic's 'See the World Differently' ad of April 2022 and their later September 2022 updated gender-identity policy release video are emphasised here; while for Bud Light we look at their 2023 Dylan Mulvaney 'Easy Carry Contest' and the backlash following its release.

Virgin Atlantic

Virgin Atlantic (2023) has always been a disruptor of the airline industry, seeking to 'come in and shake things up' with their launch into the UK market in 1984. Their focus was to inspire the public to fly, to enable their staff to have personalities, and to use their parent brand's marketing and public relations abilities to their advantage. Though over the years they have toned down their 'cheeky language' (Virgin Atlantic, 2023), they have become a leader in diversity and inclusion in the airline industry and the second most popular airline operating in the UK after British Airways in the first quarter (Q1) of 2023 (YouGov, 2023), with revenue in 2022 almost reaching the pre-pandemic levels of nearly £2,854 million (Virgin Atlantic, 2023).

Virgin Atlantic has a high share of Millennial customers and is more popular among male airline customers (at 57 per cent compared to the wider industry split of 50 per cent). They have a higher share of high-income customers than other airlines and these customers tend to have a college degree (66 per cent). Nine per cent of Virgin Atlantic customers consider themselves to be part of the LGBTQ+ community (Statista A, 2023),[3] and studies have shown that those with higher education are more tolerant of diverse sexualities and lifestyles (Dejowski, 1992; Lian, 2022; Ohlander et al., 2005). Likewise 24 per cent of Virgin Atlantic customers are innovators or early adopters of new products and technology and they tend to be centrist in their political views (Statista A, 2023).

With a thorough understanding of who their customers are and what they want from an airline, in 2022, working to make environmental, social, and corporate governance (ESG) as effective

---

[3] Higher than wider-category users at 8 per cent (Statista, 2023).

as possible, creative company Lucky Generals developed Virgin Atlantic's 'See the World Differently' ad as a launch that would kick off a series of tangible actions for the airline by focussing on the 'amazing people – customers and crew – who fly their own path' (Lucky Generals, 2022). Released in April 2022, just as air travel was beginning to pick back up post-pandemic, the sixty-second TV ad saw a group of charismatic cast and crew members happily doing their own thing as the song 'I Am What I Am' plays. The focus of the ad and the accompanying stills and digital images from home films, showcase how each and every customer and crew member are individuals and are treated as such by Virgin Atlantic. The ad highlights that Virgin Atlantic encourages everyone to be themselves in a way that sets the airline apart from other, more impersonal, airlines.

The ad has a nod to the airline's classic red lipstick and the relaxing of makeup guidelines in 2019 at the beginning of the spot, which serves to set the premise and theme as the story moves through the airport in a recognisable sequence of milestones (preparing, security, concourse, and the flight itself). This is followed by two passengers having a connection while walking to their gates, a wheelchair that is bedazzled gliding along, a professional woman setting off the metal detectors only to stick out her tongue and showcase her tongue piercings. The ad ends with the face of a female pilot at the controls as the plane glides onwards to its destination. This last image alludes to the work that is being done to make piloting a more inclusive field, though 2022 numbers indicate that of over 104,498 commercial pilots worldwide, only 8.54 per cent of them are female (Pilot Institute, 2023). These numbers are low and something that Virgin Atlantic has worked to raise by implementing a women's network group that is 'committed to supporting the advancement of women throughout Virgin Atlantic' (Virgin Atlantic, n.d.).[4]

The 'See the World Differently' ad itself was considered a success in marketing terms, landing in the top 10 per cent of ads in the 2022 Ipsos' creative database in the UK, and having a score of 185 on the Creative Effect Index and of 184 on the Equity Effect Index – these

---

[4] Ironically, in the list of major airlines with the highest share of female pilots worldwide, Virgin Atlantic does not even make the list (International Society of Women Airline Pilots, 2021).

scores are out of 200, where the averages range between 70–130 (Ipsos, 2023). As Ipsos ad-of-the-year 2022, this ad showcased how to do the social aspect of ESG well. In staying true to ESG advertising there are three principles that ads such as 'See the World Differently' adhere to: 'be true to the facts, true to the people, and true to the brand' (Ipsos, 2023).

As an ad that delivers an experience that is creative, unique, and differentiates the brand, it takes users on a journey that showcases the authenticity of real people. In doing so, it becomes the 'kind of work that not only successfully underlines that diversity drives creativity; but whose strategy and approach can serve to drive the industry forward towards a truly inclusive future' (Kemp, 2023).

One of the unique aspects of Virgin Atlantic's 'See the World Differently' campaign is its role as a kick-starter for more inclusive policy changes the company launched in following months. Because Virgin Atlantic thrives on the strength of difference, their Be Yourself Manifesto of 2022 highlights the importance of crew and customers' sense of belonging, representation, and 'being proudly themselves' across all aspects of diversity. The push for social equity in the ecosystem of Virgin Atlantic is a driving force behind their September 2022 updated gender-identity policy.

Launched with a campaign featuring a video and social media posts featuring Michelle Visage,[5] the thirty-second social campaign video shows a diverse cast of crew members and Visage dressed in variations of Virgin Atlantic uniforms that they feel comfortable in, regardless of gender, gender identity, or sexual orientation. Alongside this, crew, pilots, and ground team are able to choose whether to don the classic red, or a burgundy, version of the Vivienne Westwood-designed looks. They will also be able to opt in to wearing pronoun badges, and Virgin Atlantic will enable customers with gender-neutral passports to select that option on ticketing. In addition, Virgin Atlantic rolled out mandatory inclusivity training across its organisation, and works with tourism and hotel partners to help ensure LGBTQ+ travellers feel safe and welcome. To begin with, the uniform policy was rolled out in the UK, USA, and Israel, with other destinations considered on a risk and safety basis (BBC News, 2022).

---

[5] Singer and TV personality famous for co-hosting *Ru Paul's Drag Race*.

The longer, one-minute, forty-second campaign video includes short comments from Visage; Jaime Forsstroem, a cabin crew member; Tyreece Nye, a non-binary performer and activist, Alison Porte, a first officer; and Tanya Compas, a youth worker, highlighting what the campaign means to them, giving it personalisation and a grounding of authenticity. In doing this, Virgin Atlantic has taken an active role in moving towards the edges of authenticity by considering its customers and what they want and expect from a brand they support. This allows the brand to put down roots in a less-populated, but growing, part of the consumer's cultural landscape, enabling it to become a landmark brand within the space, which consumers can use to move their self-identity and self-projection more into alignment.

Not only was this ad a success culturally, it had hundreds of thousands of views of both the shorter and longer videos, and high engagement on social posts. Likewise, Ipsos, along with SeeHer, has found that ads with higher GEM (gender equality measure) scores, such as these from Virgin Atlantic, are more likely to drive 'choice intent and brand relationships, [which can impact] short-term sales and build ... stronger long-term success' (SeeHer & Ipsos, 2022).

Bud Light

Bud Light is a light beer offering from the larger brewer Anheuser-Busch. As a parent company, Anheuser-Busch (2023) focusses on making a 'meaningful impact in the world. [Where they ...] hope to build a future that everyone can celebrate, and everyone can share.' While the wording in their company profile indicates that acceptance and inclusivity are a key part of the brand, their corporate social responsibility (CSR) focusses on providing emergency drinking water, environmental sustainability, responsible drinking, and economic impact – all of which appeal to their Millennial customers. Recent marketing campaigns for Bud Light have tapped into the Millennial market, with nearly 50 per cent of consumers in that age range being a brand enthusiast and, of those enthusiasts, 60 per cent are men (Statista, 2023). As the second most recognised and second most popular brand in the beer market (in the USA), Bud Light performs better than the industry average in all categories except loyalty, where it did not make the top ten (Statista, 2023). Some of the reasons for this are the growth of the craft beer market and the way younger drinkers have begun to support more local breweries for perceived quality and sustainability (Carneiro, 2020). The number of breweries in the USA grew from 4,847 in 2015 to 9,906 in 2022 (Brewers Association, 2023), a 3.7 per cent upward shift from 2021–2022; while large/non-craft breweries dropped 9.8 per cent in that same timeframe. Yet another reason that loyalty may be lacking as a key performance indicator (KPI) for Bud Light is that Gen X and Baby Boomers are less keen on remaining loyal to the brand, particularly as drinkers can view beer brands as interchangeable (Bernstein, 2023).

Dylan Mulvaney and the #EasyCarryContest Instagram Partnership

Dylan Mulvaney is a US content creator and trans activist. She has 10.4 million followers on TikTok, with 491.3 million likes across her content. She has 1.8 million followers on Instagram and 8,480 followers on YouTube, though here she has only posted 7 videos.[6] As a trans content creator, Mulvaney has been posting videos of her life in her first year of transitioning on her TikTok and Instagram accounts, culminating in a video posted on 13 March 2023 that runs through her year of changes, leading to a glamourous reveal image on a red carpet with the E! logo in the top right-hand corner followed by her joyous celebrations.

In response to her celebratory video, Bud Light sent Mulvaney a custom can of Bud Light with her likeness on it. Following the gift, Mulvaney partnered with Bud Light to create a promotional campaign that supported their 'Bud Light Carry' ad. The 'Bud Light Carry' ad was a thirty-second video creative from media agency Anomaly, which featured a woman carrying five full pints of Bud Light through a crowded bar. As part of this promotion, in an Instagram post Dylan Mulvaney carried Bud Light cans to a table and talked about sports in a comedic and accessible fashion for non-sports followers. This post highlighted the fact that Bud Light was giving away $15,000 in a competition. Consumers had to post videos of themselves carrying as many Bud Lights they could on Facebook, Instagram, or Twitter,

---

[6] As of November 2023.

tagging @BudLight (Mulvaney, 2023). The winner was to be chosen based on their '[a]lignment of the brand (personifying easy enjoyment); effort into attempting the challenge; having fun and positive energy' (Calling All Contestants, 2023).

It is useful to note that this is not the first creative piece from Mulvaney that was part of a Bud Light partnership. On 11 February 2023, she posted a stitched, reaction video to Bud Light's Super Bowl ad featuring actor Miles Teller and his wife dancing to hold music while drinking Bud Light. This ad aired on Bud Light's YouTube channel on 2 February 2023, while the thirty-second spot featured at the 2023 Super Bowl, on 12 February 2023. The Instagram post by Mulvaney has half the screen taken up by the 'Easy to Hold' ad, while the other half has her reacting, while dancing in a tub with a stack of Bud Light beers behind her. The caption reads: 'only @ budlight could have a commercial so catchy it makes you wanna dance in the tub! go vote #easytoenjoy 10/10 at the link in my bio #budlightpartner'.

In both the 11 February 2023 Instagram posting and the later 1 April 2023 post, Mulvaney tags @budlight in the comment, with #budlightpartner as a hashtag, indicating that this is a collaborative promotion for the brand. While the 11 February post received only 35,481 likes,[7] the second #EasyCarryContest post garnered 195,366 likes and thousands of comments.[8] However, this second video also caught the attention of conservative individuals and outlets during what Mulvaney (2023) says 'must have been a slow news week'. While the wider reach of the second Mulvaney/Bud Light video might have had paid spend behind it to boost its reach, the amount of backlash on the ad was unexpected and was directly related to Mulvaney being a trans creator.

Reactions, Backlash, and Fallout

On 28 April 2023, Mulvaney shared a video on Instagram in which, while she does not mention Bud Light or the backlash directly, she does speak of experiencing a hard time, going offline, and how dehumanising it can be when people refuse to see her humanity. Later, in a video released on her TikTok account on 29 June

[7] As of November 2023.   [8] As of November 2023.

2023 Mulvaney broke her silence on the backlash from her second Instagram brand partnership with Bud Light. In the video she says that '[w]hat transpired from that video was more bullying and transphobia than I could have ever imagined ... I was scared of more backlash and I felt personally guilty for what transpired'. She goes on to say that she was

waiting for the brand to reach out to me, but they never did.... For a company to hire a trans person and then not publicly stand by them is worse, in my opinion, than not hiring a trans person at all, because it gives customers the permission to be as transphobic and hateful as they want.... To turn a blind eye and pretend everything is okay, it just isn't an option right now. (Mulvaney, 2023)

This TikTok video from Mulvaney came out nearly three months after the time she posted the #EasyCarryContest video on her Instagram. In it she calls out Bud Light for their lack of support and the parent company Anheuser-Busch's 'milquetoast' statement saying they work with many influencers across their brand to 'authentically connect with audiences across various demographics and passion points' (Flood & Kornick, 2023). Here Bud Light has tread the line between pushing the boundary of authenticity with some of their more conservative consumers by partnering with Mulvaney; in doing so, for this conservative group, they have aligned Mulvaney with the 'chaotic edge' of their brand's authenticity. Though most US-based Bud Light drinkers are Millennials and Gen X men (Statista B, 2023), more of half of US beer drinkers will be college graduates (74 per cent) with an income over $40,000, and 65 per cent attend a religious service nearly weekly/monthly (Brenan, 2023). Bud Light recognised that, at 13 per cent, they have a higher proportion of LGBTQIA+ identifying consumers than the industry average (Statista B, 2023), though they did not consider that 'authenticity bending' works both for and against the brand, depending on the contextualisation of the consumers, where they are in the cultural landscape, and what other factors come into play within that space.

Arguably, Virgin Atlantic came out with a much more focussed ad campaign that homes in on rights, well-being, and equality for LGBTQIA+ staff and customers, and any backlash stayed – mostly within – conservative echo chambers with some platforms, such as the Mail Online, quoting flyers who suggest 'I bet pilots would rather have a pay rise than this' and that customers would prefer lower fares

(Haigh, 2022). There was some negative commentary on Twitter, but, overall, the positive reception of the ad comes through both in the general public sentiment as well as in the award from Ipsos the campaign garnered. This is due to the fact that Virgin Atlantic took their users on a journey by including the influencers and authentic representations within the ad itself, fully aligning the brand to the presentations of those within it instead of using a paid partnership that could feel less authentic to their target consumer.

Virgin Atlantic's sales have returned to almost pre-pandemic levels in 2022 following the release of their 'See the World Differently' ad, while Bud Light has been hit by falling sales after the backlash to the Mulvaney Instagram partnership, and more loss of loyalty among consumers – especially among Gen X and Boomers. Alongside calls for boycotts of Bud Light from Kid Rock, Travis Tritt (a country singer), Ben Shapiro, and other prominent conservative voices (including Rep. Marjorie Taylor Greene (R-GA) and Sen. Marsha Blackburn (R-TN)), people shared videos online of themselves throwing away cases of Bud Light (Rep. Dan Crenshaw (R-TX)), and they actively misgendered Mulvaney online.

Sales dipped immediately following the controversy of the Mulvaney Instagram video, with tap pours down 6 per cent in the weeks of 2–15 April 2023 (Wiener-Bronner, 2023); in that same period retail store sales of Bud Light fell 17 per cent (Maloney & Weber, 2023). Overall, the sales volume of Bud Light, in the four weeks ending in 20 May 2023, declined 28 per cent from that period the year prior; and the negative sentiment spilled over to other drinks in Anheuser-Busch's InBev stable, including Budweiser, Busch, and Michelob Ultra, which all fell between 10 and 16 per cent (Henderson, 2023). Drops in sales prompted Anheuser-Busch's chief executive of InBev's North American business to issue a statement saying that, 'We never intended to be part of a discussion that divides people. We are in the business of bringing people together over a beer' (Whitworth quoted in Henderson, 2023). In some ways, the controversy did, in fact bring people together.

While the feel-good sentiment of the authenticity related to the Virgin Atlantic ad hummed along in the background, supported by the company working to make their brand more inclusive both internally and externally, the backlash to Bud Light's work with Mulvaney went beyond dropping sales for the company. Mulvaney was targeted online by trolls, stalked offline, misgendered by pundits on news channels and social media, and even actively misgendered and her body mocked by another prominent transwoman Caitlyn Jenner, who went on to criticise other organisations, such as Nike, for working with Mulvaney. Those who stood by Bud Light, such as country singer Garth Brooks who said his new Nashville bar would serve Bud Light, were criticised by the conservative right, including Rep. Matt Gaetz (R-FL), who mocked him on X.[9]

Fallout in the company saw rumours spread online that the whole marketing team from Anheuser-Busch were laid off following the backlash. This was untrue, though the company did place two marketing executives on leave: the head of Bud Light marketing and her boss (Otis et al., 2023). It cancelled an event in Missouri in April 2023 to preserve staff safety, while several brewing facilities were targeted with threats of violence and bomb scares (Maloney & Weber, 2023). In May, former President Trump (2023) weighed in on Truth Social saying that 'Money does talk – Anheuser-Busch now understands that' as a means of promoting a book on conservative buycotting;[10] while aforementioned conservative congressmen (Sen. Cruz (R-TX) and Blackburn) opened an investigation into the partnership between Bud Light and Mulvaney – claiming that Mulvaney's audience skews younger and therefore is promoting underage drinking (commerce.senate.gov, 2023).

In the months since Mulvaney's video was posted on Instagram, she has been listed as one of Forbes North American 30 Under 30 in 2024 for social media. And she has gone on to be awarded *Attitude Magazine*'s first ever 'Woman of the Year' award. The award was given to Mulvaney in October 2023, and was sponsored by Virgin Atlantic, which faced no significant backlash in showing its support for the LGBTQIA+ community in the UK and further afield.[11]

---

[9] Here Gaetz mocked Brooks for his moral stance by calling out infidelities in his relationship, see original post here: https://twitter.com/mattgaetz/status/1667527223291641856.

[10] Buycotting here is juxtaposed with the concept of boycotting, wherein consumers use their money to support companies whose values they share. For more on boycotting, see Chapter 6 on brand activism.

[11] It's worth noting that Virgin Atlantic has faced backlash for not allowing its crews to wear their preferred uniforms during the flight to the World Cup in Qatar – on the basis of risk and safety in destinations (BBC News, 2022).

Key Differences and Similarities in Approaching Gender

While Bud Light wanted to develop an ongoing connection to a younger audience who is more tolerant of minorities (sexual and otherwise) than their older counterparts (Janmaat & Keating, 2019) and move away from the 'frat-boy image' (Bernstein, 2023), they underestimated the vocality of the conservative right. Heinerscheid, the vice president of marketing who was placed on leave after the #EasyCarryContest backlash, noted that her job was focussed around reviving a brand that was in decline by targeting young drinkers. While it makes sense that Bud Light, which has had success in the past in tapping into the LGBT community in their marketing – without real backlash – would see the value in a partnership with Gen Z influencer Mulvaney, they underestimated the context in the cultural landscape in which their brand, marketing, and consumers would collide.

In order for a brand like Bud Light to fully stake out a new space in the cultural landscape, wherein they become a brand landmark for a growing area of minority spend (a global spend of $3.9 trillion (Ceron, 2023)), they need to continue to stand their ground and clear out space on the edge of authenticity where they can develop as a brand that consumers use to move about the cultural landscape in a way that enables the latter to use the brand to better align their self-identity and self-projection.[12] The 'See the World Differently' campaign from Virgin Atlantic, which also embraced diversity, has had a better reception and better traction because Virgin Atlantic are working to secure a landmark position by carving out more space around their brand for visual inclusivity.

While Virgin Atlantic made diversity and inclusion a part of their brand ethos and showcase this through their campaigns and internal guidance, Bud Light hoped to tap into a minority consumer base while not actively standing with those consumers when pressed. While Virgin Atlantic pushed on and followed up their 'See the World Differently' campaign with an arguably more visible push to showcase their policies, Bud Light chose to step away from the

---

[12] The space where we now expect authenticity to be found, not in showing our daily lives, but in pushing boundaries. This is explored in detail in Chapter 6.

backlash, not address it head on, and to instead focus on pushing out a summer ad that shows drinkers dealing with different aspects of summer in amusing ways. However, this ad seemed to fuel the anger, with one commenter noting that 'This commercial is amazing in how it shows Bud Light STILL doesn't know their customers. They need to hire a blue collar marketer asap before there comes a point of no return' (quoted in Suciu, 2023); this is in contrast to the (larger than industry average) LGBTQIA+ and high-income drinkers of Bud Light (Statista B, 2023). By retreating from the spaces in the cultural landscape Bud Light tried to stake out with their partnership with Mulvaney, the brand has lost ground and become less of a landmark for consumers across the board.

5 | The Importance of Authenticity

> When evaluating a brand's marketing success, authenticity is arguably the most valuable metric. Yet unlike other performance indicators, such as reach and views, authenticity cannot be measured or calculated.
>
> R. E. Hughes, Authenticity in marketing: how your brand can start benefitting today, *NYT Licensing* from *The New York Times*

In a world where everyone is performing a version of themselves within their cultural landscape, the concept of authenticity begins to take root and develop value for not only the consumer, but also the brands that work to develop as landmarks within those consumers' spaces. When 'the desire for authenticity is especially strong in times of change and uncertainty' (Fritz et al., 2016, p. 325), and individuals search for something that feels real, the push for authenticity in branding begins to develop. Alongside that come questions concerning what we mean when we say something or someone is 'authentic'? The question of defining authenticity is not a new one. The modern world, from marketing, management, and influencers to the attention economy is steeped in the quest for authenticity. A Google search pulls up over 1.7 billion results for 'authenticity',[1] and it's been a part of a growing body of research since the 1970s when Trilling (1972, p. 92) defined 'authentic entities' as those who 'are what they appear to be or are claimed to be'. Trilling's understanding of authenticity is a good starting point; however, the term requires more unpacking to better develop its connection to a consumer's self-identity and self-projection and how these elements work together within the shifting cultural landscape in which these pieces move.

One way of approaching the question of establishing the importance or value of authenticity is to come to an understanding of

---

[1] Date searched, 27 January 2023.

what we mean when we speak of authenticity or being authentic. This is intertwined with the recognition of what role authenticity plays in the consumer's cultural landscape and how the concept of authenticity in this space relates to the way a consumer self-identifies and projects, using brands as landmarks to move closer (or further) from their 'authentic' selves. Because authenticity is often part of the way a consumer views themselves, it is something that has become important for brands to both understand and utilise in strategic ways that can help cement the brand as a more fixed land-mark within the cultural landscape.

What Is Authenticity?

While it may seem a simple term to define, the concept of authenticity is both complex and ephemeral. The way in which a person, brand, or wider culture chooses to define the term can alter based on a variety of considerations. Moreover, within the discussion of the authenticity of an entity, differing and sometimes contradictory understandings of authenticity can apply (Newman & Smith, 2016). Authenticity has been linked to the origins of something being unquestioned, there-fore providing a sense of providence and genuineness, such as how we can define the authenticity of a work of art or luxury item. It can be a stamp of approval, often meaning authorising something as real (Van Leeuwen, 2001). It relates to the cultural context in which it exists (Nostrand, 1989), the internal state of the individual (Bailey & Iyengar, 2022), and a relationship with a brand (Cinelli & LeBoeuf, 2020). Keeping all of these different potential dimensions of authen-ticity in mind, we must also consider how history is promoted, where authenticity is considered to be a 'cultural construct closely tied to Western notions of the individual' (Handler, 1986, p. 2) and where it is the 'signature of Western exceptionalism' (Assmann, 2012).

'Many scholars either acknowledge the possibility of different meanings of authenticity but then proceed to settle on an interpre-tation that is overly general and frequently confounds the different meanings just acknowledged, or focus exclusively on one meaning at the total neglect of other possibilities' (Lehman et al., 2019, p. 2). Outside of the academy, news topics on authenticity cover authen-ticity in the classroom (Bartlett, 2023), authenticity in the work-place (Golden, 2023), culture's insistence on the performance of authenticity (Bishop, 2023), and where we go in the future with technology that can both certify authenticity with blockchain and create it with the integration of generative AI.

In their extensive literature review of how research has defined authenticity Lehman et al. (2019, p. 3) came up with a conception of the term that is built upon three areas: authenticity as consistency, conformity, and connection. The first of these, consistency, relates to the consistency 'between an entity's internal values and its external expressions' (Lehman et al., 2019, p. 3). For instance, a pair of Rios of Mercedes cowboy boots have been handmade for generations by cowboys and leatherworkers who provide (and have provided) high-end products to the equestrian market. The brand consistency (and authenticity) here lies in both the internal design of the boot for the job it promises to do and the external expression as a high-end product that does the job and also marks out a wearer as discerning. In a consumer perspective, it is about being true to oneself, where a consumer 'is authentic when they genuinely express their true inner qualities and feelings' (Bailey & Iyengar, 2022); this, in turn, links authenticity to truth and honesty.

The question then arises of how a consumer can know themselves well enough to maintain this consistency between inner values and external expression, where that consistency has also been directly linked to a consumer's well-being (Rivera et al, 2019). If it is impossible to truly know oneself,[2] then the consumer (and ultimately the brand who wants to reach them) must rely more on the complicated interplay between their self-identity and self-projection.

Relying on this interplay brings to the fore Lehman et al.'s (2019) second definition of authenticity, that of conformity. When there are as many versions of a consumer in their own mind as there are in others' minds then the place where self-identity and self-projection meet becomes authentic *because* it is mediated by conformity to the norms of its social category. Though potentially contradictory in that someone or something becomes authentic based on their perception of how they fit into a shared cultural value, this connects back to the introduction of Foucault's archaeology in asking where the consumer exists within this normative social category that overlays the cultural

---

[2] Scholars such as Nisbett & Wilson, 1977, argue that one cannot know oneself, while others, such as Baumeister, 1995, Hood, 2012, doubt that the concept of 'self' as we know it exists.

landscape. Authenticity, in this sense, gains a form of cultural capital by being acceptable within the position it holds. Continuing the example of the Rios of Mercedes cowboy boots, across their designs – higher tops, lower tops, bronco heels, square or rounded toes, simple or exotic leathers – the products remain recognisably cowboy boots and conform to the expectations of those categorical norms.

Part of what makes an entity acceptable within cultural norms is the role that authenticity plays as a 'connection between an entity and a person, place, or time as claimed' (Lehman et al., 2019, p. 1). This can be seen in how an entity – be it a consumer, product, or brand, and so on – can be linked to a referent outside of itself in a true or real sense. Is a pair of Rios of Mercedes boots, bought from their shop in Texas, more authentic than a pair of cowboy boots bought in Walmart in upstate New York? In this case, the authenticity is tied to the physicality of the shop in Texas and the value of the brand itself.

If we start from the point that authenticity is hard to pin down and is concerned with the consistency between its internal values and external expressions, how well it conforms to expected norms of its category, and how it draws connections between the authentic entity in question and an external referent such as time or place, we come to a working definition of authenticity that is valuable for understanding products, brands, and the consumers who engage with them. However, we must keep in mind that for something to be authentic it does not require all three elements of this definition to be present and the weight of the roles that consistency, conformity, and connectivity each play are related to the worth that is placed on authenticity in the consumer's cultural landscape.

Helen Simpson (2023), a social media marketing consultant, said of authenticity that '[w]e hate it because everyone says, "I want to be authentic; I want to authentically enter into this conversation".' Not everyone can enter 'authentically' into the cultural landscape because, as Simpson (2023) notes, 'it's not like it's authentic. What do you do on social …? You make a video and you edit it, and you put in filters and you put in music. Everything that you do is non-authentic.' If consumers and brands seek to perform and embody the concept of authenticity in the cultural landscape they often do so with specific outcomes in mind, which brings into focus the concept of perceived authenticity.

When a consumer or brand tries to embody authenticity, they lose some of what they seek to portray in the presentation of that authenticity. Their portrayal becomes performative, and therefore relies more on the perception of authenticity both internally and externally, in order to develop the value of the performance as authentic. As a complex derivation of some, if not all, aspects of consistency, conformity, connectivity, and the way that these elements are perceived by the consumer, authenticity works in conjunction with brand landmarks in the consumer's cultural landscape to enable the consumer to engage with the distance between their self-identity and self-perception to close, or enhance, that gap.

Authenticity's Relationship to the Consumer's Understanding of Self

The majority of consumers seek ways to find and present their authentic selves as coherent and to close the gap between self-identity and self-projection, wherein authenticity and living your authentic self have become vital cultural codes (McCarthy, 2009). However, when we define authenticity as conformity with accepted cultural expectations, we can overlook the concept that 'authenticity involved originality [... and] demands a revolt against convention' (Taylor, 1992, p. 65). And, therefore, we must not presume that all consumers want to bring their self-identity and self-projection into line, nor that part of their authenticity potentially embodies that divide. Bailey and Iyengar (2022, p. 2) suggest that '[b]eing authentic requires that [... a person or a brand] be aware of their inner states and convey them in a way that is consistent in their self-expression'. If a consumer is aware of the difference between how they are perceived by others and how they view themselves, then their authenticity can be located in how they keep these two views in balance and how they authentically inhabit this in-between space.

For a consumer, being their authentic self in the cultural landscape means having an awareness of this gap between identity and projection. Whether or not the consumer chooses to align these two versions of self, they utilise their understanding of authenticity as it relates to the consistent ways they perform outwardly their internal validation of self. In doing this, they seek brand landmarks and 'real/authentic' signs/symbols/products within the cultural landscape to move towards and utilise as a means of performing their perception of authenticity.

As the consumer proceeds to narrow the gap between their self-identity and projection, they often manoeuvre to conform with the norms of how they want to be perceived. It is important to note that authenticity as conformity does not mean that the consumer is conforming to all wider social norms, but only the social norms of the groups to which they align. For instance, a drag queen may not seek to conform to wider, Western societal standards of performance of gender as a binary. However, they are likely to seek to conform to the benchmarks of the drag queen community and economy. In conforming to the standards of a chosen community, a consumer can find validation in taking those accepted values and embracing them to develop an acceptable 'authentic' self.

Part of the process of becoming authentic as consumers conform to a group is the use of brands, products, and brand landmarks to identify where individuals exist within the wider cultural landscape in relation to those with which they choose to conform. This desire to connect with other members, brands, or products in a community enables the consumer and others to identify that consumer as authentic in relation to a particular ideal. The consumer, and those around them, can identify someone as authentic if they have the approved gear, lifestyle, and so on. For those who want to be seen as serious tennis player/sport aficionados, as well as knowing all the rules of the game, they could also gravitate towards brands that are associated with the game at a more exclusive level. Anyone can purchase a grounds access pass to Wimbledon if they wait in line, but not everyone has access to main court tickets to the women's final. Likewise, not everyone who plays at a casual level will own K-Swiss shoes and a Babolat La Decima racket, where both items are used as external referents to indicate the authenticity of a consumer's connection to the game.

Wrapped up in the conditions of authenticity are questions of how authenticity relates to the concept of happiness within a consumer. In his study on happiness, life satisfaction, and their links to authenticity, Sariçam (2015) found that there is a relationship between these three. As the consumer goes through life, they are often most naturally authentic when younger (Rogers, 1959) and remain more so when they have a good relationship with others within their cultural landscape (Wang & Graddy, 2008). This links to how the consumer navigates their landscape with respect to their self-identity and self-projection, where those who experience 'self-alienation', which can be understood as a wider discrepancy between how they view themselves and how they present themselves to others, are associated with being more unhappy (Koydemir et al., 2020).

As the consumer diminishes their self-alienation by bringing their self-identity and self-projection closer into alignment, they can develop a personal sense of uniqueness where they feel more authentic in themselves. A personal sense of uniqueness comes from the humanistic approach to psychology and personality, which 'refers to a quality of individual being, but not to an explicit ethical ideal' (Medlock, 2012, p. 39). The sense of personal uniqueness that a consumer can feel is contextual, based on their position in the cultural landscape, who they share this space with, and the self-alienation they may feel. When they feel more personally unique and comfortable within that, they become more authentic, which leads to higher levels of happiness and life satisfaction (Sariçam, 2015)

Authenticity is closely related to self-identity, self-projection, and the self-alienation that comes from the difference between these two spaces. It is often seen as a means of discovering and expressing one's true self, and to do this, consumers use brand landmarks and products in the cultural landscape to develop a sense of uniqueness. Feelings of authenticity can lead to positive outcomes, such as greater self-esteem and a sense of belonging, while feelings of inauthenticity can lead to 'negative outcomes, such as feelings of immorality and impurity' (Kovacs et al., 2018, p. 8). All of these positive and negative outcomes are mediated via the interplay between brands, consumers, and capital within the consumer's cultural landscape – which itself is shifting and unstable.

The Authenticity of Brand Personality

The brands who seek to develop a more permanent presence as a landmark within the cultural landscape often work to embed authenticity in their brand personality. As Gilmore and Pine (2007, p. 5) noted, 'Authenticity has overtaken quality as the prevailing criterion'; this concept of authenticity as a driving force in positioning a brand in the cultural landscape remains a key part of branding today – a 'cornerstone of contemporary marketing' (Brown et al., 2003, p. 21).

The growth of anthropomorphising brands by giving them characteristics such as kindness, friendliness, authenticity, and 'emotional states that people believe to be distinctly human' (Golossenko et al., 2020, p. 737), enable brands to build trust, loyalty, and attachment (Batra et al., 2012; Guido & Peluso, 2015).

Part of the way a consumer develops trust and loyalty to a brand is via the brand's anthropomorphism, wherein brands with higher levels of anthropomorphism give more recognisable self-referential cues to the consumer and make it easier for the consumer to recognise the values espoused by the brand (Morhart et al., 2015). Consumers are able to better connect to a brand that has more easily understood values, and this connection is related to how authentic the brand is perceived to be (Morhart et al., 2015).

Though related concepts, brand personality and brand anthropomorphism are not the same. According to Aaker (1997, p. 347), brand personality can be considered to be 'a set of human characteristics associated with a brand', which relate to how we mentally understand a brand in humanistic terms. Anthropomorphism, on the other hand, can be related to either a product (Guido & Peluso, 2015) or brand as a whole and 'goes beyond behavioral descriptions of imagined or observable actions' (Epley et al., 2007, p. 865). Pure brand anthropomorphism, as defined by Puzakova et al. (2009, pp. 413–414), encompass those brands that are 'perceived by consumers as actual human beings with various emotional states, mind, soul, and conscious behaviors that can act as prominent members of social ties'.

Anthropomorphism can be used to enhance perceptions of authenticity of a brand (O'Keefe, 2019) by enabling the consumer to identify with the brand and utilise its space in the cultural landscape to situate themselves in relation to the brand as a landmark. In times of change and uncertainty (from the 2008 financial crisis to the COVID-19 pandemic, wars, the cost-of-living crisis, and more), consumers desire authenticity and the continuity it brings (Fritz et al. 2016; Turner & Manning, 1988). Part of this continuity is wrapped up in how embedded the brand is in the shifting cultural landscape, because traits, such as authenticity, that are associated with a brand, tend to be relatively stable over time and unique to a particular brand (Aaker, 1997).

However, in recent times, '[d]emands of authenticity have been pitched against those of morality' (Taylor, 1992, p. 65), which necessitates asking questions of the ethics around brand authenticity and if authenticity can be bought and sold. In the world of brand personalities and influencers, authenticity can be a performative process (Heřmanová, 2022). And this performance will rely on the context in which it is developed and perceived and how the authentic nature of one area of the cultural landscape might not be considered authentic in another. If a consumer buys and collects crime fiction books to fill their library and has amassed thousands over the years, one inhabitant of the cultural landscape might look up to this as a goal, to be surrounded by books; but another might look down on that collection as trashy crime fiction – throwaway works in the view of a 'discerning' consumer who is interested only in 'higher' works of literature such as literary fiction.[3] Though showing off a library of crime fiction on a consumer's TikTok might be an authentic portrayal of self, it can be misconstrued depending on where and how it is approached and by whom.

Brands use indexical cues as objective sources to indicate that the brand is what it claims to be (Mohart et al., 2015). The consumer connects those cues to their understanding of the brand's past, what principles the brand has and how well they stand by them, how the brand relates to the consumer on a personal and emotional level, and how the internal culture of the brand is perceived (Fritz et al., 2016). Bringing together the constellation of abstract concepts that can be emotionally linked to a brand encourages the managers of the brands to stick within a framework of brand identity that has been developed over time (Holt, 2004). While this can help to solidify a brand as a landmark, embedding it within the map of the cultural landscape, it also has the potential to erode over time if the brand doesn't evolve with the landscape.

This is not to suggest that all famous brands must engage with new elements of the cultural landscape at all times. In fact, undermining the foundation of the landmark brand by redeveloping the brand with every cultural shift is foolhardy at best. Brands should, instead, continually scan the horizon in order to understand how the cultural landscape is changing, to best position themselves with regard to how they want to reaffirm their position in relation to the landscape and their consumers. Subtle shifts, activism, changes in the branding, and

---

[3] This concept of 'high' and 'low' art is considered in Chapter 2 in relation to Bourdieu's concept of social capital and habitus.

so on are relatively small alterations in the scheme of the wider market that can keep a brand relevant and standing out as a landmark, without necessarily going to extremes.

The Edges of Authenticity

Repeated exposure to marketing ads initially increases positive reactions to an advertisement or brand, until a saturation point is reached and ad fatigue sets in. When this happens the positive sentiments of the consumer become negative and brands often seek out new ways to engage with consumers in an authentic way (Chen et al., 2016; Pechmann & Stewart, 1988; Schmidt & Eisend, 2015). This often means that as consumers seek brands that best reflect them, they want a way to more closely link their self-identity to the brands they engage with through aspects of credibility that stem from an absence of 'over-promotion' (consumers do not always want to be walking billboards), being able to engage in political and cultural issues, and being more authentic than wide-reaching (Garcia, 2023).

One of the ways that 'authenticity' is manifesting is via more extreme behaviour or pushing the margins – something that draws audiences across platforms: a place where, 'in the post-genuineness internet, the margins have become the only safe place to embody realness' (Coleman, 2023). We Are Social notes, in relation to storytelling platforms like Instagram Stories and TikTok, 'First, we expected it to reveal normalcy ... Then, we expected it to reveal vulnerability ... Now, we expect it to reveal chaos' (We Are Social, 2023b). Taking part in niche communities and pushing the edges can be about consumers' purposeful decisions to gain status, to be 'the most real' subgroup. An example of this is in the rise of extreme gender roles portrayed on social media by tradwives such as Hannah Neeleman (6.4 million followers), Solie (39.1k), or Emmalee Stanton (29.1k).[4] The draw of someone on the edge of influencing a new niche culture, like Neeleman, balances 'blurring the line between aesthetics and ideology' (Jezer-Morton, 2023). However, another homesteader influencer, Beth Gantz, noted to Jezer-Morton (2023) that many of the homesteading skills pushed by tradwives have a basis in poverty and that '[p]eople turned to

---

[4] Followers as of September 2023.

these things out of necessity. To do things in the most expensive and beautiful way possible' edges on disgust.

This drive towards more extreme behaviour in order to present a self that is 'truly authentic' can 'unduly affect vulnerable groups' (Advertising Association, 2022, p. 10), which might be more likely to emulate the niche influencer. While mapping one's life around the values presented by a tradwife might not lead to an audience endangering themselves in a physical sense in the same way that influencer Jay Alvarez might as he hangs off helicopters, jumps from hot-air balloons, and so on, such influencers do develop a following of people who aspire to be like them, and in pursuing this their followers both reshape their own identity in relation to who they follow and push the boundaries of how they present themselves in this light, marking out their authenticity as part of a niche group.[5]

Becoming part of a group as can be seen as counterintuitive to being 'authentic', according to Jokilehto's (2006, p. 9) work on authenticity and heritage, where he considers authenticity as 'being truthful, i.e. standing alone as an autonomous human creation and being a true piece of evidence of something'. In communities, both in a digital and physical space, being part of a group enables the consumer to use being a part of that niche group as a way to form their own identity and self-projection. While being a part of a unique group may give the consumer a more stable sense of self in relation to others within that community, it can also lead to homogenisation of that particular niche group. While the presence of shared characteristics, be they physical, theoretical, political, and so on, may provide comfort for some consumers when they have 'found their tribe', for others, the group, and themselves within it, may lose a sense of being authentic when so many share the traits they feel sets them apart as being 'real' or unique. When this happens those consumers move to the edge, seeking out the boundaries, exploring how they can push these boundaries, and in doing so gain attention from both their niche group and groups that exist within the cultural landscape on the other side of those lines.

The boundaries that separate one group, space, or identity from another can be both physical, as in land and sea, or socially based

---

[5] It should also be noted that at the fringe of the tradwife movement there are links to white supremacy (Beddington, 2024).

elements, such as separating Taylor Swift fans from Beyoncé fans; however, the boundary lines almost always exist somewhere in the theoretical and have the potential to shift as the landscape (cultural and physical) changes. Because the concept of a boundary is a 'quite complex cultural model' (Barth, 2012, p. 20) it exists in the cultural landscape as a way to separate both physical and theoretical spaces, and as a means of movement across the landscape as consumers use these boundaries to support their concept of self-identity. We must keep in mind that most consumers are not boundary pushers, though the ones that do push and jump boundaries are likely to become more widely seen. In raising the profile and reach of those who push the boundaries and exist in the edges of authenticity, others within the cultural landscape move towards them, which effectively normalises what was once the edge. This can potentially lead to new pushing, new boundaries, and even farther edges that must then be reached for a consumer to seem (if not feel) authentic.

Consumers are not the only entities in the cultural landscape that can push towards the edges of authenticity to be their most real selves; brands also engage in boundary pushing in order to draw consumers. This can be realised in the presentation of a brand in its marketing and campaign strategies where unique and edgy advertising draws in consumers. Likewise, it can be seen in the products a brand produces, from runway fashion concepts to innovative technology. Or in the brand value proposition itself, where the ethos of the organisation is related to the concept of 'move fast and break things'. These are the start-ups and disruptors who make it part of their brand to be on the edge. Sometimes the value in edge-pushing brands is less in the products or brand's conceptual nature and is instead in the trickling down of innovation, making the brand palatable and saleable to the masses in a way that matters to the consumer sense of identity.

Authenticity Matters

There is a 'growing consumer demand for authenticity in purchased products and services' (Fritz et al., 2016, p. 324). In 2023, Millennials had a spending power of $2.5 trillion (Business Wire, 2023), and 42 per cent of those Millennials say that authenticity is the most desired quality in a brand (Statista, 2023). More widely, a 2023 Gitnux Marketdata Report noted that around 86 per cent of consumers look to brand authenticity as a key factor when deciding what brand to engage with. With this in mind, brands must first lay out the question: authentic to whom? The same Gitnux report found that though 80 per cent of brands think they deliver authentic content, only 37 per cent of consumers agree with them (Gitnex, 2023).

When the meaning of authenticity is 'context and goal dependent' (Beverland & Farrelly, 2010, p. 839), there is a vital difference in how a brand performs authenticity in relation to if they want to be appealingly authentic to a consumer or if they are staying true to their internal standards and impetus that underpin their brand identity. As audiences are more fragmented across platforms and geographies, and develop within niche spaces that are built around atomised interests and micro communities, brands must decide if and how they will engage with the less-explored areas of the cultural landscape and what value there is in developing these new narrative structures. While these areas remain unmapped in wider culture, they provide white spaces in which the brand can put down roots as a landmark that consumers can use to orient themselves and, in doing so, co-create a sense of authenticity.

The value of authenticity for organisations has been a growing area of research,[6] and 'issues of authenticity now bear down on not only all experience offerings but across all of the economy' (Gilmore & Pine, 2007, p. 2). While consumers might have once sought out an 'authentic' or unique experience from a brand, authenticity now permeates all aspects of the cultural landscape and the brands that make their home within it. With this in mind, brands must now provide more than 'authentic' products and experiences and must themselves be authentic in their business decisions, as authenticity is now what sets a brand apart (Gilmore & Pine, 2007) and what enables a consumer to identify with a particular brand at a particular moment and move towards it in the cultural landscape.

In appropriating authenticity, consumers are actively working to link the brand, product, or experience to their narrative interplay of self-identity and self-projection (Beverland & Farrelly, 2010). Authenticity is flexible for individual consumers in that if the brand

---

[6] For research into authenticity and corporate social responsibility (CSR) messaging see Pérez, 2019; Pérez et al., 2020. For research into brands and their relationships to authenticity see Bhargava, 2008, and Gilmore & Pine, 2007.

enables them to engage with their self-identity or projection in a way that suits them, they are also able to blend aspects of fact and fiction to decide how and if a brand is authentic (Grayson & Martinec, 2004). The concept of authenticity-bending is related directly to how a consumer utilises the brand to establish their self-conception at a particular, contextual point in time, and links to Bartsch et al.'s (2022) consideration that authenticity is made up of three parts. The first is existential and is tied to a consumer's self-identity; this is followed by indexical, wherein the product/brand/and so on correspond to the actual state of affairs or is true to life; and the third is iconic, wherein the consumer uses a brand's authenticity as a means of moving towards their self-projection or ideal state of being.

Sometimes it matters less to the consumer that the authenticity on display is real and true than it works in conjunction with a consumer's self-identity and self-projection. Consumers can overlook obvious breaches of authenticity, such as when they shop for a 1990s look-Halloween costume that is almost certain to be made up of modern pieces styled to look vintage. Instead of shopping for a genuinely vintage outfit on Etsy, eBay, Depop, Vinted, or in a local vintage shop, the consumer in this case employs a malleable sense of authenticity in order to project a particular vision of themselves to others at a Halloween event.

While 'authenticity' can be linked to enabling consumers to have more personalised experiences or products, it is arguable that conflating 'personalised' and 'real/authentic' is in itself a construct that commercialises authenticity by simply moving consumers into groups of one, where everyone is different in the same ways. For example, a study on rebranding an urban area of Seoul to reflect an idealised version of authenticity resulted in a homogeneous landscape where buildings may have looked authentic, but altogether and in context their similarities made them appear inauthentic within the space (Shin & Pae, 2022).

Authenticity – and the way it is valued by a cultural economy – comes in waves. Where once consumers wanted glimpses behind the shiny façade of brands, content creators, even their friends and families, and sought out those views on platforms that utilise videos, sound, and 'raw' content, we see these aspects becoming less important over time. Consider BeReal: an app meant to rival the staged and filtered looks of 'traditional' platforms such as Instagram; BeReal's user base grew exponentially between its founding in 2020 and today. In September 2022, arguably the app's pinnacle, there were 14.7 million global downloads in that month alone (Ceci, 2022). This phenomenon was driven by an American market that was craving authenticity in their social platforms and 34 per cent of users believed BeReal was authentic (CivicScience, 2022). However, research has shown that, in Europe, it takes a third of both men and women three tries to get the 'right' photo for BeReal, an app that is meant to promote spontaneous snapshots of their daily life (Sortlist, 2022), making users question what authenticity is and whether it matters. The market quickly tired of being told when and how to be authentic in what they shared online, and between October 2022 and March 2023 BeReal's daily active user numbers halved; 'ultimately, it just added another demand for self-presentation, only this time, you had to pretend to be authentic once a day' (Gerrard, 2023).[7]

As the search around how to embody authenticity is pushed to the margins of what is considered 'normal', brands and creators follow – seeking to make an impact in the edges of the cultural landscape. However, it must be noted that brands who choose to move into these unmapped areas are taking a risk. Much like there is a danger that brands may erode their landmark space if they shift their position in the landscape with every cultural change, there is also danger in setting down roots on the edge of the boundary of authenticity – delivering something 'real'. In pushing the edge, a brand can go over, lose their audience, and fold. There is a contextual limit to how much fact and fiction a consumer is willing to blur in being able to utilise a brand in their self-identity and self-projection. But if a brand times its move correctly, it can stake out a piece of the cultural landscape, root itself in place, and push the nearby edges from a solid foundation, while maintaining a sense of realness and authenticity.

Conclusion

The intricate dynamics of authenticity, especially in the digital age, highlight the multidimensional ways authenticity shapes, and is shaped by, consumer behaviour, brand strategies, and the broader cultural landscape. A central tenet throughout is the fluidity of

---

[7] BeReal stated that numbers reflecting a drop in users is inaccurate compared to their internal data, but their growth lags behind other social platforms and they are facing competition from established platforms who take advantage of their key front/back camera feature (Perez, 2023).

authenticity; it constantly shifts, evolving to fit contemporary narratives and expectations. The progression in consumers' expectations of authenticity has moved from seeking a way to view 'real life' or normalcy to desiring chaotic 'reality'. The rise of niche communities, as seen in the tradwife movement and the shifting paradigms of authenticity, underscores the ways brands and digital platforms have mediated and moulded the concept of realness in the cultural landscape. Here, authenticity isn't just a passive attribute; it's an active engagement, a strategic navigation through a landscape shaped by both self-identity and external validation.

Brands, not just individual influencers or consumers, have felt the pull of this authenticity wave. The quest for authenticity, particularly in branding, is as much a challenge as it is an opportunity. Brands constantly grapple with the fine balance between being genuine and aligning with shifting consumer expectations. The significant divergence between brands' perception of their authenticity and consumer perspectives encapsulates this dynamic. Furthermore, the malleable nature of authenticity, especially in the modern cultural landscape, is evident. Brands and consumers alike engage in 'authenticity-bending', melding and adapting authenticity to fit context, narrative, and desired identity. Apps like BeReal encapsulate this evolving demand for authenticity. Initially heralded for its unfiltered 'realness', the eventual performance of authenticity led to the app's diminishing appeal. This fluctuating embrace of authenticity reflects a broader societal ambivalence about the very notion of 'realness' in an increasingly digital age.

Authenticity is not a static, universally agreed-upon construct. Its interpretation and importance differ across cultures, platforms, and demographics. This nuanced, contextual understanding of authenticity offers both brands and consumers a lens to critically evaluate their positions in the cultural landscape and map their trajectories accordingly.

Key Points

- Authenticity has become increasingly important to both consumers and brands, especially in times of change and uncertainty.
- Authenticity itself is a complex series of relationships, encompassing consistency between internal values and external expressions, conformity to social norms, and connection to something outside of oneself.

- Consumers can use authenticity to navigate their cultural landscape, aligning their self-identity with their self-projection. This alignment can be achieved through the use of authentic brand landmarks and products, which consumers use to express and validate their self-perception and belonging within specific communities.
- Brands now are striving to create an authentic brand personality, which can be considered more important than quality in the eyes of some consumers.
- Authenticity can be pushed to its limits through extreme behaviours or niche communities in the digital space. This can lead to new cultural movements and influence a consumer's sense of self in the cultural landscape.

Discussion Questions

1. If authenticity is a cultural construct that is closely tied to Western notions of the individual, how might the concept of authenticity differ in non-Western cultures and what implications does this have for global brands seeking to maintain authenticity across diverse cultural landscapes?
2. How does the rise of generative AI and new technologies challenge traditional notions of authenticity, especially in relation to branding and consumer trust?
3. Considering the role of authenticity in branding, what are the ethical implications for brands that construct an image of authenticity that may not necessarily align with their business practices or product origins? How does this affect consumer trust? Consider Boohoo being accused of breaching the Modern Slavery Act, or Pepsi with their tone-deaf Black Lives Matter advertisement.

6 | *Brand Activism as a Power Dynamic*

Business is now expected to be an agent of change.

C. Sarkar and P. Kotler, *Brand Activism: From Purpose to Action*

In the current age of attention economy, where the consumer's attention is traded as a scarce and valuable economic entity, every piece of media (online and off) is competing for the time and attention of the marketplace (Nelson-Field, 2020). The average UK television viewer sees thirty-six TV ads a day (Thinkbox, 2022) and 44 per cent of US consumers have digital marketing touchpoints across social media, 37 per cent across streaming and video portals, and 18 per cent within podcasts (Statista, 2023). We can also factor in the addition of all the offline advertisements and day-to-day engagements with media, in all formats, that consumers are bombarded with in the cultural landscape. With this overload in mind, it has been said that consumers get bombarded by over 5,000 pieces of advertisement per day, but this number has been debunked by a variety of sources (Anderson, 2023). It is more reasonable, perhaps, to err on the side of Media Dynamics' (2014) findings that adults are 'exposed to about 360 ads per day; [and] of these, only 150–155 are even noted, and far fewer actually make a sale'.[1] These numbers will vary depending on the lifestyle of the individual consumer and how they move within culture in relation to their self-identity and projection.

Brands operating within the current environment must face rising competition from other brands where price and quality are similar, where even older, established brands are beginning to face more steep competition and are seeking ways to connect with consumers

---

[1] In this study 'media' means TV, radio, the internet, newspapers, and magazines. Out-of-home advertising is not included in this list and could potentially increase the number of ads the average consumer views in a day.

and stay relevant (Eyada, 2020). Part of staying relevant is the balance between the company's bottom line or its stakeholders and the understood value that the company is bringing to society. Notably, terms such as value and society are loaded with many implications, wherein 'value is relatively unexplored in business model research and its meaning is often open to interpretation and assumed' (Dembek et al., 2023. p. 2298) and society can be related to the wider world, a specific area, culture, or consumer demographic. While the concept of society is related to how a consumer chooses to move through the cultural landscape, using brands to better affiliate with, or avoid, different groups, the role of value is more theoretical, as something that has implications both within an organisation and the society in which it operates. Value can incorporate the brand's creation of value within the product or service and the consumer's accumulated experiences, both lived and imagined, individual and collective (Helkkula et al., 2012). In this way we can consider value as something that has a multimodal system of co-creation, in which the brand 'invents value by enabling customers' own value-creation activities' (Normann & Ramirez, 1993, p. 67).

With this point of view we can move beyond the concept of value as an inimitable resource (Barney et al., 2021; Black & Boal, 1994) and instead look at how brands can allow consumers a space in which to co-create, and therefore co-define, what value means to them. This does not mean that consumers are the final voice in defining what value a brand has, but instead the role of value as co-creation employs contextual and temporal constraints in how value is interpreted within the cultural landscape. We can break down the role of co-value creation further to encompass the position that employees take up in the space where corporate social responsibility (CSR) comes to play a role in the brand's personality and how it is perceived internally and externally. In keeping with the development of value around CSR, employees are driven to co-create value within the brand by the brand's organisational vision and social purpose (Waseem et al., 2021). This helps to satisfy the developmental or psychological needs of employees to feel they are doing good through their working lives (Glavas, 2016). Though employees potentially play a key role in directing the co-creation of value around CSR, and have a positive impact where they interact with consumers (Mubushar et al., 2020) and, specifically, when they engage in brand activism, the focus here remains on the relationship that consumers have with the brand as a whole, and employees are part of those brands.[2]

Co-creation of value for a consumer can be as simple as offering them something that makes their lives better, easier, or richer, and so on, but it also can provide them with an experience, wherein the value lies not only in the product itself, but in the 'experience of consumption' (Frow & Payne, 2007, p. 91). Brands are able to give consumers the space to co-create around their brands, but consumers do not always choose to co-create value with the brand's input. And while co-creation as a concept brings to mind equal power dynamics, the power in the co-creation of value around a brand shifts alongside the ebbs and flow of the cultural landscape. Drawing on Helkkula et al.'s (2012) propositions of value as experience highlights that value co-creation, and the experience of that space, is socially and personally subjective, is temporally based, emerges from a particular lived position within the cultural landscape, and can be real or imagined – all of which create differing power dynamics between the consumer and the brand.

This understanding of value as a co-creation of knowledge, which can be experiential, situated within a shifting cultural landscape echoes the role the consumer plays in the same spaces, where their experience lies in the journey of moving towards and away from cultural landmarks as they work to narrow the interstitial area between their self-identity and self-projection.

Value extends beyond co-creation between the consumer and the brand itself as something the two develop together, to evaluative actions by both parties. In this way, when 'people evaluate actions [such as those of a company that is working within the area of CSR], they tend to judge not only the tangible facts but also the motives they assign to other parties' (Gond et al., 2017, p. 232). The motives that consumers assign to brands alter depending on the way the brand is perceived in relation to its CSR activities, especially when a brand's activist outlook is disconnected from its real actions. Examples of

---

[2] For more research into employee co-creation of value see Merrilees et al., 2017; Chen et al., 2017; and Merrilees et al., 2021. For employee relationships to CSR see Simpson et al., 2020; Wang et al., 2020; Onkila & Sarna, 2022; Schaefer et al., 2021; and Nejati et al., 2020.

this arise when brands lean in to CSR by taking on areas of brand activism, as Nike did in 2020 after the death of George Floyd in Minneapolis. Nike was an early reactor to the social issue, publishing a short video playing on its slogan 'Just Do It', turning into 'For Once, Don't Do It', asking the public to not turn a blind eye to the issue of racism in the USA. The ad was shared across Nike's digital platforms and social accounts and was a success.[3] Nike followed this campaign up with a promise of $140 million in donations to organisations that support racial justice and equality (Nike, 2021).

This was not the first time Nike had stepped into their brand activism around equality. But at this moment in time, in the summer of 2020, it focussed the consumers on key societal issues and let them know where the brand stood. And, as positive as the ad seemed to be, with 60 per cent of people finding it empowering, many people also considered it to be exploitative (Ace Metrix, 2020). Furthermore, the cynicism of some consumers was found to be partially substantiated when articles began appearing that highlighted that the board at Nike was without a single black individual (Ritson, 2020). And though Nike did change this, it was not the only brand that took the opportunity to make their top-level positions more diverse. In 'the year after the Black Lives Matter protests, the S&P 100 added more than 300,000 jobs [and] 94% went to people of color' (Bloomberg, 2023).

Brands can stay ahead in the competition for attention by cutting prices or using promotions, but that brings with it a danger of devaluing the brand overall (Sinek, 2009). Or they, like Nike, can lean into the concept of 'doing good', embracing aspects of CSR and taking a stand on issues that may divide society. This is where brand activism comes in.

What Is Brand Activism and Why Do We Care?

Brand activism is an evolution of CSR(Sarkar & Kotler, 2020) that moves the generalised 'doing good is good' mentality of CSR as being potentially beneficial to everyone and non-controversial, towards taking on an issue that is more polarising in the cultural landscape where the consumers and brands come together (Vredenburg et al., 2020).

---

[3] With over 1.5 million views on YouTube and 16.5 million Instagram views (as of 8 December 2023).

Where progressive brands work to promote the common good, more brands are moving further towards 'justice as [a] strategy' (Kotler & Salter, 2020, p. 35). Justice as a call word for brand activism sits at the widest area of impact a brand can make within the cultural landscapes by drawing on both internal and external co-creation of value around social change. When businesses are seen as the sole institutions that people consider ethical and responsible brands become facilitators for activism and change (Edelman, 2023).

Moving from the era of the product (1900–1960s), which is about ownership, through the era of the person (1960s–2000s), which highlights individuality, we are now moving into what Smith (2020) calls the era of the public. This era of marketing is about 'society more than what you own or who you are. It will be about how you contribute. It will be about reinventing the rules of commerce to help build a better society' (Smith, 2020). It is due to this impulse towards the wider social good that CSR has developed as a core aspect of organisations and brand activism has come about as a means for brands to stake out space in the cultural landscape that enables them to put down roots and be used as landmarks by which consumers can navigate shifting terrains.

It is here that we find activist brands that are purpose-led, often around one key area in their industry, wherein they make it their mission to solve that particular issue and by doing so 'create a simple, compelling message to educate consumers about the issue at the heart of their mission' (Melloul et al., 2022). These purpose-led activist brands are creating more awareness and more expectations for brands to be moral where they were once functional and emotional (aligning to previous eras of brand expectations).[4] Globally, 63 per cent of people say they buy or advocate for brands based on their beliefs and values (Edelman, 2023). In the UK, 57 per cent of people do the same; in USA that number sits at 61 per cent; the numbers are higher for Italy (64 per cent), South Korea (65 per cent), Australia (66 per cent), South Africa (74 per cent), and China (84 per cent) (Ipsos, 2023). Generationally, Baby Boomers are the least likely to buy brands that reflect their personal values (58 per cent) and Millennials are the most likely to buy based on their values (64 per cent), while Gen Z comes

---

[4] For more information on the role of emotional branding see Cossío, 2021; Akgün et al., 2013; Rossiter & Bellman, 2012; and Gobe, 2010.

in at 60 per cent, which may be accounted for by their smaller, but growing, share of purchasing power,[5] which is now more than double what it was in 2018 (Pollard, 2021).

With the growth of Gen Z's purchasing power, brands must pay attention to the significance Gen Z and Millennials put on brand activism, where, if they do not agree with a brand's morals, they not only will not purchase but will encourage their friends and family to boycott brands as well (Fromm, 2022). This is directly linked to what Ary Ganeshalingam (2023), global CMO for Change Please coffee, notes as the new age of moral brands, wherein for a brand to have 'moral authority it must (a) possess moral identity, (b) possess potential to influence via power and platform, and (c) be perceived by stakeholders as moral' (Agarwal & Malhotra, 2019, p. 393). If a brand manages to obtain and hold moral authority in their positioning within the cultural landscape alongside activist issues, they can benefit from 'positive moral emotional reaction[s]' (Romani et al., 2013, p. 193), which generate feelings of gratitude in consumers, making them feel good about themselves and the brand that allows them to feel that way.

One of the ways that brands engage with consumers is by facilitating moral cleansing, whereby in providing a 'social good' or taking an activist stance on a societal issue, brands allow consumers to engage with the brand as a way to compensate for their own perceived lack of moral action (Sachdeva et al., 2009). This 'doing good' by using the brand makes a consumer feel morally better, which can lead to feelings of awe, gratitude, and elevation (Xie et al., 2015). As consumers calculate a sense of moral balance based on all the morally relevant actions they could, or did, take in a given time span, they often want to stay on the morally balanced or positive side of the decision-making process (Zhang & Du, 2023).[6] Moral cleansing and choosing moral, or good, actions as a means of offsetting less moral actions help to enable the consumer to feel the 'warm glow' of satisfaction (Nunes & Schokkaert, 2001). And, in doing so, consumers are motivated by eliminating the gap between their self-identity and self-projection, in which morality plays a part (West & Zhong, 2015).

---

[5] Gen Z's purchasing power, while growing, is over 85 per-cent less than that of Baby Boomers at the same age (McCants, 2023).

[6] It should be noted that not all consumers have the same attentiveness to morality or the morality of the choices they make, and therefore not all consumers will feel the same need to balance their moral decision-making.

All levels of morality, gratitude, and a sense of being part of a wider community that brand activism bring into play, are mediated by the shifting of the cultural landscape around what is and is not culturally, politically, and morally acceptable. The brands that are able to establish themselves as landmarks within the landscape provide a beacon by which the consumers can navigate the (sometimes unreliable) geography. As brands move towards the era of the public, where morality is evidenced by brand activism, which itself is a means by which brands put down roots in a particular space within the cultural landscape, we can better understand the temporal and cultural aspects that bound that influence the emotions of the individual consumer, which play a key role in moral judgement of the 'doing good' aspects of a brand's brand activism (Dedeke, 2015).

Activism as a Branding Strategy

If all elements and outward influences on a consumer and brand relationship are the same, consumers who agree with a brand's stance on social issues will have a positive response to that brand,[7] feeling a sense of goodwill and connection (Verlegh, 2023). As a brand makes activism part of their business model they need to take a public stance on an issue. It is the public nature of brand activism that distinguishes it from other behind-the-scenes work that brands have taken part in for decades, which can include lobbying efforts, such as those by Meta, Amazon, Apple, Microsoft, and Google, which combined spent upwards of $60 million in 2022, potentially to combat anti-trust and anti-tech legislations that could hit their bottom line (Feiner, 2023).

Brand activism goes beyond 'doing good' or 'doing one's part' and proactively works to make changes in wider society. If a company adds a Pride flag to their logo for the month of June (in the USA, UK, and parts of Europe) but makes minimal effort or does not take any pragmatic approaches to actually working towards equality, this is a form of shallow activism that seeks to earn consumer credibility instead of change (Rusch, 2023). While many brands now see the value of the pink pound/dollar, which holds an estimated

---

[7] Here, the term 'social' is used as a catch-all term for any outward-facing issues in society such as political, economic, or racial injustice, and so on.

$3.9 trillion dollars in purchasing power (Ceron, 2023), there has also been a growth of backlash against LGBTQ-identifying people worldwide.[8] Brands sometimes try to straddle the line, appeal to both sides, and lose no potential customers. For example, in 2022 Seattle Pride cut ties with long-supporting brand Amazon due to the brand's donations to politicians who back anti-LGBTQ legislation and a desire by Amazon to have the parade named after its sponsorship, and yet Amazon remained quiet in the first week of Pride on their Instagram accounts – in a reverse from previous years (Cantor, 2023). This is rainbow-washing. Akin to green-washing, this happens when brands try to step into brand activism in a superficial way that gains public approval for activism, while sometimes undermining the activism they say they support; however, this can potentially expose them to legal questions (Rice, 2022). It is therefore valuable for a brand to ensure that the issues it supports in its activism align with its core values and the mission of the company.

Embedding activism into the core business model and branding of an organisation can help grow the business and have a wider social impact. Brands can do this by ensuring the alignment of activist activities with their core values and by understanding the needs of their key stakeholders (from staff to investors, consumers, etc.), and how those stakeholder relationships might alter based on which areas of activism the brand focusses on (Korschum, 2021). In working to better understand these relationships, we can begin to see how power dynamics ebb and flow around brand activism. Because consumers are now more likely to hold brands to account based on the stances the brand takes, or not, on sociocultural issues (Romani et al., 2015), the power of deciding the success of a brand is less about the brand developing and selling goods or valuable products and services and is more about the acceptance or rejection of the brand's values by the consumers.[9] A shift away from where the consumer expects the brand to be on sociocultural issues can potentially alter the way a consumer

---

[8] As of 14 December 2023, in the USA alone there were 508 anti-LGBTQ bills on the table (ACLU, 2023).
[9] It should be noted here that in this research the focus is on business-to-consumer brands, though there is also a growing area of research and focus on the way that brand activism manifests and is implemented in business-to-business (B2B) brands. For more research into B2B brand activism see Kapitan et al., 2022, and Markovic et al., 2023.

chooses to interact with the brand and, in this shift, consumers can mobilise others to follow suit in leaving a brand behind.

Brands must manoeuvre within the complex cultural landscape, where taking an activist stance can cement a brand as a landmark and might be used by consumers to navigate their way to, or away from, the brand. Splitting the market can be a concern for brands of all sizes, but in a market where differences in pricing and quality of products are hard to discern consumers begin to ask 'not what is being sold, but who is selling it' (Korschun, 2021, p. 13). Brand activism, then, can invite scrutiny of a company, wherein the consumer makes a decision based on a brand's mission, values, personality, and marketing, and on whether that brand aligns with their own values and social concerns, and, finally, how authentic the brand is in their activism.

Brands Can Be Activists Without Being Authentic, But Should They?

The role and value of brand authenticity is covered in depth in Chapter 5; however, it is worth revisiting here as specifically related to concepts of brand activism, as consumers and other stakeholders are increasingly expecting brands to take a stand on sociocultural issues and, at the same time, are more sceptical that companies may be using activism in insincere and manipulative ways (Markovic et al., 2023). Just because a brand is acting in a socially responsible, or even activist, manner does not mean that consumers view the brand as socially responsible or good (Alhouti et al., 2016). In order to reap the rewards, brands need their sociocultural stances and activism to be seen as authentic.

Perceived authenticity in brand activism is when a brand's purpose, values, outward-facing activist marketing and messaging, and corporate practice and strategies are aligned (Vredenburg et al., 2020). Consumers now care less about the sincerity of a brand and more about its authenticity, as the former is internally focussed while authenticity is seen as a more 'true expression of core beliefs' (O'Conner et al., 2019). Brand attributes such as credibility, commitment, and heritage all play a role in the dimensions of authenticity and how consumers perceive the brand (Mirzaei et al., 2022), as do elements of nostalgia and cultural symbolism (Napoli et al.,

2014). But, most importantly, consumers expect brands to practise what they preach, and if a consumer detects that a brand is being inauthentic not only will they boycott the brand and tell others to follow suit, they often do so by calling the brand out in a public manner (Bakhtiari, 2020).

Consumers are moving towards brands that take a stance on socio-political issues because there is a lack of landmarks in the cultural landscape that enable a consumer to find meaning in aligning their self-identity and self-projection. Likewise, 'consumers can be motivated to express their sociopolitical orientation and belonging through ethical behaviour that includes both boycotting and promoting products' (Schmidt et al., 2021, p. 43). Brands that are able to root themselves in the cultural landscape have the opportunity to position themselves where they can authentically engage in issues that are relevant for their brand and are less likely to be perceived as merely an 'adaptation to social trends rather than a sincere and genuine action' (Kubiak & Ouda, 2020, p. 33). Not all brands need to take up the same activist issues, nor do they need to necessarily fight over positioning in the cultural landscape. It is this differentiation between activism and positioning that enables clusters of brand landmarks to develop. Oftentimes these clusters will develop around heritage brands, which are branded representations of past, present, and future timeframes (Pecot et al., 2019) wherein authenticity plays a key role in the positive brand association consumers have (Halwani, 2019). These positive brand associations are seen as more authentic when brands have continuity in their activism over time (Ferenius & Kotras, 2021).

Those brands that are able to transcend time by continually engaging with current socio-political issues in a recognisably authentic way will create structural narratives that allow consumers to draw near to the brand. The more consumers who draw near to a brand, the more visible that brand becomes in the landscape. 'This territorial ownership, combined with the ability to influence a mass of consumers is the source of a brand's market power' (Dawar, 2004), and the power a brand has here is supported by the brand's engagement with consumers who believe in the authenticity of the brand's actions and activism.

It is not enough for brands to simply express their support for an issue in order for consumers to perceive their activism as authentic;

the latter need evidence that the brand's activism is correlated to their internal values. Ferenius and Kotras (2021) found that brands that work to make their take on activism different from other brands, and link that activism to the heritage of their brand, are more likely to be perceived as authentic. Because authenticity is a complex construct that relies on how well the brand aligns the promises it makes towards activism and its corporate practices (Cammorota et al., 2023), there remains a need for brand transparency around how brands integrate activism both internally and externally.

The demand for transparency from the brands with which consumers engage will continue to grow (Lyon et al., 2018), and though not all brands need to be loud about their activist activities, such as by leading marches or funding large marketing campaigns, they do need to be visible enough that their consumers are aware of their activities. For example, World of Books, an online, second-hand book dealer, is a B-Corp,[10] and leans in to sharing reading and education for all. To this end, they pledged to donate a million books to good causes by the end of 2025 and became carbon neutral in 2022. They not only seek to sell second-hand books, they actively work with Ziffit, a used-good sales site, to encourage their customers to buy into the wider recycle and reuse network. Furthermore, they work to ensure authors get a share of sales through their AuthorSHARE initiative,[11] and internally they have a 0 per cent gender pay gap. All of these activist activities work to support each other. Stakeholders, such as consumers, corporate managers, and outside partners, are all provided with the invitation to not only applaud World of Books' activism, but to take part in creating this value alongside the brand.

---

[10] 'B Corp Certification is a designation that a business is meeting high standards of verified performance, accountability, and transparency on factors from employee benefits and charitable giving to supply chain practices and input materials' (B-Corp, 2023). In order to reach B-Corp status there are a number of goals that an organisation must reach, demonstrating their adherence to the key standards of the certification.

[11] This is a distinction from how authors would normally get paid royalties in that copyright in books (and other items) work under the first-sale or exhaustion doctrine, which means that after the initial sale of a physical item there is no longer a need for permission from the copyright holder to sell it onward. This means that royalties are paid to authors on new books sold, but not via second-hand sales, which sets World of Books' AuthorSHARE Initiative apart.

Capitalism and Activism as Bedfellows

Understanding how value is defined among stakeholders is key to developing a strategy that grows the value of a brand. In this sense, value does not always mean growth of the company or growth of profit, or that the value a company creates exists in a fixed ratio where company value grows at the expense of social values. Instead, Edmans (2023) suggests that brands should consider a pie-growth mentality, which stresses that the total amount of value is not fixed and, by growing the value to society, the brand can increase its returns. This concept of pie-growth works when profits become a by-product of serving a purpose (Edmans, 2023). Making money and doing good are not necessarily in opposition. Returning to Nike's 'For Once, Don't Do It' ad, after they posted it, it was reshared by rival sporting goods giant Adidas, and Ace Metrix (2020) found that consumers' positive purchase intent after this ad was on par with the 2018 Colin Kaepernick campaign – where sales went up by 31 per cent.

Growing the value of a brand via activism also plays a role in who a brand can recruit to work in the organisation. '[E]mployees want to work for companies that support the causes they deem important' (Ferrell & Ferrell, 2021, p. 16) and 20 per cent of applicants refuse job offers when a company's values did not align with their own (McCalla-Leacy, 2023). This number grows to one out of three when we look at Gen Z, and over half would take a pay cut to work with a brand that reflects their values (Bupa, 2022). This need for an employee's values to align with that of the brand they work for relates directly to how employees are also consumers in the cultural landscape working to anchor themselves among brands and people who share their values and in doing so narrow the gap between their self-identity and self-projection. Having employees who believe in their brand's values, and the activism those values inspire, means these workers are more likely to stay with the brand (70 per cent) and tell others about it (Cote, 2021).

Though there is risk in taking a stand on social issues, there is more risk in not speaking out (Quinlan, 2018). Some brands might consider that it is better to not engage with brand activism in order to not alienate their target consumer, or to be taken as inauthentic, but brands might be doing more harm to themselves than good by staying out of hot-button topics and issues and may 'grossly underestimate the risk of inaction' (Korschun, 2021, p. 14). Some insights go further and suggest that 'silence is seen as negligence or condoning unjust social dynamics' (Datawords, 2020), and since consumers have a willingness to make product choices that are more costly if the outcome is advantageous to other people, it makes sense for companies to work to grow social good (Pelligra & Vásquez, 2020). Even missteps are tolerated by consumers when a brand is making its first inroads into brand activism, as long as the brand remains transparent (Vredenburg et al., 2020).

If we start from the point of view that profits are a by-product of an organisation with purpose – which goes beyond corporate strategies into why the brand exists, what it does, and what it aspires to become (Mayer, 2021), we can begin to consider how brands can engage with activities such as brand activism to advance the brand's purpose while simultaneously growing their profits. Brands such as Sweet Cherry Publishing focus on diversity and inclusivity as their purpose, and to this effect, over half their team and leadership is comprised of the 'global majority' (Sweet Cherry, 2023). Focussing on inclusivity, their newest imprint, Every Cherry, specifically caters to people within the Special Educational Needs and Disabilities community. The books that Every Cherry publishes are retail items and not charitable products, and, in fact, many of their first releases are reworkings of out-of-copyright texts without royalty costs. However, this does not diminish the authenticity of the purpose of Every Cherry. Instead, by generating profit, Sweet Cherry is able to invest more in Every Cherry as a tangible attribute of the company's mission for diversity and inclusivity.

Other organisations that nurture purpose and profit at the same time are Ben & Jerry's, which is a 'leader in change' that also sells ice cream (Sharon, 2022), and Lyft, a ridesharing platform. Being open and loud about their activism helps consumers to know what a pivotal part of the Ben & Jerry's brand this is. The brand's core values are made up of human rights and dignity, social and economic justice, and environmental protection, restoration, and regeneration; which, in turn, relate to their progressive values on equality, waste reduction, chemical use, and peace and justice (Ben & Jerry's, 2023). As Ben & Jerry's has made their values align with their activism, the brand comes across as authentic and, as a by-product of striving to fulfil their purpose, the brand continues to speak out and see 'strong growth' (Beard, 2021). Lyft likewise, in 2017–2018, saw strong growth in the aftermath of President Trump's 'Muslim Ban' when they committed $1 million to the American Civil Liberties Union (ACLU) to help protect immigrants' rights in the USA. They have raised more than $3 million for the ACLU through their Round Up & Donate campaign (Lyft, 2019). Through this focus Lyft's percentage of the US rideshare market went from 22 per cent to 29 per cent (whereas Uber dropped from 74 per cent to 69 per cent).

Because 'economic responsibility is laced with an ethical dimension' (Carroll, 2021, p. 6), purpose and profit do best when tied together. Brands do well by doing good and could increase their profits by engaging in activism and ethical behaviours that directly relate to their purpose (Camilleri, 2022). This increases a consumer's willingness to buy from the brand (Becker-Olsen et al., 2006) and can help the brand maintain the balance of power between the brand – including the way it portrays itself, its purpose, and its products and services – and the power of the consumer, who has the ability to expand and move opinion and loyalty away from a brand.

When It Goes Wrong

Even as consumers and brands move towards taking a visible and active stance on social issues, brands still have a concern that they might alienate part of their consumer base. Only 30.2 per cent of CMOs in 2022 indicated that their brands would take a stand on politically charged issues,[12] as there is more likelihood of losing existing consumers than gaining new ones if the brand's stance does not align with the consumer's self-identity or self-projection (Hydock et al., 2020). Because consumers tend to believe their own point of view, or moral compass, is superior, they are not likely to alter their stance on a social issue due to a brand's activism (Mukherjee & Althuizen, 2020). This, instead, could lower the connection and loyalty that a consumer feels for the brand (Tuškej et al., 2013).

While '[p]eople are surprisingly tolerant, as long as they feel that the brand otherwise has their interest in mind, that the brand is not too pushy about the activism, and that its intentions appear to be honorable' (Korschun, 2021, p. 14) sometimes this is not the case and overall

---

[12] This is an unusually high percentage in the history of the CMO Survey, which has run since 2008.

negative feelings for the brand prevail and cause backlash, sometimes leading to anti-brand action. These anti-brand actions are the behaviours of consumers who feel a sense of dissatisfaction with the brand. And, while some dissatisfaction can be overcome, such as when the dissatisfaction stems from product or service issues, those that are sociopolitical and rooted in the authentic values of the brand are less easy to separate out. When consumers move into an anti-brand state they may share negative feelings via word of mouth, organise boycotts, or even spread wider hatred of the brand (Pöyry & Laaksonen, 2022).

Triggers that cause backlash can be around the authenticity of the brand to be able to step into that activist arena, the wider political associations of the cause, and the way that the brand implements the campaigns that are based in their activism (Pöyry & Laaksonen, 2022). The role of authenticity in brand activism is discussed in detail earlier in this chapter, while there is a risk that discussions around socially charged topics may inadvertently associate a brand with a political stance even if that stance is not explicitly stated. An example of this is 84 Lumber. In 2017, during Super Bowl 51, building supply company 84 Lumber ran an ad that showcased a mother and daughter travelling north through Mexico to reach the American border. Their harrowing journey is interspersed with images of men on a building site making a wooden structure. The mother and daughter finally reach the border, only to find a solid wall; right before they give up they notice a light shining through and find that the building work that was being done was to create a large door in the wall. The takeaway was 'The will to succeed is always welcome here.'

While it was noted that Fox refused the full ad for being too controversial (Hill, 2017), a shorter version was played during the game and was watched by 111.3 million people. The ad directed people to the company's website to see the full version; the subsequent traffic initially crashed 84 Lumber's website. While the ad gained national attention, it also garnered backlash from more right-wing and conservative consumers, so much so that 84 Lumber released a statement the day following Super Bowl 51, stating that:

We do not condone illegal immigration. The journey of the mother and daughter symbolizes grit, dedication and sacrifice. Characteristics that we look for in our people at 84 Lumber. President Trump has previously said there should be a 'big beautiful door in the wall so that people can come into this country legally'. We couldn't agree more. (Hill, 2017)

The purpose of the ad was to grow recruitment, an aim that was arguably lost among the following discussions online, which ranged from support to hatred to confusion. It was even noted that 84 Lumber's president voted for Trump and the '"door" represents legal immigration' (Framke, 2017). 'The advertisement's messages embody a constrained polysemy where nearly all interpretations related to immigration are plausible' (Galarza & Stoltzfus-Brown, 2021, p. 53). As one of the most expensive Super Bowl ads ever (coming in at $16.2 million (GOBankingRates, 2021)), the return on investment has worked for 84 Lumber, which saw a 103 per cent growth between 2019 and 2022 (84 Lumber, 2022). This campaign can be seen as a stance that showcases the power of a marginalised community that has a will to succeed; by drilling into that narrative, 84 Lumber was able to stay on top of the wave of power that comes with tapping into a base that historically and contextually has scale but no power to change wider socio-political issues.

84 Lumber is one example where backlash eventually levelled out and the brand continued to grow, but US retailer Target was hit with backlash around its annual Pride collection in 2023, which resulted in the retailer moving Pride displays to the back of the store and a loss of support from both conservative boycotters and LGBTQ+-identifying consumers, culminating in a drop in sales of 5.4 per cent over the three months through and following Pride (in June) (Aratani, 2023). With LGBTQ+ equality as the top social issue on which brands have taken action, at 59 per cent (CMO Survey, 2023, p. 62),[13] it is not likely that conservative boycotts will stop progressive social issues from remaining at the heart of brand activism. However, it is important for brands to take a firm stand that authentically aligns with their brand values and purpose. From this profits can follow. If brands such as Target work to appease all sides by still hosting Pride merchandise but moving it to a less visible location in stores, they alienate both groups. Consumer attitudes towards the brand decreased when they did not agree with the brand's position, but when the brand apologised for any offense and changed its stance both proponents and opponents of the brand thought less of it (Ghosh, 2021).

While there are many examples of activism that has gone wrong for a brand, there are ways to mitigate alienating consumers though

---

[13] Up from 40 per cent in February 2021 (CMO Survey, 2023, p. 62).

narrative storytelling that enables the brand to showcase their position on a social issue and yet still leave room for the consumers to be
persuaded instead of repelled. When a brand tells a story, it creates
narrative transportation that enables consumers to get lost in the
tale and it becomes an effective means to persuade (Key et al., 2021).
This can further change the attitudes and intentions of consumers (Van Laer et al., 2014). While not all storytelling can convince
consumers to change their point of view on a social issue, brands can
potentially make inroads by telling sophisticated stories that tackle
issues directly (Nike's Black Lives Matter (BLM) campaign), making
use of valid statistics in addition to stories, and moving away from
the personal/individual by embracing the era of the public (Polletta
& Redman, 2020).

Conclusion

As brands have transcended traditional marketing paradigms to
embrace their roles as agents of societal change we see a growth of
brand activism in the cultural landscape. This shift is not simply a
response to an increasingly cluttered marketplace but a reflection
of a deeper understanding of value co-creation between brands and
consumers. As consumers navigate a complex cultural landscape, seeking authenticity and moral alignment with the brands they support,
the proliferation of brand messages and the volume of advertisements
indicate that being visible is no longer enough. The attention economy has forced brands to innovate not just in their messaging but in
their core values and actions. Brands like Nike have demonstrated the
potential of brand activism to resonate with consumers and stimulate
dialogue on social issues. However, this same activism invites scrutiny,
requiring a commitment to authenticity and a consistent alignment of
public stances with internal practices, purposes, and values.

However, brand activism is not without its pitfalls. Missteps in
authenticity or alignment can lead to consumer backlash, damaging
brand reputation. The case of Nike's response to the BLM movement
illustrates the delicate balance brands must maintain between taking
a stand and ensuring their actions are not perceived as performative or exploitative. The future of brand activism seems inextricably
linked to the concept of 'doing well by doing good'. The emergence
of purpose-led activist brands reflects a societal shift towards ethical

consumerism, where the purchase is not just a transaction but a statement of personal values and societal engagement. This trend is particularly pronounced among younger consumers, who are more likely to make purchasing decisions based on brand alignment with their personal beliefs.

The power dynamic at play is one of mutual influence and shared responsibility. Brands wield significant power in shaping societal narratives and consumer perceptions. At the same time, consumers hold brands accountable, using their purchasing power and public platforms to endorse or reject brand actions. This intersection of capitalism and activism presents both opportunities and challenges. Brands that navigate this terrain with strategic foresight, moral conviction, and authentic engagement can thrive, contributing to a more socially responsible and ethically conscious marketplace. As we move further into the era of the public, the brands that will emerge as landmarks within the consumer's cultural landscape will be those that effectively leverage activism, not just as a marketing strategy but as a core element of their identity and corporate ethos.

Key Points

- Consumers are bombarded with a high number of advertisements daily, creating a competitive environment for brands. Brands need to find meaningful ways to engage with consumers.
- Brands are increasingly seeking to connect with consumers and remain relevant through brand activism, which goes beyond the company's bottom line to include societal value creation.
- Consumers are increasingly expecting brands to be socially responsible and take a stand on social issues. This is a shift from traditional CSR to a more active and engaged form of brand activism.
- Authenticity in brand activism is critical. Consumers are sceptical of brands that use activism as a marketing tool without genuine commitment. Authentic brand activism requires alignment between a brand's purpose, values, and corporate practices.
- Brand activism influences consumer behaviour, with a significant portion of consumers, especially among younger generations, preferring to purchase from brands that reflect their personal values. Brands that successfully engage in authentic activism can build a strong, loyal customer base and potentially grow.

Discussion Questions

1. How do generational differences impact the expectations and responses of consumers to brand activism and what strategies should brands employ to appeal to diverse age groups while maintaining authenticity?
2. Considering the concept of value co-creation, how can a start-up tech company in the fintech space call on their consumers to work together to foster a sense of shared social responsibility?
3. How can large multinational brands in areas that are contentious (such as energy or defence) effectively align their public stance on social issues with their internal practices and values?

Case Study 2

Activism
Kate Spade and Change Please

If we can just get a small proportion of coffee drinkers to simply change where they buy their coffee, we could really change the world.

Cemal Ezel, CEO and Founder of Change Please

Brand activism is linked to corporate social responsibility (CSR), as noted in Chapter 7. It is often less oriented towards the good for a major part of society and with what is considered widely 'correct' and instead seeks to take a stand that is 'correct' for the brand's values and purpose (Månsson & Stéen, 2022). Because of this, brand activism can be directed towards a smaller target audience and make a larger impact in that group. The reach of a brand's activist message will rely on the size of the brand, the campaigns they are running around their activism, and the associated reach of their messaging. For brands to ensure that their brand activism rings as true and authentic to their current and potential consumers, they must ensure that the '[b]rand activism conveys the values and morals that a brand prioritises, affording consumers the opportunity to evaluate the degree of self-brand connection based on their values and morals' (Lewis & Vrendenberg, 2023, p. 265). It is this feeling of connection to the brand's values that consumers look to when they are moving around the cultural landscape, utilising brand landmarks in order to move in a way that brings closer together their self-identity and self-projection: 'Brand activism therefore goes beyond mere product provision through attributing brand-related action with abstract moral concerns related to rightness, goodness, or virtuousness' (Koch, 2020, p. 594).

By stepping away from a neutral stance on a socio-political issue and taking a public stand in recent years (Pavlovica & Lendeng, 2023), brands have been drawing attention to issues that are linked to the heart of who they are (Garg & Saluja, 2022), and in doing so they make themselves more visible to both potential consumers and those who might support or boycott the brand for the stance they have taken on a particular issue. Authenticity in a brand's activist activities plays a key role in how the activities are received by consumers, and, in being perceived as authentic, brands are putting down roots in the cultural landscape and drawing inspiration from the landscape around them and the people who move into that shared space (Södergren, 2021). At a time when brands must work harder to differentiate themselves from their competitors within the market, tapping into the values that consumers hold dear is a way to develop a connection and loyalty between consumers and the brand.

Consumer loyalty is expressed when individuals continue to rebuy and reuse products from a brand even when the market suggests that other options would be more beneficial, in some way, to them (Oliver, 1999). Loyalty to a brand is linked to the emotions that a consumer feels for a brand, and '[i]ntensity of emotion is related to purchase behavior' (Franzak et al., 2014, p. 18). When a brand is able to create a positive emotional engagement with a consumer, they support a connection and potential growth of loyalty. Consumers are more likely to remember ads that draw out an emotional response (as opposed to a rational ad demonstrating benefits) (Cahill et al., 1996), and there was a proliferation of emotion-led campaigns in and around the turn of the twentieth century. During this period Gobé's (2010) work on emotional advertising defined four pillars of emotional branding as relationships, sensorial experiences, imagination, and vision. While emotion remains at the heart of connectivity between brands and consumers,[1] there has been a shift from how brands use emotion to communicate about products to how they use emotion to inspire consumers.

This inspiration finds its footing when branding and marketing move into the era of the public that relies on brands doing more than selling a product or service, or tapping into emotion, or, in many cases, more than having a solid CSR programme that underlies the social good they do. Brands must take a visible stance on socio-political issues that are directly related to their brand values and purpose in order to be read as authentic in the cultural landscape. Brands such as Change Please,

---

[1] For a wider understanding of emotional branding see Akgün et al., 2013; Rossiter & Bellman, 2012; Kim & Sullivan, 2019; and Mingione et al., 2020.

which are developed with social good and a specific socio-political purpose at the heart of their mission, have a different means of putting down roots in the cultural landscape than brands that have focussed more on a specific social purpose, such as Kate Spade.[2] However, both of these brands tap into both the emotional and inspirational side of brand activism in order to make their brands memorable for the consumer and to help the latter develop a feeling of connectedness to the brand in the crowded markets of coffee and fashion.

Kate Spade: A Brand with Activism Close to Home

An iconic brand that sold 'whimsical, affordable luxury to women' (Grimmer & Mortimer, 2018), Kate Spade was founded in the early 1990s as a handbag brand that was named after its founder Kate Brosnahan Spade. By tapping into a mid-level luxury market that gave women something to aspire to when they were not quite able to buy the, often prohibitively expensive, traditional luxury brands, Kate Spade set the standard with her line of colourful handbags. Within a few years of founding, Kate Spade had a shop in New York City and her brand had begun to take a position in the cultural landscape as a rite of adulthood for American women. Her work was 'a bridge between the early female icons of the sportswear era, and those of the current lifestyle age' (Friedman, 2018).

As a brand that developed a deep connection to woman coming of age and going into the workforce, by 2023 Kate Spade had expanded to 205 locations in North America and 192 internationally (Tapestry, 2023). For many years the brand was synonymous with the founder,[3] Kate Spade, who 'was a designer who did more than support the notion that it was okay for women to have multifaceted lives' (Latham, 2018). Within five years of opening Kate Spade was a $28 million brand that had a designated space within the cultural landscape that consumers used to navigate the cultural space and their own sense of self-identity. In 1999, Spade sold 56 per cent of Kate Spade to Neiman Marcus, and in 2007 Spade sold

[2] Kate Spade is sometimes referred to as Kate Spade New York, which indicates the luxury end of the brand. Often Kate Spade New York is just referred to as Kate Spade, which is what I will do in this case study.
[3] Kate Spade began the brand with her then partner, future husband, Andy Spade, but it was her name on the company.

the remaining shares. In 2007, Liz Claiborne purchased the brand;[4] and in 2017 Kate Spade was purchased by competitor Coach for $2.4 billion (Petroff, 2017). Highlighting the economic and business direction of the brand provides a sense of growth and showcases how Kate Spade staked out space in the cultural landscape that allowed consumers to utilise the brand as a landmark.

, Since 2013, the Kate Spade line On Purpose has been working with employees of Rwanda-based Abahizi Dushyigikirane, Ltd, which is an employee-owned handbag manufacturer that is also a B-Corp. The company provides the women who work with it with life-skill educational opportunities and health support (On Purpose, 2023). As part of this partnership, On Purpose supports holistic empowerment and well-being, giving employees access to mental health support. It also invests in infrastructures including yoga and trauma-recovery programmes (On Purpose, 2023). This focus on female empowerment and mental health has been a feature of the brand since the beginning. It forms the core of the brand's activism and seeks to inspire consumers. On Purpose's focus on the empowerment of African women is just one facet of doing well by doing good, where, for the Abahizi Dushyigikirane brand, '[a]side from simple economic gains, artisans report high levels on several indicators of psychological well-being' (Salas, 2017). Kate Spade continued to balance purpose and profit, and measured the 'impact of their work by tracking social metrics systematically and objectively in partnership with the Akilah Institute for Women' (Trone, 2015).

Kate Spade's work to empower women continues with the On Purpose partnership, and in 2018 attention was focussed more closely on the role of women's mental health in Kate Spade's brand activism and social impact when Kate Spade, the founder of the brand, died by suicide. In the aftermath of her death, the stock of Kate Spade's parent company, Tapestry, went down by 2 per cent (Thomas, 2018). Even though Kate Spade, the founder, had not been part of the brand in over a decade, the brand that still carries her name was affected by her death. In their communications from June 2018, the brand said that even though, as their founder, she was no longer a part of the organisation, they recognised her input and honoured the 'beauty she brought into this world' (Kate Spade New

---

[4] Now known as Fifth & Pacific.

York, 2018). Outpourings of condolences from celebrities such as Chelsea Clinton and Ivanka Trump highlighted both the meaning the brand had in their lives and impact of suicide, along with where to get support. In addition, on the day of Spade's death, the American Foundation for Suicide Prevention put out a statement in support of her family, noting that '[t]here is never a single cause for suicide' (AFSP, 2018).

In the USA, deaths by suicide peaked in 2018.[5] In June of that year, the Google search term 'suicide' was at its highest rate in Google's history (Suicide, 2023), which coincided with a spike in the search term 'Kate Spade' (Kate Spade, 2023a). In 2018, the Mind, Body, Soul initiative was launched by Kate Spade New York, to support the mental health and well-being of employees. The following year, in 2019, the Kate Spade New York Foundation 'updated its mission to include mental well-being as an area of focus' (Social Impact Report, 2019. P. 20), tapping into aspects of the emotions brought the fore by Spade's death, and to inspire their employees to take charge of their well-being and their own mental health. This push in CSR in relation to Kate Spade's wider brand activism around mental health enabled consumers to feel connected to and motivated by the brand in a way that felt compelling and authentic.

In 2018, Kate Spade reaffirmed its commitment to its activist work around women's mental health, where 'a woman's mental health is foundational to her achieving sustainable long-term empowerment – and that it should be prioritized in the global empowerment agenda' (Kate Spade, 2023b). With this in mind the company is investing money into supporting women's mental health and empowerment. In 2022, its impact model put mental health at the centre, and it hosted events raising awareness of mental health. It continues to keep mental health on the radar through its social media content (not just around World Mental Health Day in October) and public engagement. With the Christmas holidays, Kate Spade not only focused on selling gifts and gaining market share, but also included marketing content about the difficulties around the season and how members of Kate Spade's Social Impact Council deal with their own well-being concerns.

---

[5] The number of suicides in 2018 in the USA peaked at 14.2 out of every 100,000 people (US Department of Health and Human Services, 2022).

The Kate Spade Social Impact Council was launched in 2022 as 'a group of leaders who champion the integration of mental health into women's empowerment, address stigma, and provide access to resources' (Kate Spade, 2022). It focuses on integrating mental health into the empowerment agenda. Kate Spade, and the associated Kate Spade Foundation, partner with a series of organisations that further their drive for the mental health of women by working with Find Your Anchor (suicide prevention and awareness), Lower East Side Girls Club (Center for Wellbeing and Happiness), National Council for Wellbeing, and Girls Who Code, amongst others. Each of the partners with which Kate Spade engages speaks directly to the brand's mission of empowering women, with mental health at the centre. It does this consistently, with a focus on brand activism around mental health developing more strongly year on year.

The brand activism that Kate Spade undertakes comes across as authentic to its brand and its consumers, wherein authenticity in its values and activism is significant enough that it can overtake quality in a consumer's selection process (Oh et al., 2019). By focussing on how it could help its consumers deal with mental health concerns in the wake of founder Kate Spade's death by suicide, the company drew consumers into a brand narrative that cemented its space as a landmark brand that consumers can use in moving around the cultural landscape. In doing this the brand creates a space where consumers can co-create value around the brand. Examples include the NAMI Bucks County Bingo event on 1 February 2024 that used Kate Spade prizes to draw in people and to raise awareness for mental health and suicide (NAMIBUCKS, 2023). A further search of X with the phrase 'Kate Spade mental health' brings up hundreds of connections between mental health and the brand posted by both consumers and partners of the brand.[6]

The authenticity of the brand's activism resonates with consumers and encourages them to support the brand, both through their purchases and in recognising the brand as a safe space. In this way, the brand's activism works together with its purpose, values, and mission; thus, while brands may not be set up as activist brands, they can move into that space and in doing so established long-term roots in the cultural landscape.

---

[6] Search completed on 27 December 2023.

Change Please: A Social Enterprise

Unlike many legacy brands that have found themselves in a place where they need to make a stand on socio-political issues in order to stay relevant to modern consumers, Change Please was founded in the UK in 2015 as a social enterprise with a focus on addressing these types of issues, with particular concentration on the challenges of homelessness. Change Please utilises the daily ritual of coffee consumption as a vehicle for social change. It is an example of a social enterprise that 'acts as a catalyst for social change [... with a focus on] creating social value rather than generating private economic gains' (Gupta et al., 2020, p. 209). In the case of Change Please, this began when founder Cemal Ezel found himself disillusioned with his work in commodity trading, which led to the creation of Change Please. With a business model that focusses on training homeless people as baristas and getting them back into the world of work, Change Please marries doing well while doing good in a way that enables the brand to put 100 per cent of profits back into the training and supporting of trainees (Change Please, 2023a).

The business model of Change Please works to support trainees out of homelessness by helping them get a bank account and a place to stay, and teaching them transferable skills. By 2022 Change Please had helped 434 trainees through their programme and had launched in the USA, Australia, and France (Change Please, 2022). In 2023, forty trainees graduated from the Change Please programme, with 70 per cent of graduates securing ongoing work or returning to education (Change Please, 2023b). Because the level and type of support required varies for each trainee, the programme at Change Please is individually structured to help each trainee have the best chance of succeeding.

As a social enterprise, Change Please is set up to enable consumers to understand the core of its brand activism and how it directly relates to its purpose and values as a key part of its brand personality and messaging. The work that Change Please is doing is closely linked to the phrase 'eating for change' (Johnston & Cairns, 2012) wherein consumers choose to buy products that better align with their cultural and/or social values, even if less convenient. 'It is a viable and meaningful alternative to conventional modes of participation' (Shah et al., 2007, p. 233) yet allows consumers to take a socio-political stand for what they believe in. By having physical shops where consumers can buy their coffee and interact with trainees, Change Please helps consumers to co-create value with the concept that changing the world is as simple as changing where a consumer buys coffee – making it simple to make a difference.

However, Change Please is aware that their coffee must also be at least as good, or better than, other coffee on the market, because 'consumer ethics are perhaps best thought of as a luxury' (Eckhardt et al., 2010, p. 434). Refined or elite preference or consumption habits are expressions of the consumer's cultural and economic capital (Lee, 2021), wherein they use their consumption choices to indicate their position within the cultural landscape. And while tapping into the emotion that doing good brings out in consumers, if we consider ethical consumption to be a luxury, even when buying a cup of coffee, brands need to harness the power of the rational, especially in digital and social marketing. By making it simple for a consumers to choose Change Please by appealing to their rational side by unemotionally stating the value that they provide the community by buying their coffee at a Change Please outlet, the brand also draws in consumers who feel they are ethical consumers and 'foodies', and further increases its perceived status (Lee, 2021).

Johnston and Cairns (2012) note that when we consider the dominant narratives around 'eating for change' we often overlook, or are overwhelmed by, aspects of the systemic inequalities in which some areas of 'change' are being promoted above others. Brands such as Change Please, while working across a variety of socio-political activism areas, foreground alleviating homelessness as their mission and purpose. Tapping into this focus on one area of brand activism, and the halo around this, facilitates a shared journey between the brand, the trainees, and the consumers who buy the products. This, in turn, allows for the co-creation of relationships that prioritise human outcomes, which are seen to be fundamental to harnessing trainee agency within the brand and the authenticity of the brand's wider activism (Deloitte, 2023).

Partnerships Are Extensions of Brand Activism

When a consumer becomes a political category a brand has to continually re-evaluate where it exists in the cultural landscape and how that location relates to the positioning of its consumers. Some of the ways brands successfully do this is in establishing suitable partnerships that support their core missions. The best partnerships, for both participants and in terms of perception, tend to be where a clear narrative is created and the contributing role of each partner is clearly understood. Much like people judge others based on who their friends are, as the latter can provide credibility and validate ongoing commitment levels (Lee & Bruckman, 2007), consumers judge activist brands by whom they partner with to draw attention to their activism goals. In recent years, social enterprises and activism brands alike have moved to develop partnerships to expand their reach and find the answer to socio-political problems that cannot be solved by a single sector (Dong & Rim, 2022). For most corporations, partnerships around brand activism are seen as win–win (Austin, 2000), except when the partnering brands have values that differ.[7]

For Change Please, its partnerships reflect the values mission of the brand and serve to support the core aspect of the brand, which is around helping trainees back onto their feet with wraparound care that extends beyond training them to be baristas. It is this sense of wraparound care that makes Change Please's partnership with HSBC and Colgate a natural and authentic extension of the good they do. This partnership is socially valuable for all three brands as it moves the 'doing good' from inside the walls of the organisation out into the visible spaces within the physical consumer landscape. It has done this by repurposing two London buses that work across London boroughs of Hackney, Lewisham, and Croydon to help homeless people receive dental and hair care, NHS care and social support, alongside digital and financial literacy training that can be followed by helping them start a 'no fixed address' banking account (Change Please, 2023b). In working to direct the power of organisations such as the NHS, HSBC, and Colgate to help those that are at the core of Change Please's activist purposes, the brand lends authenticity to larger organisations.

While Change Please harnesses the power and reach of larger multinationals, Kate Spade, through the Kate Spade Foundation, as mentioned, partners with smaller organisations to support its mission of 'empowering women and girls by enabling opportunities for agency

---

[7] For instance, the dissolution of the long-standing partnership between Shell and LEGO, which was at the heart of a successful Greenpeace campaign (2013/14), was due to the mismatch in company values over environmental policies.

and employment, by uplifting communities, and by creating accessible resources for their mental health' (Kate Spade, 2023). As an international brand, Kate Spade has spread its various types of activism across different parts of the world in order to better direct its social impact in a way that directly strengthens its mission and purpose. After the death of their founder, Kate Spade focussed more on supporting the mental health of women and girls and, in doing so, kept its social impact authentic when partnering with smaller organisations to support its work at a more local level.

It is this ability to work at a local level that helps to engage audiences and to allow them to buy into, or support, a brand's activism. Brands of all sizes can take advantage of the value of local partnerships within the cultural landscape, whether they are a large multinational giving funding and support to local organisations (such as Kate Spade or Colgate), or if they are more local-facing brands that receive funding and support to develop community-based solutions (such as Change Please). And though consumers often acknowledge that brands might get involved with activism activities in order to link their brands to a good cause, they also interpret this as ways for the organisations to generate conversation around their brand in relation to the cause they are championing (Németh et al., 2019). The reputational value of all brand activism partnerships relies on the social context of the cultural landscape, the consumers' concepts of power and justice, and the reputation of the partners in the relationship (Mutch & Aitken, 2009), wherein it is less valuable to the activist brand to partner with a corporation that does not have a stellar reputation within the area of brand activism they are seeking to partner.

Many of these corporate–social enterprise/not-for-profit relationships are 'met by a sceptical yet pragmatic public, willing to support the partnerships so long as corporates are seen to be fair and just in their dealings with the non-profit partner' (Mutch & Aitken, 2009, p. 92). In the case of Change Please, it is utilising the power and reach of its corporate partners to support its activist goals, whereas Kate Spade is a corporate that enables many smaller partners to utilise their power to do work that coincides with Kate Spade's social impact goals. In both cases, the roles of legitimacy and authenticity come together to further the brands' mission and values while also building up their presence in their area of the cultural landscape. And in doing so, Change Please and Kate Spade are making themselves available to consumers as land-marks for them to use in navigating their space and identity.

Conclusion

Brand activism, as highlighted through case studies of Kate Spade and Change Please, represents a transformative shift in the relationship between consumers, brands, and societal values. The convergence of activism and branding not only redefines CSR but also encapsulates a deeper commitment to authenticity and purposeful engagement within the cultural landscape. Different brands can activate their values to resonate with consumers and effectuate social change that aligns with their mission, values, and purpose as an organisation. On the one hand, Kate Spade's journey from a whimsical fashion icon to a beacon of women's mental health advocacy underscores the profound impact a brand can have when its activism is rooted in genuine commitment and aligned with its heritage. The brand's ability to navigate the tragic loss of its founder by reinforcing its dedication to mental health exemplifies the potency of authentic brand activism in forging emotional connections and fostering community engagement.

Change Please, on the other hand, showcases how brand activism can be embedded in the very foundation of a business model. By leveraging the consumer's ritual of coffee consumption as a catalyst for social change, Change Please demonstrates that brand activism need not be an adjunct to business but can serve as a core driver of both mission and profit. Change Please's focus on alleviating homelessness through tangible support systems personifies how brands can actively participate in shaping a more equitable society.

These narratives illustrate that the value of brand activism lies in its ability to move beyond transactional relationships towards creating shared values and collective identity. When a brand takes a stand on socio-political issues, it not only distinguishes itself within a saturated market but also invites consumers to engage with the brand beyond the product, participating in a larger conversation about societal progress and individual empowerment. The role of partnerships in brand activism emerges as a critical factor in amplifying impact. Strategic alliances, whether with global corporations or grassroots organisations, extend the reach of brand activism, enabling a collaborative approach to addressing complex social challenges.

It is important to recognise that the success of brand activism hinges on the perception of sincerity. Consumers today are more discerning than ever, seeking out brands that not only claim to uphold certain values but demonstrate consistent and tangible commitment to those principles. The authenticity of a brand's activism is therefore not just a matter of public image but an imperative that can significantly affect consumer loyalty and market position. The role of brands as activists and partners will become more pronounced, shaping both consumer behaviour and societal outcomes. This paradigm shift signals a future where brands and consumers coalesce around shared visions for change, using the marketplace not just as a platform for commerce but as a catalyst for the common good.

7 | *Ownership as Power*

The body is not large, beautiful, and permanent enough to satisfy our sense of self. We need objects to magnify our power, enhance our beauty, and extend our memory into the future.

> M. Csikszentmihalyi, *History from Things:*
> *Essays on Material Culture*

As consumers, we prefer to possess objects that help us to define our identities both to ourselves and to those around us. This 'sense of ownership towards objects is present in individuals by nature and/or by nurturance' (Kumar, 2019, p. 244) and is related to the concepts of capital accrual, performance, and identity. If 'we are what we possess' (Tuan, 1980, p. 472) then the brands that consumers move towards in the cultural landscape are means of not only telling themselves and others of their past and the changes they have been through in the journey to where they are now, but also connect them to those around them by virtue of products that function as threads of their history and family, and by grounding them in the landscape by becoming places to which they can move and return (Belk, 1988).

While there are visible markers of ownership of a branded item, such as an Hermès bag or Adidas tracksuit, there is a difference between legal ownership – as recognised by society and the rights of ownership that are protected by a legal system – and psychological ownership, which is held by and within the individual consumer (Pierce et al., 2001). Legal ownership and psychological ownership can come together when a consumer both owns an item physically and feels a sense of possessiveness and ownership of the brand, 'as if they have control over the brand' (Chang et al., 2015, p. 595). This does not necessarily mean that the consumer who feels they own part of a brand has any tangible hold over the brand itself in the form of stocks, voting rights, corporate governance, and so on. Instead, this feeling of ownership is more related to how the brand enables the consumer to ground their sense of self-identity and self-projection, which in turn increases the sense of personal and cultural meaningfulness of the brand (McCracken, 1986).[1]

The sense of ownership over a brand extends beyond those consumers who legally or psychologically feel a brand is theirs and works internally within the corporate structure of the brand itself. When employees of a brand feel ownership over their work within that brand, they 'demonstrate a positive attitude and altruistic behaviour with respect to the organisation' (Chiang et al., 2013, p. 56). This leads to feeling they are important to the organisation they work for, which, in turn, enhances the work they do for their company as they display high levels of affective commitment (Liu et al., 2012). This, in turn, can influence the way a brand is perceived in the wider cultural landscape with regard to how authentic the brand is seen to be, whereby the perception of the authenticity of a brand may also 'trigger the emotions of brand ownership' (Kumar & Kaushal, 2021, p. 6). This can become more apparent as the brand seeks to position itself at the edge of authenticity to stake out a new space where consumers can come together around the brand's products, attitudes, and values.

The most visible consumers who feel a sense of ownership over a brand are more likely to move towards that brand as a means of self-identity and projection; in that journey they are more predisposed to share supportively about the brand and have more positive purchase intentions (Kumar & Kaushal, 2021). However, lurkers are owners too (Kumar, 2019). Lurkers in digital spaces are those who are within digital communities and read messages, but do not take part. Much like in the digital communities where lurkers make up the majority of users (Barnes, 2018), in the cultural landscape most consumers are lurkers who do not engage with those they pass, with content creators, or explicitly with the brands they use as landmarks. But this does not mean they do not feel psychological ownership, or have legal ownership, of branded products. In fact, much like in

---

[1] We are leaving aside issues of inequality here to focus on the role of the 'feeling of ownership' instead of the reality of legal ownership; however, it should be noted that inequality relates directly to social power, which includes economic and political power and can be the direct result of the ownership and control of capital (Luria, 1976).

the physical world, where consumers may not directly interact with those they pass by, those 'lurkers' can influence how other consumers perceive a space, a brand, and so on. In all the choices a consumer makes, and in the performative nature of society, they use brands to perform their sense of self. Because all performances have audiences, even if that audience is made up of only the performer, 'all people are simultaneously performers and audience members' (Abercrombie & Longhurst, 2003, p. 75). Every touchpoint that a consumer has with a brand in the cultural landscape adds up to that brand's perception for that customer (Davis, 2000)

Brands develop through interactions among various stakeholders across the cultural landscape. Each stakeholder and position within the landscape possess varying degrees of authority, influence, and power over the brand (Mingione et al., 2020). Stakeholders, here, is being used as a catch-all term for all parties that have an interest in, are affected by, or have interaction with or say over a brand. They can be consumers, the organisation that owns the brand, the employees that work for and with a brand, suppliers, communities, governments, and more (Conmy, n.d.), but can also include those consumers and other organisations with cultural capital, such as influencers or platforms where the brand either advertises (social media, TV, radio, etc.) or has a presence because their consumers move in that space. When consumers are stakeholders and feel a sense of ownership over a brand, the brand itself needs to take into account that they do not solely own the brand anymore; to an extent the consumer owns the brand (Davis, 2000). As stakeholders, these consumers 'increasingly acquire power by influencing brand value and meanings' (Mingione et al., 2020, p. 1). This is especially true in the age of the global village, where reviews of brands and products and word-of-mouth marketing play key roles in influencing purchasing decisions.[2]

This empowerment of stakeholders results in brands needing to no longer just sell directly to the consumer, but also to communicate and negotiate with them in the cultural landscape (Siano et al., 2022). These negotiations take place around four areas identified by

---

[2] Askalidis and Malthouse (2016) found that the average conversion rate of a product with review can increase to an average of 270 per cent, higher (380 per cent) for high-priced items and still high (190 per cent) for low-priced items, indicating that the power to sell items does not always come from the brand itself and, instead, often builds from the bottom up.

Haarhoff and Kleyn (2012) as meaning, experience, physical, and code/text, and can be a collaborative process (Merz et al., 2009; Tewari & Mittal, 2014). It can also be a 'non-collaborative process' (Kristal et al., 2018), which can potentially harm the brand. Those brands that have tight control over their messaging are those that want to manage the subjective way consumers perceive the brand (Haarhoff & Klein, 2012).

Brands such as Burger King try to create a balance in how their brand is perceived by the consumer through the way they create and develop structural narratives via their marketing messages. By utilising tools such as rhetorical questions to provoke customers to agree with them in their social media marketing (Losi et al., 2022), Burger King mixes colloquial language (Rudito & Anita, 2020) and (on television) earworms to situate their brand narrative.[3] As part of their work to situate the brand, Burger King draws on references from the cultural landscape to facilitate consumers' ability to see where the brand is in relation to other cultural markers and show them the way to the brand position in the landscape. This can be seen in their advertisements that reference 'news pieces' such as the McDonald's burger that did not decompose after twenty-four years (Salaky, 2020) – the Moldy Whopper ad – or social posts that draw on Pacman imagery, pulling out a sense of nostalgia that can appeal to a 'consumer's emotions, attitudes, and memories' (Crespo-Pereira et al., 2022, p. 109). In times of uncertainty (in relation to world events, personal events, or other crises) nostalgia can help consumers feel safer and more secure (Gross, 2018).

By working to both firmly control their brand image in what they produce, and in controlling for the narrative of consumer experience by tapping into pop culture references and nostalgia, brands such as Burger King seek to direct the consumer's subjective understanding of, and relationship to, their brand. In the current cultural landscape a brand's narrative direction becomes more important as brands put down roots and consumers utilise brands to not only develop their

---

[3] Earworms can be defined as 'catchy pieces of music that repeats through a person's mind' (Gao, 2021, p. 2) or 'automatic mental singing without an accompanying sense of agency' (Killingly et al., 2021, p. 456). Brands have been taking advantage of earworms for decades by their use of jingles (Singhal, 2011) and their relationship to sonic advertising (for more information on this topic see Beilina, 2022; Kemp et al., 2023; and Gustafsson, 2015).

self-identity and self-projection, but as landmarks by which they navigate the cultural landscape itself.

One of the key events that take place when a brand finds space within the landscape to put down roots is the 'splitting of ownership from control' (Soederberg, 2010, p. 74) in the way the brand is understood by the consumer. When a brand has found its space in the cultural landscape, whether that be in a populous area filled with other brands and consumers, or on the edge of the landscape at the place where brands can push the edges of authenticity, it begins to look outward to present itself within the landscape. Brands do this by utilising a variety of marketing techniques, online and offline. It matters less, in this case, how an organisation markets their products, services, and ultimately their brand, than the fact that they are now at a place in the brand's lifecycle where, in putting the brand out there, they are giving over some aspects of control of the way a brand is perceived to the cultural landscape and the consumer. In doing so the power dynamic between brands, consumers, and the spaces they take up in the cultural landscape, begins to shift.

What Does Power Mean in the Consumer's Cultural Landscape

Power means different things to different players in the cultural landscape. For organisations, brands 'are thought to represent powerful forces shaping the identity politics of our age' (Power & Hauge, 2008, p. 125); their power is inherent in the 'pact' they make with the consumer that promises the consumer that they are the brand that will best help them align their self-identity to their self-projection (Stobart, 2016). From the brand's position in the cultural landscape, power is developed via strong intellectual property rights, differentiation between themselves and competitors, advertising, and management over time. '[B]rands, with trademarks as their legal anchors, are important sources of corporate power and have facilitated a significant expansion of this power' (Griffiths, 2018, p. 75). They do this by positioning their brand within the consumer landscape in a way that will benefit their brand and goals.

Most brands seek to develop growth and share in the marketplace and, when an organisation has a strong brand, it can cultivate its power by 'improving profits, cash flow, and share' (Diorio, 2019).

Beyond the role that the product or services provide for an organisation, the intangible assets related to a brand account for 48 per cent of
the world's stock market value (Haigh, 2022).[4] These non-monetary
assets without a physical substance (IFRS, 2023), that is, the brand,
must be identifiable, controllable (in its original state), measurable,
and able to accrue value for the organisation. The value here can further be defined as brand equity, brand love, brand commitment, and
other forms that tie a consumer to a brand.

This intangible relationship between the consumer and a brand
is at the heart of the brand's power within the cultural landscape,
where the 'strongest brands own a positioning in [both] the consumer's mind' (Davis, 2000, p. 4) and the space the brand occupies
physically in that landscape, in relation to the consumer. Because
the cultural landscape is one that is ever-shifting as the edges of the
landscape alter, as brands build and fall into decay, and as socio-
political concerns change the flow of consumers and ideas, the
power that a brand has to put down roots in a specific location is
partially dictated by the social dynamics of the community in which
they build and serve. Power here, then, is used to describe the acts
of one group (brands) moving other groups (consumers) to act in
relation to a product or service within a specific space physically
and culturally (Hunter, 2017).

Power itself has been used interchangeably with '"strength", "ability", or "wealth"' (Leitch & Merlot, 2018, p. 85) and can equally refer
to brands, organisations, or individual consumers. Power is rooted in
the ownership, control, and utilisation of capital, and it cannot be dis-
entangled from the relationships or relational contexts in which power
circulates (Leitch & Merlot, 2018). This context, the current and ever-
fluctuating cultural landscape, invites both the pyramidal approach to
power, wherein there is an apex and a top-down approach to brand
management, and cultivates the understanding that the summit (organisation owning a brand) is not the source from which the power of
a brand comes. It is, in fact, given to the brand by the 'lower' class of
consumers through a multitude of complex interactions. Power in this
sense, comes from a balancing act between the brand and the consumer, and this 'power is constantly being transformed along with
them' (Foucault, 1980, p. 159).

---

[4] In the USA this number is closer to 90 per cent (Haigh, 2022).

As individual consumers, the power to make decisions about their self-projection and self-identity lies in the amount of capital they possess. This power is directly related to where they are and where they are going within the cultural landscape and the ability they have to make those moves in the currents of socio-political overlays. While individual consumers may have varying degrees of power here, in relation to capital, when they come together as wider communities they possess more '[p]reemptive power' (Stone, 1988, P. 83); wherein they have power 'as a capacity to occupy, hold, and make use of a strategic position' (Stone, 1988, p. 83). Because communities, and the cultural landscape itself, are composed of a range of different and interrelated elements, these become places where social changes can occur (Stone, 1988). This affects different parts of the landscape, including which brands can enter a community and put down roots,[5] and can give rise to feelings of either 'not in my back yard' (NIMBY) or 'yes in my back yard' (YIMBY).

The term NIMBY, and its counterpart YIMBY, are often used in relation to planning and community development projects where NIMBYs are 'the brand of people that rejected common interest projects, only to optimise their own private interests' (Mulder, 2012). While these terms are normally associated with planning and the development of housing or infrastructure projects, the terms are also helpful in understanding the power dynamic that is held by a community and those within that community in deciding what brands are able to put down roots in their local spaces. Brands that put down roots in a space in the cultural landscape, either physically (in building a storefront – digital or physical) and/or theoretically (pushing a brand into a community through targeted advertising), must also negotiate with those that do and do not want them to take over space nearby. While some consumers will see brands putting down roots in their neighbourhoods as a barrier to their movement within the cultural landscape – making their journeys to align their self-identity and self-projection longer – other consumers will embrace the brands as landmarks. These brand landmarks can both serve as markers in the cultural map for other, like-minded consumers to draw closer, or for local consumers to find their way home, or indeed, move away.

---

[5] Here, we are not differentiating between online or offline communities, as both spaces exist and play a role in the accrual of capital in the cultural landscape.

When communities are tightly knit around what they consider acceptable as activities and brand movement into their regions within the cultural landscape they are more able to mobilise as a unit to exert their power through the minute practices that comprise every-day life (Foucault, 1980). These micro practices are made up of the daily movements of consumers – of how they position themselves in the cultural landscapes in relation to their identity, each other, and the brands that provide landmarks for navigation. Power, here, 'gets hold of its objects at the deepest level – in their gestures, habits, bod-ies, and desires' (Fraser, 1981, p. 278). It is this interplay between the power held by the consumers and their communities – within the acting out of their daily lives, wants, and needs – and the power of the brand to recognise those daily micro practices and to provide a prod-uct or service that addresses the desires therein. And, though brands can move into a community space and put down roots, the consum-ers maintain power within their choices to engage with that brand or actively move away.

This is not to say that brands cannot be used as landmarks if individual consumers do not engage with their products or services; even the utilisation of a brand as a navigational tool through which they can move through the cultural landscape imbues both the brand and the consumer with power in relation to one another. The power dynamics developed here are 'both intentional and non-subjective' (Foucault, 1978, p. 94). Because power is continually renegotiated between all parties within the cultural landscape, it has a 'directly productive role' (Foucault, 1978, p. 94) that comes from below, which is not distinguished by the binary of those who make the rules and those who follow.

Business Scenario: Uber in Denmark

Uber operates in over 10,000 cities across the world (Uber, 2024); yet none of them are in Denmark. In November 2014, global ride-sharing service Uber started giving lifts in Denmark and began facing difficulties almost immediately. With over 2,000 drivers and 300,000 app users in the country, it seemed like a great market for the company to move into, not least as forty employees of Uber's infrastructure soft-ware team were based in Aarhus (Skydsgaard, 2017). Though many local and foreign users appreciate the ability to summon a car via an app, the Danish government did not appreciate that Uber 'operated just like it does in the USA. The company simply did not care about existing legislation' (Lindahl, 2020).

With opposition from taxi driver trade unions and some parts of the political establishment, Uber set up regardless. For this action, it was reported by the Danish Transport, Building and Housing Authority to the 'police for being in breach of legislation' related to transporting people without proper licensing (Lindahl, 2020). Uber lost. In 2017 Denmark put into place new regulations to set caps at issuing new licences to drivers of taxis to 125 a month, drivers must have a taxi meter and seat-occupancy sensor for airbag activation (Rodionova, 2017). Uber argued under new regulations it would take years to get all Uber drivers licensed and would raise the barrier of entry due to the costs involved.

In the years between Uber's Denmark launch and when it left in April 2018, 1,500 Uber drivers were reported for violations of the regulations. The following debate led to Denmark slightly deregulating its taxi market, but it still required drivers and cars to be licensed. Because of this, Uber ceased providing ride-sharing services in the country. Ownership as power in the dynamic between the Danish government, Uber, and the consumers who interact with both parties shifted from Uber, as it moved into the country, to the Danish government, who saw the flouting of taxi regulations as a detriment to the wider community. As Uber left, it was noted that 'getting around Copenhagen before Uber launched there wasn't that hard' (Mack, 2017), and the brand had struck upon an apathy from consumer communities who did not oppose the Danish government's NIMBY stance to the brand.

Branding as an Imposition of Will

When brands are set up, there are different paths that organisations follow in defining what their brand assets will entail. Managing the customer in addition to the product or service available from the brand 'begins well before the customer realizes a need for the products' (Gupta et al., 2008, p. 949) and is part of the flow of information between the brand and the consumer. The organisation that creates a brand often focusses on the brand's distinctive features, which serve a twofold purpose: to distinguish the brand from other competitors in the marketplace; and to indicate how the brand should be perceived by the potential consumer (Ianenko et al., 2020).

The second point narrows in on the role that brands play in guiding the consumer's brand knowledge, which plays a part in 'the mental representation of brand awareness … and brand image' (Swaminathan et al., 2020, p. 25). Brand knowledge leads directly into the brand's equity, which is valuable for creating brand awareness, shaping the consumer's attitude towards the brand, and establishing corporate ethics, all of which are elements the brand can influence or control by developing a narrative brand structure that provides consumers with an easily navigable path through the cultural landscape (Lemon et al., 2001). Awareness relates directly to the ways that a brand shares its message with consumers, and in this case is platform agnostic.[6] Through advertising messages, brand ambassadors, reviews, and consumer/brand interactions, the brand helps guide the consumer's attitude towards the brand. In properly aligning their brand messages with their space in the cultural landscape the brand can facilitate emotional ties between themselves and the consumer – who often seeks to use the brand to 'signal identity to self and others, [… as brands help to] elicit [a consumer's] daydreaming, emotions, and aspirations' (Bagozzi et al., 2021, p. 586). By using their placement in the landscape and advertising to grow a sense of emotional connection between the brand and the consumer, the brand can help direct the consumer's attitude towards the brand, providing them with a narrative structure to follow. Both awareness and the way a consumers feels about and towards a brand are influenced by the way the brand itself functions in the era of the public(Smith, 2020),[7] where a brand's stance in regards to sociopolitical themes will alter how a consumer views the brand.

---

[6] In this theoretical consideration of branding in the cultural landscape, the platforms a brand utilises to speak to their consumers and potential consumers via advertising is less relevant than the spaces within the landscape in which they root themselves and how they tell that story to consumers. There are many studies on the roles of online advertising and brand equity that do the topic more justice (see Alhaddad, 2015; Rios & Riquelme, 2008; Alanne, 2017; and Fachreza et al., 2023). Likewise, for more information on the effect of comparative online/offline advertising on brand equity see: Kurniawan, 2020; Bayer et al., 2020; and Pauwels et al., 2016.

[7] For a more detailed explanation of the 'era of the public' see Chapter 6 on brand activism.

Providing a narrative brand structure for the consumer gives them an easy path to follow in relation to the brand, its placement in the cultural landscape, and how they move around the space in relation to their self-identity and self-projection. In addition to creating this trail for consumers to easily move across the landscape, brands can also control the way they differentiate themselves from others. This brand differentiation can be considered 'the engine of the brand train [... wherein] if the engine stops, so will the train' (Agris quoted in Aaker, 2003). It is therefore valuable for the organisation to consider how they will position their brand as different from the others that populate the consumer's cultural landscape. Even if the points of differentiation are meaningless with regard to the quality of the product or services themselves, and even if cost is higher than similar brands, consumers value the role that differentiation plays (Carpenter et al. 1994). Brands that are able to differentiate themselves from other products via their presentation, identity, and marketing, are able to ground themselves within the cultural landscape in such a way that consumers come to expect a certain level of service. Different elements of a brand's identity, such as colour, logos, and fonts, serve as quick cues for customers to quickly recognise one brand over another (Hoek & Gendell, 2010), or one region of the landscape from another. This differentiation works not only in the locality of the consumer, but also in horizon scanning by the consumer as they begin to plot how they move through the cultural space.

Signposting of what the brand offers, how it differs from other brands, and what the narrative structure of the brand entails, together provide pathways through the landscape that are imprinted with the brand's identity. The elements of brand identity are the 'building blocks that contribute, creatively, to enhancing brand presence' (Ward et al., 2020, p. 394). As consumers and brands coexist in the 'modern aspiration economy' (Andjelic, 2020, p. 2) that contributes to the changing dynamics of power in the cultural landscape, brands not only imprint their concept of identity and ownership in the spaces they put down roots, but there is also a consumer movement that coincides with the era of the public and relates status, aspiration, and identity to 'social capital, environmental credits, and cultural savviness' (Andjelic, 2020, p. 2). The change of the format of capital in the cultural landscape is part of a wider shift in our cultural understanding of 'value' in a time when the purchasing power of younger generations (Gen Z) is up to 86 per cent lower than that of Baby Boomers when they were the same age (Gupta, 2022).

Due to this change in how consumers and society define the concept of 'value' in relation to brands, consumption, and culture, brands are not the only entities that have the power to define a brand. While brands do have control over the creative aspects of differentiating their brand from others, and they can work to control the advertising a brand does and if/how a brand seeks to take part in aspects of authenticity and activism, they do not control the message once it is in the cultural landscape. Consider, for instance, when Twitter became X and the full-time internal moderation team was cut in half (Brewster, 2024) – issues of proximity began to arise on the platform. Ads for major brands such as Adobe and Gilead Sciences (among others) were seen to be running alongside tweets from an account 'promoting fascism' (Duffy & Fung, 2023). By appearing next to such controversial/inappropriate content consumers' favourability and trust for the brand dropped by 71 per cent and 70 per cent respectively (IAS, 2024, p. 7). Over half of consumers are unlikely to engage with (56 per cent) or recommend (52 per cent) the brand; furthermore, 51 per cent are likely to stop using a brand whose ads appear near inappropriate content (IAS, 2024, p. 8). Because the cultural landscape is comprised of shifting elements through which consumers must navigate, even if the brand develops signs and a narrative structure for consumers to follow, they cannot own the entirety of the community noticeboards and right of ways.

How the Power of a Brand Is Derived From and Embedded in Its Role as a Landmark

'Iconic brands function like cultural activists, encouraging people to think differently about themselves' (Holt, 2004, p. 9). This sense of 'thinking differently' is directly related to the interplay that a brand has with a consumer's sense of self-identity and self-projection, wherein consumers use brands as a way to form who they are and who they want to be seen to be. This imbuing of identity from a brand to a consumer's sense of self is filtered via a brand's products, where those products are 'a conduit through which consumers can experience the stories that the brand tells' (Holt, 2004, p. 36). The power that a brand holds is its position within the consumer's cultural landscape and the structural narratives that it can provide via its advertising highlighting the pathways and roads that lead consumers closer to them.

It is this ability to put down roots in the cultural landscape, or 'mythmaking', as described by Holt (2004), that gives brands their power. Much like in the physical landscape, a brand must choose a location in which to base itself, whether that outlet be branded stores, such as those that sell only items from one brand (Tiffany & Co., Audi, or L'Occitane), or retail outlets that bring together many brands under one roof (Harrods, Target, Belk, or Sephora). Each choice the brand considers makes a difference in how they position themselves in both the physical and cultural landscapes. These spaces do not exist in isolation, and there is power and capital involved in a brand's ability to claim real estate, which feeds into how they relate to the communities they enter into. While an exclusive luxury brand may be able to enter into a space of wealth and privilege such as Bond Street without pushback, brands that are seen to not align with desired capital (of all forms) of the area, such as a Poundland, may not be welcome. Likewise, brands that possess more capital and are more exclusive may not want to have space in the part of the landscape that does not align with their strategy, goals, and narrative.

Though, in the above consideration, brands choose a place to put down roots and the consumer communities in that area have the power to accept or reject that,[8] that power is not equally held or distributed. Consumers and brands that are rooted in areas with less capital, which are often less affluent or less connected, have less power over which brands are allowed to put down roots in their neighbourhoods. Closely linked to the role of gentrification in the physical world, which has been called 'the consequent transformation of an area into a middle class neighbourhood' (Smith & Williams, 1986, p. 1), those who call these spaces home often do not have the power or voice to push back. This can lead to displacement (Easton et al., 2020) or the social cleansing of a space (Cameron, 2003).[9]

---

[8] See the section on NIMBY and YIMBYs earlier in this chapter, 'What Does Power Mean in the Consumer's Cultural Landscape'.

[9] For more information on these concepts in the physical world see Qiang et al., 2021; Hepburn et al., 2024; Zuk et al., 2015; and see Forouhar et al., 2022; and Pastak et al, 2019, for more information on the role that commercial gentrification plays in changing urban neighbourhoods.

The power that a brand holds, then, is in relation not only to its ability to direct its capital to develop a narrative structure for consumers that can guide how a consumer understands and feels about the brand in a way that enables differentiation from its competition, but also in how it uses its power to choose a space in the cultural landscape to put down roots. This choice of location can potentially alter the make-up of the neighbourhood as the brand becomes a landmark that can be utilised by consumers for navigating the cultural space. The power to do this is checked by the power that consumers, within a shared location, hold and exert on the brand's ability to distribute its message and to put down pathways for a consumer to easily move towards the brand as they engage with closing the gap between their self-identity and self-projection. This power balance is held in place not only in the movement of a brand into a location, but in the daily movements, decisions, and purchasing power of consumers; all of which are overlaid with shifting socio-political contexts.

The creation and ownership of a brand is both a collaboration and juxtaposition between brands and consumers, consisting of community spaces, structural narratives, brand equity, landmarks, and the consumer's self-identity and self-projection. While organisations ostensibly develop and create brands in order to tell the story of their brand, develop a narrative structure for consumers to follow, and differentiate their products or services from other brands, once their brand and narrative structure is out in the world it is no longer directly controlled by the organisation.

Conclusion

In the consumer's cultural landscape, brands emerge as multifaceted entities that intertwine with the very fabric of identity, ownership, and power. This landscape, ever-shifting and filled with socio-political nuance, provides a stage where consumer–brand interactions unfold, each wanting and needing different things from the other and the spaces they inhabit. The notion of power within this context is complex and multifarious. For brands, power is woven through the narrative structures they create and the spaces, both physical and metaphorical, they occupy. By putting down roots and seeking to become a landmark brand, they have the power to alter consumer behaviour and perceptions and play a key role in how a consumer narrows the gap between their self-identity and self-projection. However, this power is not unilateral; it is reciprocal and often contested. As brands exert their influence in the cultural landscape, they simultaneously invite consumer agency, allowing consumers, and the communities in which they reside, to assert their own narratives upon the brand, shaping its meaning through their use and interpretation.

Legally, ownership is clear-cut, guarded by the rigidity of laws and rights. Psychologically, it is a personal, sometimes intimate, claim over a brand and a manifestation of a consumer's identity and experiences within the cultural landscape. The ownership consumers can feel over a brand can extend beyond the tangible to the essence of the brand itself, as consumers embed personal and communal narratives into the brand's identity, further complicating the concept of true ownership. Employees, too, play a role in this interplay of power and ownership. Their investment in the brand's success, driven by a sense of belonging and importance, not only reinforces the brand's internal culture but also radiates outward, affecting consumer perception and authenticity.

For the consumer, the brand serves both as a beacon and a mirror, helping them to recognise, and potentially narrow, the space between their self-identity and self-projection, and providing pathways through the cultural landscape. Brands with this power become landmarks, touchpoints that offer both direction and meaning. This relationship is dynamic; as consumers move through the cultural landscape their interactions with brands accumulate, contributing to a brand's equity. As brands establish themselves within the cultural landscape, they face the dual challenge of asserting their narrative while remaining open to the consumer's story. The separation of ownership from control becomes evident as consumers become co-authors of the brand narrative. This separation, in turn, indicates a shift in the traditional power structures within the consumer's cultural landscape.

Key Points

- Ownership is not just a legal right but also a psychological state that contributes to a consumer's sense of their self-identity and self-projection, and how they move to bring them into alignment.

- Brands serve as markers and extensions of consumers' identities, reflecting their personal histories, relationships, and their place within the social fabric. Consumers' attachment to brands can lead to a sense of ownership and control over the brand, irrespective of legal rights.
- The power a brand holds is derived from its position within the cultural landscape and its ability to influence consumer behaviour.
- Brands must consistently communicate and negotiate with consumers, including understanding the difference between imposing brand messages and co-creating narratives with consumers.
- There is a separation of ownership from control as brands put down roots within the cultural landscape. This creates a shift in power dynamics as consumers become co-authors of the brand's narrative structures, influencing how the brand is perceived and experienced in the cultural landscape.

8 | The Transience of Power in the Cultural Landscape

It is therefore not surprising to find that, at any given moment, perceptions of power turn out to be both misleading and fleeting; and that
the calculations of power are even more delicate and deceptive than in
previous ages.

S. Hoffmann, Notes on the elusiveness of
modern power, *International Journal*

Anywhere that consumers, brands, and culture interact, power
dynamics come into play. Some aspects of power are directly related
to the control and movement of capital in and across the cultural landscape;[1] other concentrations of power are found in the brands that
choose to put down roots in the cultural landscape, the relationships
those brands have with the communities in which they enter, and the
consumers who both call these spaces home and who encounter these,
now occupied, spaces as they move across the landscape. The ebb and
flow of consumers and capital in an ever-shifting cultural landscape
'forces us to consider the assemblages of power that actively channel
and direct flows across multiple spaces' (Raeymaekers, 2019, p. 60).
When a brand is able to make a place for itself and develop a narrative structure that allows consumers to use it as a navigational beacon, the brand has accumulated power to become a landmark part of
the cultural landscape.

Within an organisation there is often institutionalised power that
is developed and upheld by a belief in a course of action for the
brand, or North Star,[2] a sense that those who have the most say in the

---

[1] The topic of capital in the cultural landscape is considered in depth in
Chapter 3; while a more complete understanding of the cultural landscape is
developed in Chapter 1.

[2] The North Star metric provides an overall direction that is directly related to
the value to give to a consumer; focussing on the product/service and what it

organisation are on the right path, and the development and growth of networks to solidify the positions of those who are able to make internal decisions (Ocasio, 1994). Within this place of power, represented by the space a brand owns within the cultural landscape, the brand develops and solidifies its identity within that space and creates a means to connect with consumers via its messaging. An example of the way a brand might move to reinforce its identity and ownership within a space is when it embraces aspects of glocalisation, whereby a global outlook is applied to local conditions – a concept closely related to micro-marketing (Robertson, 1994). Multinational brands such as McDonald's and Starbucks are prime examples of those that are able to utilise their global positioning as navigational landmarks for consumers, while also tapping into the wants and needs of their local audiences by providing region-specific offerings. Glocalisation is accounted for in the North Star of each, where McDonald's focusses on making 'delicious feel-good moments easy for everyone' (McDonald's, 2024), while Starbucks hones in on connection with a mission that states, 'With every cup, with every conversation, with every community – we nurture the limitless possibilities of human connection' (Starbucks, 2024). In adapting their brand offerings to the local communities, brands are able to embed themselves and become more easily accessible for those consumers to use in navigating their self-identity and self-projection in the cultural landscape.

This can, however, go wrong for a brand that is not able to consolidate its institutionalised power, as happened for Starbucks in 2017. With the brand's new focus on their North Star to ensure that Starbucks baristas develop an emotional connection with consumers, there was backlash from baristas as they felt they were not given the tools to make those better connections (Taylor, 2017). Without addressing issues such as understaffing and how long it takes to create drinks, Starbucks' North Star project 'landed with a thud' (Holden, 2017) and there has been further diluting of what the brand can look like as it solidifies its hold on the 'third space' between home and work in the face of changing values and working patterns (Rainey, 2022). This situation has recurred again in light of the war between Israel

gives to a consumer enables a brand to drive engagement and create a strategic direction for the brand. For more information on the North Star metric see: Ellis, 2017 and Chen, 2022.

and Gaza, where Starbucks Workers United Union (a collective of US Starbucks workers) posted (now deleted) on Twitter/X 'solidarity with Palestine'. It was not authorised by the union itself (Meyersohn, 2023). This has sparked backlash at Starbucks stores worldwide and Starbucks currently has a lawsuit against the union for using its name and logos. The Starbucks Workers United Union has filed a counter-suit against Starbucks. The back and forth between the organisation and the union playing out in the public eye alters how consumers react to the brand as a whole, sometimes steering clear of Starbucks, sometimes boycotting it and its physical locations.

When a brand is able to harness their space within the shifting land-scape, and the changing values of the players that populate it, brands 'create a powerful transnational appeal as they represent a set of shared norms that not only resonate across (most) cultures, but also speak to the experiences of (most) individual [consumers]' (Asmar et al., 2023, p. 26). Whether on a micro, community level, or at the macro, city/country level, brands that are able to put down roots and tap into the culture of the consumers and communities they wish to speak to are in a position of controlling power in that space. The power a brand holds is directly related to where the brand exists in the cultural landscape, and how much ownership the brand claims over the resources that are val-ued within that community or space; this leads to a hierarchical power structure between brands, consumers, and spaces (Rucker et al., 2012).

Because power relations are linked to controlling resources that ebb and flow, as the mapped edges of the cultural landscape expand and contract, perceived differences in power become apparent in the asymmetric control of value propositions through a lens of capital exchange (Rucker et al., 2012). These changes in power dynamics can be temporary, such as when a branded product becomes the new 'it' item, as did velour Juicy Couture tracksuits or the Von Dutch trucker hats in the early 2000s (which are making a return – as much fashion is cyclical in nature),[3] and then fall out of favour. Or they can last over generations in ways that are often associated with heritage brands (Burberry, Jaguar, Hunter Boots, Liberty).[4] The relationship, either

---

[3] To further explore how fashion is cyclical and the power of designs returns in different ways in different periods, see Cho, 2019; Tripp, 2021; and Ewens, 2022.

[4] It can be noted that these brands are all part of the 'luxury' market. This is often because a brand like this may have a 'longer history, track record, core values, use of symbols and particularly ... organisational belief that its history

real or imagined, that a consumer has with a brand as they move around the landscape plays a role in helping the consumer form their sense of identity, wherein their self-identity and self-projection come into alignment. The moves that the consumer makes are informed by their sense of self, the cultural capital they hold and desire, and narrative structures laid out by the brands in these shared spaces. In drawing these narrative structures, or 'affective boundaries', in wide parts of the cultural landscapes, brands are able to delineate 'who is included and who is excluded, as well as indicate a power relation' (Dahlman, 2023, p. 15).

Becoming a landmark brand that consumers can use for navigating their cultural landscape links to what O'Reilly (2005, p. 582) considers to be branding as a 'socially constructed text'. This can be achieved by 'manipulating symbols to which they [the consumer] respond[s]' (Palmieri, 1963, p. 200); and, furthermore, by the acquirement of knowledge as it relates to the productivity and relational aspects of power (Cooper, 1994; Dore, 2010). Though it has been noted that power is transient (Palmieri, 1963), it is only relatively recently that brand messages go beyond one-directional outputs to what can be seen as an increase in conversations between brands and consumers. The dynamic where a brand has always been more powerful than a consumer is changing (Saldanha et al., 2023), and the empowerment of consumers as stakeholders signifies a shift in the traditional power structures. Consumers' collective voice can alter brand value, making it imperative for brands to engage in a dialogue with consumers, to negotiate meanings and to co-create experiences.

The Role of the Consumer in Assigning and Removing Brand Power

Because power is impermanent and subject to circulation (Ocasio, 1994), it shifts and moves across the cultural landscape, gathering in places where brands put down their roots, and also among communities of consumers, wherein power shapes how consumers value themselves in relation to others (Rucker et al., 2012). The power dynamic

is important' (Urde et al., 2007, p. 4). As Urde et al. point out, there are differences between brands with heritage and heritage brands, in that heritage brands use their history as a part of their brand's value and positioning in the cultural landscape.

that exists between brands and consumers is played out in the spatiality of the cultural landscape and between the shifting socio-political constructs that move across the space. Where it used to be that brands put down narrative structures that developed pathways for the consumers to use to draw near to the brand, consumers are now more prepared to take advantage of the '*productive* nature of power's modern exercise' (Sergiu, 2010, p. 58; original emphasis).

Consumers are able to do this by a combination of connectivity within their wide communities and relationality with themselves (their self-identity and self-projection), other consumers, brands, and the topography of the landscapes in which these elements come together and diverge. And, '[o]ut of all of the areas where the brand is built, it is important to pay close attention to the consumers and the perception of value they assign to the brand' within this space (González-Mansilla et al., 2023, p. 242). In the traditionally hierarchical method of branding, wherein the organisation creates a brand to develop and market their product/service, the points of sale are a means of top-down, brand-to-consumer product flow that is facilitated by the brand's structural narrative and often not consented to by the consumers (Leitch & Merlot, 2018). However, brands at the apex of this hierarchy do not alone form the source of power that a brand has; this power is a relationship between the brand at the top and the consumers below, where power is found in the 'relationship of mutual support and conditioning' that upholds the system (Foucault, 1980, p. 159).

The power to maintain the current system of brand and consumer relationships is multidirectional and moves from below (Foucault, 1980, p. 201). The flow of power between brands and consumers has been accelerated in digital settings; with access to social media consumers are now perceived to be equally as powerful as brands (Saldanha et al., 2023). This change can be seen as challenging to brands that have historically retained control over how their messaging fits into their narrative structure (Tewari & Mittal, 2014). However, most brands have taken on board this relational change in power dynamics and often now work to co-create value with consumers around what Boyd et al. (2014) call 'consumer empowerment'. This manifests in three different ways: a strategic approach, an information-based approach, and the influential approach, that is, one consumer's perceived influence over other consumers. Within the strategic approach brands engage with consumers to allow them to create ideas and to choose which of these ideas work for them (Fuchs & Schreier, 2011; McShane & Sabadoz, 2015), providing consumers with a sense of ownership of the brand's product and services. We can see this when works of fiction are written on Wattpad and readers make suggestions that the author brings into the story, enabling the reader to feel connected to the work in a new way.

The informational approach to the co-creation of a brand is focussed on the brand providing enough information to the consumer so that they feel a sense of understanding of the brand's product/service and can make an informed choice (Pires et al., 2006; Tiu Wright et al., 2006). This comes to fruition for brands like Barbour, where the heritage and story information they provide via their narrative structure is enough to secure brand attachment/loyalty from the consumer.

The value that is created when consumers are able to influence one another is an example of the movement of power from above (the brands), to below (the consumers), and back again (Boyle et al, 2014). This expression of power is highlighted by influencer culture and the visibility of consumption in the digital age, where a TikTok influencer like Charli D'Amelio has large amounts of power in suggesting products and services to her nearly 150 million followers.[5] However, the influence of one consumer over another can have a negative effect. This power dynamic can be illustrated by cancel culture where 'cancelling is an expression of power' (Saldanha et al., 2023, p. 1072) that is gathered by consumers and used against a brand in a public space.

With the 'progressive empowerment of stakeholders' (Siano et al., 2022, p. 372), there is a gradual loss of control by brands over their branding and messages, especially in a hyper-connected world, where brand meaning is co-created (Swaminathan et al., 2020).[6]

---

[5] Influencers such as Charli D'Amelio work with a variety of brands from Prada to Hollister; she has used her status as one of the most highly paid influencers ($17.5 m per annum) to launch a TV mini-series and cosmetic collaboration with Morphe Cosmetics (Santora, 2023). In doing this, D'Amelio expands her reach and power in the cultural landscape in a way that is both reliant on, and has power over, brands.

[6] There is a growing body of work on the co-creation of brand experiences based around branded experiences developing consumer/brand engagement. For a starting point into the research in this area see: Merrilees, 2016; Stach, 2019; Ramaswamy & Ozcan, 2016; Nysveen, et al., 2014; and Merz et al., 2018.

While Kusume and Gridley (2013) define the co-creation of value as being focussed on the creation and sustainability of an emotional connection between consumers and a brand, this is a somewhat simplistic understanding of a concept that forms part a complex relationship between brands, consumers and their identity, and the cultural landscape and the socio-political shifts that take place within it. While open-source co-creation of products and services might enable consumers to personalise products (making their own customised pair of Converse shoes, for example), and lead to the consumer moving closer to the brand in the cultural landscape, this co-creation is still within the control of the brand, which can decide what personalisation they allow and what consumers' ideas for products/services they take on. This type of brand co-creation is comfortable for the brand.

Brand co-creation that is less comfortable happens when the consumer takes control of the brand's message – disrupting its narrative structure and the pathways to the brand's space within the cultural landscape. The process by which brand knowledge is created and shared, especially across 'instant' platforms such as social media, can happen outside the brand's ability to monitor and control it. The value of 'immediacy over veracity' (Leitch & Merlot, 2018, p. 91) plays a role in the consumer developing a resistance to brand messaging and enables them to apply their own meaning to a brand's narrative structure and choose how to use it in relationship to their self-identity and self-projection, where they are and where they want to be in the cultural landscape, and what socio-political factors are at play in a particular time and space.

When a brand's messaging is out in the world, it is almost too late for the brand to manage how it is perceived. Though brands may have taken the time to lay out a narrative structure for consumers to follow, brands must be prepared for consumers to make use of that messaging as they will, and to either use the narrative structures laid down by the brand, or to ignore the easy paths and follow their own way towards the brand, or to actively tear down the paths made by the brands, making the paths harder for other consumers to follow. With this in mind, the power that a brand has within the cultural landscape is to put down roots and become a landmark that consumers can use to navigate, even if the consumers are not navigating towards the brand itself.

Power Shifts across the Cultural Landscape and Their Impact

The influence that consumers have on each other and that brands have on consumers and the spaces they inhabit, ebbs and flows, and though 'there is no single dominant social relation, this does not mean there is no order at all' (Joseph, 2004, p. 159). In fact, order and structure are often provided by the landscape in which these interactions take place. The cultural landscape exists in a liminal space between the physical and the digital worlds and its topography and borders are continually shifting. The narrative structures that a brand develops to enable consumers to move towards them must exist within the constructs of the spaces available to it. In the cultural landscape we may see this as brands using advertisements to create narrative structures that lead directly to the brand and the neighbourhood in which it is situated, but these neighbourhoods also play a role in who can put down roots within them and how their spaces are traversed.

The complex interplay between the moving parts of the cultural landscape allows power to move through both 'hierarchical and independent layers; [where] these layers intertwine visibly and invisibly, below-ground as well as aboveground, horizontally and also vertically' (Van Dijk, 2020, p. 2802). Power here can change direction when it comes into contact with individuals, communities, other brands and structures, and in relation to the socio-political context that flows across the landscape. For instance, when a luxury brand puts down roots among other luxury brands, power is stored up within that agglomerated location as that space becomes a brighter landmark that consumers can use to know where they are within the landscape and navigate accordingly. Even among consumers who will never use or purchase a luxury handbag, car, coat, or other items, the grouping together of luxury brands indicates something of the power and economic and social capital that is likely to be imbued in these grouping of luxury brands. Likewise, groupings of brands that are more everyday and utilitarian in nature also can provide narrative structures and beacons within the landscape.

Power among brands is often concentrated in particular spaces, as brands tend to set down roots in locations where they are more likely to be welcome and find consumers who want to make use of the interplay of capital that being near/using a brand's products and services bestows. Brands that have multiple locations in the cultural landscape rely on the 'permanent and expanding monopoly of portions of society's knowledge' and the intangible assets (power) that knowledge brings (Rikap, 2021, p. 1). As brands grow, they can exert more power in the cultural landscape, though they can also be at risk from power growing from below (consumers) to directly affect their organisation in the form of boycotts, cancel culture, or other forms of 'non-collaborative co-creation' (Kristal et al., 2018).

Brands and the cultural landscape they inhabit influence each other's development and value (Cova & Paranque, 2016). Sometimes this comes in the form of a backlash where power of image control is taken from the brand and the process becomes one of brand destruction (Gyrd-Jones & Kornum, 2013). Kristal et al. (2018, p. 342) found that brand attacks are often driven by 'risk-affecting', high-equity brands,[7] and that '[b]rand meanings created by non-collaborative co-creators are starting to compete with the [originally indented] brand meanings'. This shift in power from the brand to the consumer's view of the brand can alter based on the brand's position in the cultural landscape, the capital and reach of the consumer, the consumers' former attachment to the brand, and how quickly a new vision of the brand spreads (Jain & Sharma, 2019).

Because brands within the cultural landscape are 'fluid and open entities that are co-created through social processes involving multiple stakeholders' (Saleem & Iglesias, 2016, p. 44), the way they interact across physical and digital spaces alters the power dynamic between themselves and consumers. When consumers utilise a brand as a means of discovering how they can best align their self-identity and self-projection they do so by drawing near a brand by either purchasing and using the product or service, by means of conspicuous consumption, or even by drawing near to the space in the cultural landscape in which the brand has put down roots. This drawing near is especially relevant in a digitally connected world where consumers can maintain (some) anonymity as they present themselves in a cultural space. By drawing near to a brand, even if they do not, or cannot, engage directly with the brand, they can join in with consumer communities that are made up of both users and aspirational users of the brand.

---

[7] High-equity brands are often associated with luxury or expensive items where consumers are happy to pay a higher price for a product or service from a particular brand when they could get a similar product or service from elsewhere at a lower cost.

Drawing near to a brand is directly connected to the concept of 'reflected glory', which is the 'tendency to strive for prestigious affiliations' (Aadland et al., 2020, p. 29), or, at the least, to have some aspect of status granted to the consumer by being near to places where power sits. As consumers take the paths laid down by the narrative structure of the brand's messaging and funnel towards the position the brand takes up in the cultural landscape, they develop as a group. As they develop social ties with each other they are less likely to utilise the brand itself to confer status on other community members (Aadland et al., 2020). The growth of brand communities is both a benefit to the brand, in that there is a group of consumers with a shared set of identity values that integrate with the brand, and has the potential to be detrimental where, as the community grows, so does members' knowledge of each other, the brand, and the spaces different players take up in the cultural landscape, which can lead to consumers choosing other brands. This growth of community is also an amalgamation of this knowledge and power.

Some brands rely on their ability to control the power that amasses near them; however, studies have repeatedly shown that when consumers group around a brand,[8] the brand is 'no longer the sole creator of value' (Kristal et al., 2018, p. 335). When groups of consumers come together around a brand they create communities and if they use their growing knowledge of each other and the brand to wield the power that knowledge entails, they can come to 'take greater control over the association that characterizes the brand rather than the brand team which actually supports the brand' (Veloutsou, 2009, p. 128). At the point of critical mass of consumer power it can become trickier for the brand to maintain not only control over, but also the goodwill of, the consumers if, for example, the brand is seen to do something that goes against the consumer communities' understanding of the brand's values.

Sometimes consumers use their power to widen the pathways to a brand by taking advantage of the brand's narrative structure, which

---

[8] For more detailed considerations of different strands of brand co-creation and co-ownership see Kou & Powpaka, 2021, for brand pseudo-ownership; Payne et al., 2009, for consumers as co-creators of experience; and Zwick et al., 2008, Sarasvuo et al., 2022; Biraghi & Gambetti, 2017; and Ramaswamy & Ozcan, 2016, for what co-creation means and who participates in it.

can lead them and others directly to the brand. At other times, consumers can cause harm to a brand with relative ease. They can wield their mass to cancel a brand, or can wield, more directly, consumer brand sabotage, a form of deliberate, aggressive behaviour from the consumer towards the brand (Kähr et al., 2016, p. 25). This can lead to brand hate, where negative emotions (anger, contempt, disgust, and dissatisfaction (see Fetscherin, 2019; Kucuk, 2018)) and events can lead consumers to act against a brand. This is especially the case when consumers are in communication with one another, as they are more likely to share information about negative brand experiences (as opposed to positive ones) (Ritcher, 2018).

Brand sabotage, cancelling a brand, brand hate, and the negative feelings that a consumer, or consumer community, has not only encourages a consumer to move away from the brand in the consumer landscape, it could potentially alienate the consumer from the community that congregates around the brand. 'Empowered by new technological possibilities' (Kähr et al., 2016, p. 25), consumers can not only move away from the brand, but they can actively disrupt the brand's narrative structures, which form part of the pathways leading to the brand. However, it is not the case that brands that face backlash from consumers are removed from the cultural landscape. If a brand is able to put down roots within a space and carve out its area so that it can be seen by consumers as part of the topography, it can remain utilised by consumers as a landmark by which consumers can navigate the landscape and their own identity.

The Power of Having Access To, and Use of, Platforms and Spaces

The spaces that brands and consumers have access to in the cultural landscape are both physical and digital in nature and exist beyond the limits of textual boundaries. A brand's access to physical spaces is linked to the capital they can bring to bear on a physical community, and its networks, to either move into a grouping of like-minded, similar brands (as in a luxury village shopping area), or to move into a neighbourhood where it may be the only brand of its type – pushing the edges of its (and the community's) perceived authenticity. This movement into particular tangible spaces is underlined by governmental regulations and the limitations of physical topography and spaces, both within the brand's store and the areas in which consumers can congregate around it.

The agglomeration effect is when brands seek to locate close to competitors in order to potentially increase their market share. Though there is the potential for consumers to choose to enter another store, overall the effect of being located in a grouping of like-minded brands is positive for each (Pasidis, 2013). Brands that cluster together can share narrative structures as pathways to the grouping of brands. While there might be competition among brands in how they highlight their products/services using the limited infrastructural resources (signs, size/shape of stores, etc.), the combined volume of the cluster works as a more visible landmark in the cultural landscape by which a consumer can navigate.

In the digital age, there is both more and less agglomeration of brands. There is more in that the main platforms by which brands seek to reach consumers are shared across a huge variety of brands, and less in that within digital locations each community space can feel like an island unto itself. In this liminal space between where brands are both clustered and spread out across the cultural landscape, 'brands are social processes represented by constant online textual interactions in a stakeholder network and brand meanings as dynamic online textual expressions of what stakeholders have in mind about a brand' (Vallaster & Wallpach, 2013, p. 1505). The value of brand meaning in digital spaces is underlined by the platforms and spaces in which a brand chooses to develop their narrative structures and the interplay between those locations, networks, and structure with how a consumer chooses to perform their identity (which in itself is a complex process of self-identity and self-projection in a space that has less limitations on the physicality of self-presentation).

How players in the cultural landscape and the digital suburbs engage with the concept of identity is tied up with the perception of authenticity. The perceived authenticity of a brand and where it puts down roots in the cultural landscape are directly related to how much power it holds and how it can wield said power within its space. If a brand moves to the edge of authenticity, near the outside of the known topography of the cultural landscape, it maintains more power to say how that space will be developed and who can put down roots near the brand, than if it situated itself within a community grouping of brands – or a brand node (Pitta & Katsanis, 1995; Till et al., 2011) – with similar equity and capital.[9] However, this is not always the case as some brands are able to move into a community and, in doing so, can gain more power than their neighbours. What matters in determining where the power flows within and around a brand is the brand's possession of different types of capital and how it seeks to both develop a narrative structure leading to it and situate itself in relation to other brands nearby.

With this in mind, brands can be seen as evolving 'dynamic entities, actively contributing to the lives of consumers' (Füller, 2016, p. 357). This process is made easier by the connectivity of the consumers' daily lives and the growth of digital suburbs,[10] which encompass the continuum from the physical to digital landscapes inhabited by both consumers and brands. The power dynamic in this space is a balancing act where new practices that are consumer-centric are coming to the fore (Leitch & Merlot, 2018), such as speaking directly to the consumer instead of via intermediaries (Weber, 2009), and providing a brand community space where like-minded consumers can draw near the brand and to others with similar focusses. In physical locations brands are subject to external forces that have a say in whether the brand can set down roots within a particular community. Likewise, in digital spaces, brands and consumers alike are subject to the regulations of the platforms on which they build relationships. The intermediary platforms 'mediate between infrastructures and individual users, as well as between infrastructures and society sectors' (Van Dijk, 2021, p. 2806). In mediating, the platforms transform the content presented on them into a structure that works within platform constraints.

It would be easy to consider that, in the digital sphere, power is concentrated in the platforms; however, we should take into account how platforms are now embedded 'in a complex array of markets'

---

[9] A brand node relates to the parcels of stored information that a consumer has about a brand. They may have strong or weak connections to other nodes; for example, 'favourite snack' may link to 'chocolate and peanut butter', which can draw lines to 'Reese's'; or 'best car' might link to a cluster of nodes comprised of 'Audi', 'BMW', 'Ford', or 'Genesis'. Each individual consumer will have different nodes they connect, based on their personal experiences, but these can also be influenced by outside pressures such as society, economics, and more.

[10] For more information about digital suburbs, see Chapter 1.

(Prey, 2020, p. 2) and are an interface between users.[11] In this consideration, platforms are multisided markets (Nieborg et al., 2022) and the power is balanced in a tetrad of players: brands, platforms, consumers, and governing bodies. While this is a somewhat simplistic take on the power dynamics in digital spaces, it serves to showcase how power can move across these spaces with fluidity as long as the balance remains stable, with power flowing from brands to consumer and back again through the prism of the platform's constraints. When power begins to amass in one of the corners of the tetrad, the balance tips the system, and that is when capital moves and changes the shape of the tetrad.

The cultural landscape is able to absorb the new tetradic shape a shifting power dynamic brings to the fore by altering its topography. As this new digital power dynamic moves across the cultural landscape, its edges can either be softened or sharpened by the ebb and flow of sociopolitical overlay within different spaces. This is most evident in the heart of cities, where social-political considerations have a larger say on what can or cannot be done within that power tetrad (consider the role of the General Data Protection Regulation (GDPR) across the EU). Likewise, in the digital suburbs and leading out to the digital wilds, there may be less regulation and wider proliferation of dark platforms (dark net), which have their own internal power dynamics.

Conclusion

As brands establish themselves within the cultural landscape, they face the challenge of putting down roots in a space in order to become a landmark brand, developing a structural narrative that can serve as a pathway for consumers to use to navigate their way towards the brand. Brands do not operate in isolation; they coexist with and are shaped by the communities they serve. The communities, in turn, are made up of consumers who now have the ability to amass their power and speak directly to a brand. The concept of glocalisation, a blend of global outreach and local adaptation, showcases how brands can tailor their products or services to meet regional tastes while maintaining a universal appeal. This approach allows brands to ingrain

---

[11] 'Users', in this instance, refers to the widest definition of those who make use of platform spaces, including consumers and brands.

themselves into the local fabric, becoming landmarks not just in physical spaces, but in the cultural landscapes of their consumers.

However, the dynamic is not unidirectional. Consumers, now more than ever, wield significant influence over brands. The wider access to digital spaces has begun to democratise the flow of power, enabling consumers to shape a brand's structural narratives and assert their expectations through different channels. This shift is evident in the rise of cancel culture and the phenomenon of brand sabotage, where consumer communities can exert their influence to uphold or dismantle a brand's standing in society. The cultural landscape itself is a stage for the performance of power. By integrating themselves into the fabric of consumer life, brands can become part of a community's identity (both internally and externally). The success of a brand in anchoring itself within this landscape is a testament to its ability to understand and align with the collective narrative of its consumers.

As the landscape evolves, so too does the nature of power. The separation of ownership from control becomes evident as consumers become co-creators of the brand. This becomes more apparent in the digital ecosystem where brands are simultaneously clustered on major platforms yet isolated in their unique digital spaces. The dynamics of power in digital spaces can be seen as a tetrad wherein brands, consumers, platforms, and regulators all have a role in balancing the power dynamic within a particular space. The stability of this power structure is susceptible to shifts that can reshape the cultural topography, influenced by socio-political forces and the evolving digital marketplace.

Because the cultural landscape in which brands and consumers interact is a dynamic ecosystem, it remains marked by a constant flux of power and ownership. Brands are not merely commercial entities but cultural symbols that embody and reflect the values, aspirations, and identities of the consumers with whom they engage. This symbiotic relationship underscores the notion that power is not a static commodity to be owned but a fluid resource, shaped and reshared through interaction and interpretation.

Key Points

• Power dynamics are influenced by the movement of capital and the strategies that brands employ to integrate into local communities and cultural spaces.

- Power is not only held by brands but is also dynamic and can shift to consumers as they interact with and navigate these spaces.
- Glocalisation can allow brands to become navigational landmarks for consumers.
- Facilitated by digital connectivity, consumers can engage in dialogues with brands, negotiate meanings, and co-create brand experiences, effectively becoming stakeholders with the power to alter brand value.
- Consumers are now more involved in the branding process, contributing to the narrative structure and value of brands. This shift challenges traditional brand control and requires brands to engage in strategic, information-based, and influential co-creation with consumers.
- Power in the cultural landscape is impermanent and circulatory, gathering in places where brands and consumer communities interact, and is always shifting in balance.

Discussion Questions

1. How do global brands use glocalisation to balance global consistency with local relevance, and what are the implications of this approach for the power dynamics between the brand and local cultures? Consider also the balance of power between the organisation and franchisees (including the consumer experience).
2. Analyse the impact of a current socio-political event, such as conflicts or social movements, on the consumer perception of brand power and identity. How should brands navigate their messaging during such events? Is there more danger in staying silent?
3. If power in the cultural landscape is transient, how have digital platforms shifted the balance of power between brands and consumers, particularly with the rise of phenomena like cancel culture and brand sabotage. Consider the example of 'United Breaks Guitars' as a starting point.

Case Study 3
Shifting Power
Skype, Burberry, and Old Spice

The relationship begins when both the brand and consumer are on equal footing.

J. DeLane, 4 reasons why consumers view brands as relationships, *Digital Branding Institute*

Brands are no longer able to simply choose a space in the landscape to put down their roots and develop their brand as a part of the community unopposed. Though they may be able to exploit the exchange of capital to gain entry into a space, economic capital is not the only form of capital that comes into play in the delicate balance of power in the cultural landscape. And while ownership, in many ways, is a form of power,[1] it is transient in nature and subject to interplay between consumers and the communities they are a part of, the topography of the cultural landscape itself, and the shifting flow of socio-political considerations within a particular space and time.[2]

The increased growth and adoption of digital technologies as a means of extending the cultural landscape into a series of digital cities and suburbs has added further fulcrum points into the balance of power. These relate to the amalgamation of power in the platforms, which both allow for direct communication with consumers via brand communities and brand spaces, but also give parts of the brand's narrative structure over to consumers. As the power of brand ownership shifts from the brand alone to become an entity that moves from the top of the hierarchy to the bottom and back again, a brand becomes 'the sum of all the individual experiences that customers have with it' (Rakestraw, 2022). The experiences that consumers have with a brand are both deeply personal and often emotional (Carrol & Ahuvia, 2006; Langner et al., 2016;

---

[1] For a detailed consideration of ownership as power see Chapter 7.
[2] For a fuller discussion of the transience of power in the cultural landscape in relation to brands see Chapter 8.

Magids et al., 2015). As such, a consumer's reaction to brand messaging is not always clear cut. Instead, the way a consumer reacts is both individual, in that they take themselves into account in relation to the brand and the space they currently inhabit in the cultural landscape, and collective, in how they navigate the other players and the socio-political context in the spaces between their self-identity and self-projection. While a brand can utilise data to better understand its current and potential consumers, it must also take into account the influences that the community mass holds and the (potentially volatile) effect of the power/knowledge complex that is found within groups.

If organisations can no longer maintain complete ownership and control over their brand, they must find ways to work with and within consumer communities to co-create value that both engages with consumers on their own terms and provides a structural narrative that leads towards the brand. This is not always a straightforward process of simply providing narrative pathways or becoming a visible enough part of the cultural landscape that consumers can utilise the brand to navigate. Brands such as Old Spice have been able to ride the ebb and flow of power from the brand to the consumer, and have been able to successfully harness this movement to reposition themselves within the cultural landscape and develop narrative structures that draw in a new consumer group. Not all brands successfully manage to maintain the equilibrium of power. Burberry and Skype are two such brands that have, over different periods in their lifespan, found the transience of power works against their brand. While Burberry found its classic branding being taken up by a less traditional consumer group, Skype was unable to develop a narrative structure that was useful to and picked up by consumers. Burberry has managed to maintain its 'dual markets' over the years, while working to shift its consumer market back to the spaces in the cultural landscape in which they can better exert ownership, but Skype has done considerably less well with engaging with their consumers and has continued to experience a rocky descent.

Narrative Structures and Rocky Landscapes

Back in 2003, when peer-to-peer sharing of files was beginning to really get off the ground,[3] Skype was launched as a free voice-calling

---

[3] By 2003, when Skype was founded, Napster (a peer-to-peer digital file sharing platform for audio) had already been closed for two years after, arguably,

platform that users could utilise to make calls via their headsets and computer. The idea was based on the concept that the more people who used Skype, the more reliable the connection would be for everyone; furthermore, it allowed for free international calls (Aamoth, 2011). Just two years after it was founded, Skype was purchased by eBay for $2.6 billion in one of the largest exits in European tech history. After a few rough internal years, eBay sold Skype to Silver Lake ($2.75 billion); Silver Lake then sold it on to Microsoft in 2011 for $8.5 billion. With a seeming monopoly on internet-based voice and video calls, Skype was a disruptive technology that successfully integrated voiceover internet protocol and peer-to-peer sharing in a way that changed the technological landscape and unseated the hierarchy of communications (Roa et al., 2006).

Since Microsoft purchased Skype their marketing campaigns have grown, beginning with their 'It's Time for Skype' (2012), which mocked other social platforms as falling short of creating a true connection, and moving to memorable advertisements that leaned heavily into the emotional connection of users across their platform. Notable ads include one titled 'Stay Together', featuring two young women, both born with only one arm, growing up sharing a connection with each other from across the world via Skype – eventually leading to their emotional meeting in person. The ad highlights how connectivity is at the heart of the organisation and was honoured at the 2014 Cannes Lions Awards. More ads followed in the next few years showcasing ways that Skype could be used to boost connections (in the 'This Is My Family' campaign in China, 2014) via new tools such as live translations (shown across the UK in the 'Guide' campaign, 2015).

However, by 2017 Microsoft had integrated several features into a Skype redesign that saw its core product diluted to a point that ratings in the US app store dropped from 3.5 to 1.5 stars, and which had users feeling as if Skype was trying too hard to be like other platforms such as Snapchat (Chowdhry, 2017). By the time the global pandemic hit in 2020, it seemed that Skype was due a rebirth into the cultural landscape in a new context that saw much of the world locked down and working from home. But, this was not the case. In March 2020,

pioneering peer-to-peer file sharing on a mass scale with (often illegal) sharing of MP3 files (Carlsson & Gustavsson, 2001).

Microsoft indicated that 'Skype had 40 million daily active users, up 70% from the previous month', but this fell short of Microsoft's other connectivity software Teams, which in April 2020 had 75 million active daily users (Novet, 2020). 'Even backed by the world's largest software company, Skype is falling by the wayside' (Novet, 2023), with Zoom owning 57 per cent of the global videoconferencing market in 2023 (post pandemic), followed by Microsoft Teams (24.5 per cent); Skype owns 1.18 per cent (T3 Technology Hub, 2023).

In the space of a handful of years during the 2020s Skype quickly lost its dominance over the videoconferencing space. This was not due to consumers hating the brand or disagreeing with its morals and values. Consumers did not cancel Skype, but neither were they able to connect with the brand, which stayed focussed on the era of the person without also beginning to move into the era of the public. This is partly due to Skype being under the wider umbrella of Microsoft, with less of its own structural narrative for consumers. Because of this inability to maintain the pathways the brand originally laid down for consumers, it is harder for consumers to see the roads to follow to move towards the brand. The power dynamic here has not been a swift downfall of Skype, but instead has been a slow movement of power down from Skype to consumer communities and back upwards to other brands, such as Zoom, as the knowledge/power dynamic shifted in the cultural landscape.

Skype is far from the only brand that has not been able to maintain their narrative structures in a way that allows consumers to easily navigate towards their brand. Both Old Spice and Burberry Inc. have had times in their history when the power of their brand moved beyond their control and shifted how they were seen by consumers. The difference among Old Spice, Burberry, and Skype is that Old Spice and Burberry recognised that though they might share ownership of their brand with consumers, a large part of balancing the power dynamic between their brand and consumers was in how they positioned themselves within the cultural landscape and the narrative structures that they built so that consumes can easily move towards them.

Founded in 1856, Burberry is a global fashion brand with a 'deep British heritage' (Burberry, 2024). It is known throughout the world for its iconic trench coats, Burberry check (1920s), and the equestrian knight logo (dating back to 1901). From its single store in Basingstoke, England, the brand has grown to be a large international player in the luxury fashion market with a global brand value of $6,445 billion (Interbrand, 2023); though in some ways Burberry kept parts of its 'working-class' roots as a brand that was sold via Kays catalogue and paid for via weekly payments up until 2001 (Weston, 2022). By the late 1990s, Burberry was languishing – as a brand that was associated with middle-aged men – and its profits had dropped from £62 to £25 million by 1997 (Moore & Birtwistle, 2004). In the ensuing years, Burberry worked to redevelop the narrative structures of their brand by putting down roots in a prestigious location in the physical landscape (New Bond Street, London), stepping into a luxury agglomeration space that utilises other brands' narrative structures to support its own.

Furthermore, in the UK in the early 2000s Burberry leaned into cool and modern marketing, using Kate Moss and Britishness as a focus. While this altered the narrative structures of the brand to cut the average age of a Burberry consumer, Burberry did not take into account that 'the same image also enticed a cross section of working class consumers to the brand' (Weston, 2022, p. 182). This new approach of branding Burberry as younger and British attracted an unexpected group of consumers: chavs. Chavs is the term 'commonly used to pathologize young, white, British, working-class people adopting specific markers of style and dress ... and it is associated with a range of denigratory characteristics' (Le Grand, 2013, p. 215). Around 2004, chavs who chose to wear branded items, such as Burberry, linked doing so to keywords such as confidence, money, image, spending, and peer pressure; while non-chavs viewed those who wore branded items as being thugs, fake, tacky, criminals, unstable, and so on (Mason & Wigley, 2013). By the mid 2000s the Burberry's brand was leaking further to include football hooligans and thuggery, and wearers were being turned away from establishments.[4] This 'effectively polarized Burberry's image in the UK' (Weston, 2022, p. 191) and altered how it was perceived in the cultural landscape. Burberry's nova check is unable to be 'read apart from its hierarchy and power' (Rodgers, 2022) where the ownership of the brand is a balancing act. But Burberry redeveloped their offerings and the narrative structures of their brand to rebalance the power distribution of their brand image.

---

[4] For more information on this see *The Herald*, 2003; *The Drum*, 2003; and Finch, 2003.

Reinvention and Storytelling

In ways that Skype has been unable to emulate, Burberry, a brand that 'once fretted over the wrong kind of customer' (Lex, 2016), has 'executed one of the most successful brand identity transformations of all time' (Desai, 2021). After 2006, with a new CEO at the helm, Burberry focussed on its reinvention as a luxury brand. In doing so, they worked to trim down the twenty-three licensees around the world who were each doing something different with the brand in their location. While the cultural landscape does directly interact with the physical and digital landscapes, there is a movement across these liminal spaces that can ignore physical distances. If a consumer seeks to buy a Burberry trench coat in Japan, they should be able to utilise the brand's narrative structures to find the brand and move towards it in this space. What differs in the landscape will be the socio-political overlay that ebbs and flows over the cultural landscape as it corresponds to the different physical locations.

With this in mind, Burberry set out to ensure that all of their narrative structures led to the same places and provided the same experiences for their consumers. This meant trimming down their lines, closing some factories, and ensuring that all decisions on lines went through a single location and a 'fashion czar' (Ahrendts, 2013). This 'ambition to be a true luxury brand remains … the strategic positioning for Burberry' (Akeroyd, 2022, p. 7) and has seen the brand's economic and cultural value grow to where the brand has again become a landmark in the cultural landscape.

Another brand that has managed to see the balance of power shifting away from their control and was able to harness that shift to reinvent itself and develop new structural narratives that appealed to a new consumer is Old Spice. Old Spice was founded in 1937 and before the 1970s focussed on shaving products, but gradually increased its offerings to include the aftershaves, deodorants, and body washes that are often associated with the brand. When Procter & Gamble bought Old Spice in 1990 they purchased a brand that was mostly associated with an aging generation, with a target age of 40–60 (Houraghan, 2023). From 1985 to 1995 the brand focus was on 'the family man', showcasing what a man should be, drawing on aspects of patriarchal cultural that shows a man as into sports and as a good husband, father, and provider; this led further into an Old Spice man as a hero and a man's man (Liu, 2022).

In 2009, sales were down and competition from other, cooler brands (such as Axe (with its iconic body spray)) meant Old Spice was losing market share. Old Spice needed to reposition their brand in a way that would speak to both male- and female-identifying consumers, because women played a large part in the marketing of men's personal hygiene products (McNeill & Douglass, 2011). And, 'women purchase as much as 70 percent of the shower gel for men in their households, but using body wash struck some men as unmanly' (Newman, 2010). In order to address this key insight, in 2010 Old Spice launched 'The Man Your Man Could Smell Like' as an online campaign on Super Bowl weekend and then on television shortly after, focussing on environments where couples would be watching together (Wieden & Kennedy, 2010). The use of a 'new Old Spice guy', Isaiah Mustafa, was an instant hit. In the thirty-second spot, Mustafa is speaking directly to the women saying that even though their man is not him, they could smell like him.

The ad and the recorded reactions to it were wildly popular. With a goal of increasing body wash sales by 15 per cent, 'by May 2010, sales of Old Spice Red Zone Body Wash had increased 60% from the previous year. By July 2010, sales had doubled' (Wieden & Kennedy, 2010). Though the 'The Man Your Man Could Smell Like' campaign played on the concept of 'overselling toxic masculinity and sex to both male and female consumers' (Liu, 2022, p. 2897), Old Spice Red Zone products remained in the top ten best-selling men's grooming products in the USA through the mid 2010s and into the 2020s, where Old Spice was the third leading body wash brand (Drug Store News, 2014; *happi Magazine*, 2023). By addressing the old and stuffy brand image that they had maintained for decades, Old Spice, by tapping into valuable consumer insight, was able to redevelop their narrative structures to take into account the role that both male- and female-identifying consumers play in creating a brand community in the cultural landscape.

Both Old Spice and Burberry were able to understand that the narrative structures leading to their brands needed to be clear and well signposted if they wanted consumers to be able to use their brands as landmarks for navigating the cultural landscape in ways that Skype have yet to emulate. Old Spice and Burberry not only are able to tap into new markets with their revamped narrative structures, but they are better positioned within the cultural landscape to move into new spaces at the boundary edges by working with other brands to extend the edges of their authenticity.

Collaborations at the Edge of Authenticity

As we have moved into the era of the public and as the roles of brand activism and authenticity have become more important to consumers as indicators of brand value, we have also begun to see brands develop collaborations in interesting and unexpected ways. It can be argued that this move towards collaboration has been led by the fickle nature of Gen Z (Power, 2023), whose consumption habits differ from previous generations. Unlike Gen X and Boomers, Gen Z (and Millennials to a lesser extent) are redefining what they expect from brands and are using their power as consumer communities to bring this to bear on the marketplace. 'Gen Z doesn't think of luxury as a name brand that they want to slap onto their bag or their shirt and wear as a badge' (Spagnuolo, 2020); they expect their brands to provide a story or narrative structure that they can use to navigate their identity within the cultural landscape.

This change in consumptive power brought about by Gen Z is partially due to how Gen Z relate to themselves and other players in the cultural landscape. They want brands to connect them to other people, where 'connection is the new currency' (SproutSocial, 2019). Brands have always served as a lynchpin in culture. They are meeting places where like-minded consumers can gather together, something that has become more prevalent with the growth of brand communities in digital settings. But as all brands move to develop narrative structures that enable consumers to move towards them and come into contact with other consumers in relationship to the brand, this simple means of connectivity is no longer enough. The spaces where brands cluster can feel too busy and inauthentic as they become more popular among consumers. Consumers, especially Gen Z, are seeking out authenticity and novelty in their connections with other consumers and the brands that bring them together.

What this looks like in the cultural landscape is a movement towards the edges of the map where the edges of authenticity can be tested to create new spaces that come into existence where brands push their boundaries. One way that this is taking shape is with brand collaborations; or, more specifically, unusual brand collaborations. 'Collaborating companies don't have to be alike in any way, just creative and willing' (Power, 2023). By moving towards the edges of what is known or expected, brands are able to tap into a new market and solidify their relationships with their current consumers. With this in mind, in 2022 Old Spice collaborated with fast-food chain Arby's to create a limited edition Meat Sweat Defense kit that set about answering the question: Do Old Spice products battle even the meat sweats and keep their users fresh?

The two brands created marketing creatives that showcased the meaty Arby's sandwiches with Old Spice 'Meat Sweat Defense' deodorant and anti-perspirant. The kits came with roast beef sweatshirts, a moisture-wicking towel, a headband, and an Arby's gift card (Kelly, 2022). The $60 kit sold out in under three hours (Hypebeast, 2022). The two brands also released a commercial that shows Isaiah Mustafa (famous as the face of modern Old Spice) climbing a large Arby's roast beef sandwich and proclaiming the value of Old Spice meat sweats defence. One of the results of this was a 15 per cent increase in sales of Old Spice in 2022 (Happi Magazine, 2022).

This is not the first time that Old Spice has moved towards the edge of authenticity with their collaborations. In 2019, Old Spice partnered with Danner, a boot brand that focusses on exploration and adventure by making several ranges of long-lasting boots. To highlight Old Spice's Fresher Collection, which featured outdoorsy scents, Danner created hiking boots that were a walking advertisement for both brands. The soles of the boots were mismatched to leave imprints that read: 'take only photos' on one and 'buy only Old Spice' on the other. The 'boots sold for $400, USD[with] 100% of [the] proceeds' going to organisations focussed on restoring trails in Danner's native Oregon (Hypebeast, 2019).

While Old Spice moves towards the boundary of what their consumers might expect with the collaborations, brands such Burberry lean in to collaborations with more focus on their brand heritage and the overall narrative structures being developed. Many of the Burberry collaborations are with artists across a range of genres. One thing that all of Burberry's artistic collaborations have in common is their cultural capital or value as 'high art'. Dancers, poets, and digital artists maintain the same levels of cultural capital that Burberry focusses on as a luxury brand. Though the bulk of Burberry's collaborations are within a similar framework of cultural capital, they have also collaborated with brands that help push them towards the edge of authenticity.

In May 2022, Burberry collaborated with American skate-boarding and lifestyle clothing brand Supreme. Some items with Burberry's iconic colouring and designs were sold exclusively via Burberry, while other pieces sold through Supreme. The items sold included a nod to the Burberry Nova Check baseball cap that was so closely associated with chavs in the early 2000s. This playful link between the brands allowed Burberry to focus on their heritage designs and patterns while also linking with a popular American brand, allowing Burberry to move into new parts of the cultural landscape by developing a shared space with Supreme.

With the boundaries of the cultural landscape being moved as brands and consumers push outward into new spaces, so also are digital frontiers. Burberry, in 2022, moved into a new digital space with a collaboration with Minecraft. The free downloadable content (DLC), 'Burberry: Freedom to Go Beyond', allowed consumers to explore 'an alternate reality of London taken over by a malevolent entity called Nexus' (Anderca, 2022). In this collaborative space, the user is invited to restore the natural environment in the digital world while coming into contact with digital representations of the Burberry brand, each of which have different powers. Likewise, as a user, consumers can choose the Burberry look for their avatar that fits their self-projection in that space. Burberry and Minecraft went further and brought collaboration into the real world by producing a capsule collection of Burberry items with Minecraft icons and styles. A part of this collaboration also sought to attract younger consumers who care about brand activism. The brands donated $100,000 to Conservation International's forest protection and restoration programmes to link the game-play of saving the 'natural' environment in the digital space to that in the real world, tapping into the doing well of luxury brand Burberry, to do good in a tangible way at the edge of the consumer's cultural landscape (Anderca, 2022).

Conclusion

The shifting power dynamics within the cultural landscape present a complex terrain for brands like Skype, Burberry, and Old Spice. As brands are unable to maintain complete control over their brand image, the interplay among economic, cultural, and social capital becomes increasingly prominent. This shift is not solely a challenge but an opportunity for brands to redevelop their narrative structures and reposition themselves within the evolving topography of the cultural landscape. Burberry's ability to traverse the balance of preserving its heritage and navigate the association with an unexpected consumer group, while being able to embrace new narrative structures in the form of collaborations, has allowed the brand to maintain its status and expand its reach. Similarly, Old Spice's revitalisation through a clever use of consumer insights to refocus their brand demonstrates an understanding of the importance of consumer perception, ensuring that the brand speaks to all those involved in the purchasing decision. However, Skype's decline in the face of emerging competitors like Zoom and Microsoft Teams illustrates the consequences of its inability to adapt within a changing cultural landscape.

A brand's power is not a static attribute but a dynamic one, heavily influenced by consumer experiences and the ever-shifting socio-political context that overlays the cultural landscape. This underscores the concept of consumer–brand co-creation, where value is not unilaterally imposed by the brand but is shaped through consumers' interactions and experiences with it. Burberry's and Old Spice's ability to harness and direct the flow of power back into their brands through strategic marketing and collaborations exemplifies this interactive process. These brands have not only adapted to the shifts in power but have leveraged these shifts to develop stronger connections with consumers and stake out new territories in both physical and digital realms at the edge of authenticity. The brands that can engage with their consumers and help them navigate the cultural landscape via their narrative structures, while remaining flexible and responsive to the changes in the cultural landscape, will likely emerge as landmarks.

9 | *TL;DR*
The Application to Industry

Top down approaches to changing behavioral norms result in changes that are difficult to sustain, even though such changes may be easy to bring about.

R. H. Kilmann et al., Issues in understanding and changing culture, *California Management Review*

In a cultural space where consumers can become such a powerful 'signalling force' that they directly influence and alter a brand's identity, brands need to reconsider how they interact with consumers across the totality of the cultural landscape (Black & Veloutsou, 2017).

Brands are symbolic representations of self that are continually being renegotiated by consumers as they try to align their self-identity and their self-projection (who they are versus who they want to be seen to be as) in the cultural landscape. The signs and symbols that represent a brand serve as landmarks or touchpoints in the space that enable the consumer to know where they are in the landscape. The narrative structures that a brand helps to develop and put down are key parts of its marketing, to both let consumers know their brand exists and provide easy passage to draw near to the brand. As consumers become increasingly empowered to signal their values and exert influence, brands are compelled to navigate this complex environment with a renewed sense of purpose and adaptability in order to maintain a balance in the power dynamics within the cultural landscape.

What the Cultural Landscape Looks Like to Brands

Throughout this book the focus has been on where the power changes hands between brands and consumers in the cultural landscape, and it has considered how consumers and brands move across the landscape and develop narrative structures, digital suburbs, and communities. The way a consumer sees and experiences the landscape is from the ground level, they see and walk the paths laid down by brands within the context of socio-economic and political contexts that continually shift. In this perspective, that of consumers, brands are landmarks within this cultural landscape that they can use to navigate. The navigation is both a movement towards where they want to be in the space and a means of better aligning their self-identity and self-projection through the brands they utilise as symbolic resources (Elliott & Wattanasuwan, 1998).

Brands play a key role in the movement and identity of a consumer. While the consumer often remains at the ground level, brands have the advantage of size and height to stand above the landscape. Some brands have a large physical presence that can be seen from miles away, but in the liminality of the cultural landscape the physical size of the brand and its outlets, or the number of sales, do not directly translate to the visibility of the brand.

The equation of 'size does not equal visibility' in the cultural landscape is related to the movement of context within the space. For both consumers and brands, the cultural landscape is a mapped space with settled topography and boundary edges that remain blurry. The blurriness of the known edges of the cultural landscape is due to the continual renegotiation of power dynamics that happens at the edges of authenticity. These negotiations work to balance the elements of power in the spaces and develop and maintain the narrative structures of the brands that serve as roads and pathways across the landscape, leading to brands.

Much like the physical landscape has transportation networks that facilitate the movement of people and goods, the cultural landscape is modelled in a similar fashion. The cultural landscape exists in a liminal space between the physical and digital worlds, where activities in one (such as the launching of a new videogame) have repercussions in the other (the access to the product from anywhere, and the development and growth of brand communities online). While consumers are using brands in the cultural landscape to navigate the space and better align their self-identity with their self-projection, brands are rooted in a spot and when they move they must consider how future navigation will take place.

The role of perspective in the landscape is important in the cultural landscape; while consumers are often on the ground level and brands have a higher overview of what the landscape looks like, how it is changing, and how consumers are moving, brands are not able to see the landscape in its entirety. Regardless of where they put down roots, the brand's perspective is still somewhat limited, and while they have a right to speak from the position that they hold they are not the only ones in that space. Consumers who draw near to a brand in the cultural landscape, and who develop communities related to the brand, also have the right to speak from the position near the brand; and it is in this growth of communities that power can amass.

With this in mind, the brand must take into account whether they have the right to put down roots in a particular space and what the consumer communities within that space expect from a brand. When a brand moves into a brand cluster there is often less pushback as long as the brand has the capital (either economic or cultural) to blend into the cluster. In these spaces that are set aside for brands, the power belongs to the other brands and the consumers who are willing to come to that space. When a brand seeks to move into a space where they are the only brand around, they must consider whether the consumer community in that space is open to the brand and if that space within the cultural landscape is one that other consumers will move towards. In the physical world this concept is closely tied to concepts of gentrification or the choice of a brand to move to the edges of a community so the brand has more space and freedom to develop.

Business Scenario: Dollar Stores

Dollar Tree, Dollar General, and Family Dollar are all brands that an average consumer in the USA will be, at least, aware of. These stores sell household goods, toys, and some food items in physical spaces of 'under 10,000 square feet, ... sometimes literally offering items for one dollar or less' (Chenarides et al., 2024, p. 853). While the American consumer market values choice, in recent years it has become more apparent in media that over 39 million Americans live in food deserts: often rural or inner city locations where 'access to stores that sell healthy, affordable foods is limited or constrained' (Chenarides et al., 2021, p. 1). Dollar stores have used this lack of availability of fresh food to move into neighbourhoods. Classified as 'essential', as they sell some food, dollar stores have put down roots in spaces where they can fill a gap in the market and be a space to pop in and grab something without going into town (in the case of a rural setting).

However, in more urban food deserts, it can be argued that dollar stores utilise 'predatory tactics to undermine grocery stores, [and] they target Black communities and rural towns in particular' (Mitchell et al., 2023). The dollar stores see the cultural landscape as a means of identifying where there is space to put down roots in a community. As 'America's fastest growing retail options' (Lopez, 2024) the brands are not waiting to be welcomed into a community space. Instead, they see a physical space where people are less likely to have money, are more likely to be people of colour, and they move in – sometimes triggering the 'not in my back yard' (NIMBY) network (which has had some success in blocking dollar stores from moving in). From the brand's perspective, these locations are not only valuable in that they are often in less-expensive real estate areas, they are places in the physical and cultural landscape to which other brands might not want to go. Dollar stores provide a service to consumers in a space where consumers might not have easy access to household items and foodstuff, but in doing so they compound the negative social capital of an area. This, in turn, may keep other brands, and consumers who have the economic capital to go elsewhere, away from their position.

Brands Can Become Landmarks and Maintain Their Position in the Cultural Landscape

Before a brand puts down roots in the cultural landscape they must first fully understand their brand image and equity, the consumer, and the space in the cultural landscape where they will be best positioned to work with consumers to develop narrative structures that allow for the growth of brand communities. Without a complete grasp of these three elements a brand will not be able to develop into a brand landmark that stands the test of time and the shifts in the cultural landscape. This is not to say that all brands are meant to be international landmark brands. In fact, some brands work best when they are developed to work for and with specific consumers in a specific location, such as the family-run restaurants and local shops that play key roles in the communities they serve. What matters here is less the size of the brand under consideration than the value of developing capital for that brand and what that means in terms of the habitus shared by the brand and consumer.

Brands should first consider what capital they have in terms of brand image and equity. Capital might be the economic capital of a wealthy brand, the symbolic capital of a heritage brand, or the institutional capital of a well-respected organisation. It could be all of these, just one, or none. Capital in the cultural landscape is a shared network of meaning, and brands must first take stock of the capital they think they have (be it in monetary, cultural, or institutional terms) and consider how their understanding of that capital is shared within the landscape's context. Context here is key, alongside individual experiences, in that they inform the development of the habitus of the brand and the consumer.

Most, if not all, brands will have solid insight into who their target audiences are, and they will focus on those consumers and potential consumers. But consumers can be complex, multifaceted individuals with tension between their self-identity and their self-projection. While a brand cannot be expected to fully understand the habitus of every individual consumer, they are expected to understand the differing habitus that overlays the position in the cultural landscape they choose to set down roots. For consumers, capital works as access to both the narrative structures of a brand and the ability to use those structures to move towards a brand. Access to a brand's narrative structures, in the form of engaging with advertisements and seeing physical or digital shopfronts or brand community groups, is not the same as a consumer having the capital to use those structures, enter the shop, or take part in a brand community.

In all these activities, there is an exchange of capital involved, and if one form is not accepted for another (economic for cultural, for example), then a brand can remain out of reach for a consumer. There is always a cost in the transfer of capital. This is something that must be negotiated by the brand itself within the context of the cultural landscape, which itself is ever-changing as the tide of socio-political and economic influence alters the individual perspectives of the consumer.

Brands Can Negotiate Shifts in the Cultural Landscape

Changes in the cultural landscape include the growth of digital suburbs, the development and decay of narrative structures leading to brands, how well brands can utilise their knowledge of the landscape, and the power brands have in enabling consumers to locate their identities within a brand's space. Knowledge of the spaces they inhabit is key to a brand. This does not simply mean where the brand is located in physical spaces (in strip malls or in standalone storefronts), but it relates to how a brand situates itself in the liminal cultural landscape. If being part of an agglomeration of similar brands is formed by the brand understanding the space they occupy as one that draws consumers to them, that is one consideration (an example is the way car dealers often group together in the USA). Another is how to stand out and lay down individual narrative structures that lead to the brand.

In order to find the space to put down unique narrative structures, brands can consider moving towards the boundaries of the mapped areas of the cultural landscape. This does not mean that the edges are completely unknown to either brands or consumers; instead, they are spaces that provide more room for the brand to stand out and push the edges of authenticity. Authenticity is mentioned many times in this book, but perhaps it should always be 'perceived authenticity' that we discuss. In this push to be more authentic, more real, brands and consumers have begun to move to the edges of authenticity. This manifests in pushing the limits not just of the inhabited spaces, but of all areas of the cultural landscape. We begin to see more extreme forms of 'authenticity' where only those that are 'truly authentic' push those boundaries in ways that make society uncomfortable, but sit up and take notice. Because there can be a competitive element to authenticity, the edges are continually shifting outward.

When the desire for authenticity is strong in society, especially in times of uncertainty (Fritz et al., 2016), brands need to consider how they are perceived and how to better solidify the brand elements that consumers grasp onto and that strengthen the brand's narrative structures. There is value in a brand working to ensure they are perceived as authentic as it helps consumers feel they can follow the brand to the edges of the cultural landscape as a natural way of growing with the brand. There is a direct link between a consumer's self-identity and self-projection, and how a brand helps them to close the gap between these two forms of their identity, which allow them to live more authentically. This works because brands are closely associated with how consumers see themselves, even down to their gender identity.

Some brands make it part of their core values to be inclusive of all gender identities, such as Oregon-based gender-neutral clothing brand WILDFANG. However, all brands could benefit from closer consideration of how every aspect of their brand image, from logo to colours, to content and how they advertise, are viewed through a gendered lens. This is not to indicate that all brands need to focus on being gender-neutral, but, because everything in society is gendered (Martin & Slepian, 2018), brands should take into account how their brand is perceived. Not only do consumers often choose brands and products that align with their own gender identity (Lorber, 1994), but this can lead to brands being seen as a 'safe space' for consumers to find and develop communities. By creating a space within the brand to allow consumers to be themselves and feel respected and safe, consumers become more attached to brands and are willing to give more of their capital to them. The role that a brand plays here in the alignment of a consumer's self-identity and self-projection relates to how the brand is perceived in a gendered fashion, by a gendered consumer group.

The landscape shifts in relation to gender dynamics. Being aware of how consumers, within and across generations, perceive gender identity and fluidity should directly affect how brands work to identify where they should put down roots in the cultural landscape and what their narrative structures need to look like to make it simple for consumers to draw near and lean into their symbolic values for their own identity.

What the Shifting Elements of Power Mean to the Consumer

Brand activism has become a key element that pushes brands to better consider how they interact with consumers and where they choose to put down roots in the cultural landscape. Closely linked to concepts of authenticity, consumers now expect brands to take a stance on socio-economic and/or political issues. Brands need to approach this from the point of view that capitalism and activism are bedfellows as a standard, and that consumers are often the ones pushing the boundaries further and expecting more of brands. Therefore, brands have the opportunity to take this into their own camp, rebalancing some of the power dynamic that has shifted to the consumers via them boycotting and buycotting brands based on brands' activist stances. Brands can go further than consumers expect, and in doing so brands become a brighter beacon for the consumer to use to navigate the cultural landscape. However, brands need to keep in mind that though they can develop activist activities that are not authentic, there is the potential that consumers will see through this and reject the brand based on that 'perceived inauthenticity'. Therefore, it is more productive for a brand to develop activist stances that stay true to their core values.

In addition to tapping into an authentic stance of 'doing good', brands who seek to be a landmark in the cultural landscape, used by consumers to navigate, should cultivate a feeling of ownership among consumers, while also being aware that power is a balance between those who provide (the brand) and those who demand (the consumer). People like to possess things, whether physically or psychologically. A Ferrari is as much a car to own as it is a state of mind for a consumer – even if they do not (or could not) own one. With this concept of ownership as both mental and physical, brands need to become more comfortable with the separation of ownership from control.

When a brand is able to allow partial ownership to be held by the consumer, they can collaborate with consumers to create something new that increases brand affinity and love and can also draw in new consumers who also want to feel that sense of ownership and community. The co-ownership of a brand helps to develop new narrative structures as pathways that highlight to consumers how they can find a brand in the cultural landscape. This is especially useful for brands in crowded marketplaces such as the sneaker market (now brands from Adidas, Nike, and Converse are all offering personalised trainers), drinkware (YETI), or clothing (SPOKE London). Having consumers on your side, as a brand, can help keep narrative structures up to date and maintain a balance of power across the digital and physical landscapes.

Power, for consumers, is closely linked to the amount, and different types, of capital they possess. Different groups of consumer communities can pool their power and have a say in where brands can put down roots. Likewise, communities with less capital have less say – brands need to consider the value of context in deciding where to put down roots and what narrative structures might be developed in the future – these can be in co-ownership of a brand or collaboration with other brands to bring consumers to a space in the cultural landscape that they might not have considered before. This process can open up wider narrative structures and draw in other brands to develop a cluster of brands in a particular location. This agglomeration of brands can be a bright navigational landmark for the consumer, even if the individual brands in the cluster are themselves less easily seen. The power to be a part of a larger landmark may outweigh the need for the brand to be at the edges of the landscape, where the brand is often required to develop its own narrative structures and draw in consumers without benefit of other brands' magnetism. A brand's power is rooted in its ability to use its capital to create narrative structures for consumers that not only differentiate the brand from its competitors but influence its strategic choice of where to establish its cultural identity.

Business Scenario: Share a Coke

In 2011, in Australia, Coca-Cola debuted a marketing campaign that drew in consumers with the promise of co-ownership of the brand where individuals could find their own or friends' names on bottles and cans. Taking the internet by storm, the 'Share a Coke' campaign 'swapped out the Coke branding on bottles and cans with the 150 most popular monikers in Australia' (Coca-Cola, 2014). Jeremy Rudge, creative excellence lead at the time, highlighted that there were countless conference calls and much nervousness in meetings with internal stakeholders who were concerned about the risks of letting a consumer feel a sense of ownership over a product or brand. The concept was all about sharing the brand with someone. The focus was on giving the Coke to someone else, and the sense of sharing 'broadened the appeal' (Rudge, 2014).

With '50% of teens and young adult having not enjoyed a Coca-Cola in the previous month alone' (Ogilvy, n.d.), the 'Share a Coke' campaign tapped into popular culture in a way that pushed Coke up the Google searches, infiltrated all social channels, and was picked up and shared further by celebrities and individuals alike. That summer they sold over 250 million named drinks, 'in a nation of just under 23 million people' (Coca-Cola, 2014). The traffic to Coca-Cola's Facebook site increased by 870 per cent, while their Facebook page increased by 39 per cent and young adult consumption increased by 7 per cent (*Marketing Mag*, 2012).

The campaign did not stop in Australia; it has run in over eighty markets and won a variety of marketing awards, including seven

Cannes Lions awards and Mumbrella insight and campaign of the year (Ogilvy, n.d.), launching in the UK market in 2013 (with 150 names) and the USA in 2014 (with 250 names). In addition to individual names, Coca-Cola offered drinks labelled 'mom, family, friends, wingman, bestie, etc.' to feel more inclusive. The company quickly found that the names they had were not enough and consumers were very engaged with the campaign and wanted more. With this in mind, Coca-Cola set up a website to allow people to personalise virtual bottles and share them across social media. Likewise, there was a 'Share a Coke' tour across both the UK and USA, which enabled consumers to personalise mini-cans on the spot.

One of the key factors that allowed the 'Share a Coke' campaign to be so successful across a variety of markets was that Coca-Cola gave up a bit of prime logo real estate on their products in order to brand products with a consumer's name. While the brand did stay true to its design and even created a similar font to their Spencerian script (which was trademarked), they allowed a sense of shared ownership with the consumer. Since consumers 'want to feel unique' (Grimes, 2013), allowing them to own a small, personalised branded product while also encouraging them to share that product with someone tapped into the sense of self-identity and self-projection in the cultural landscape that is so important for them. This campaign is credited with a 0.4 per cent year-over-year sales growth for Coca-Cola, reversing a downward trend in sales and enabling Coca-Cola to share ownership as a means of balancing the power dynamics between the consumers, the brand, and the spaces and platforms they share (Esterl, 2014).

TL;DR

Brands can tap into their role as landmarks to increase brand loyalty; this translates into a consumer purchase decision. Power shifts. Brands must develop an identity that is elastic enough to take into account the rise in consumers able to assign and remove power from a brand. What is the balance between a rigid brand that has an unmovable sense of what their brand identity is and a brand that has a fluid identity that changes as their consumers and the cultural landscape does? The terms 'rigid' and 'fluid' have meanings from both the consumer and brand perspective. For instance, for the consumer in China, Eckhardt and Bengtsson (2015) indicate that Häagen-Dazs is considered to be for lovers. There is an unmovable sense that this brand is not for a group of male friends hanging out or for parents taking children out for a treat; it is instead for romantic dates. An inflexible brand identity develops out of the social norms around a brand, the context of the cultural landscape, and the work that a brand itself does in leaning into a fixed brand identity. The more structural narratives that Häagen-Dazs develops via advertising and marketing that veers into that identity, the more consumers come to expect that identity to remain firm.

From the brand's perspective, the rigidity of sticking with an identity allows for control over how the brand is presented to consumers and indicates a steady mark of ownership. It helps a brand to build a recognisable legacy that helps them in creating narrative structures that allow consumers to move towards them and develop brand communities around them. However, this does not mean that brands should remain static. Even large multinationals undergo rebranding. The Co-operative in the UK has been around for nearly 200 years, but in the mid-2010s they rebranded to the Co-op, utilising a less corporate blue and taking into account the colloquial nickname the food shops often went by even before the rebrand. The logo was a reworking of the brand's classic 1968 logo, drawing on a sense of nostalgia (Banks, 2016). The tone of voice changed and in 2017, a year after the rebrand and rework of their membership scheme, profits were up (Co-op, 2018).

While a sense of control over brand identity is something that brands often want to keep a tight rein on, there is a benefit in brands embracing a sense of fluidity in their branding in order to ensure that they are moving with the consumer as they alter their point of view when moving around the cultural landscape. Often concerning for brands is the sense of loss of ownership over their brand identity when they move to become more fluid. But ownership is a state of mind for a consumer and the more a consumer feels this sense of co-ownership of a brand, the more likely they are to develop a positive attachment.

Brands must strike a balance between fluidity and rigidity. They can achieve this in a number of ways:

1. Work with consumers to develop the brand identity and, if appropriate, lean into consumer concepts, tapping into that feeling of co-ownership.

2. Understand that ownership of the brand is constantly being rene-gotiated between the brand and the consumer and this plays out in the cultural landscape, both physically and in digital spaces.
3. Decide what parts of the brand identity are most fluid and what must remain inflexible in order to provide stability as the brands develops into a landmark in the cultural landscape; while core products or services may need to stay the same, some brands can benefit from being playful with their trademarks and logos, tapping into the function of logos as brand ambassadors (Pearson, 2013).
4. Be up to date on the knowledge/power dynamic that exists between brands, consumers, and the spaces where they interact – again, both physical and digital.
5. Be aware of the need to develop the structural narratives to make it simple and safe for consumers to move towards the brand as they navigate the cultural landscape.

Even if power shifts and flows, brands must maintain the core knowledge of the brand itself and the space in the cultural landscape that it inhabits (and those that it seeks to inhabit). This knowledge includes a comprehension of who the brand's consumers interact with, how consumers use the brand to align their self-identity and self-projection, how far the digital suburbs extend, and where the brand's consumers call home.

Knowledge here is power. Even if the balance of power shifts to the consumer, the knowledge the brand has about the consumer and the cultural landscape can be leveraged to restabilise the power dynamic. This can be maintained in several ways: knowledge of the cultural landscape, knowledge of the consumer, and knowledge of the brand – including where the boundaries are for the brand at the edges of authenticity. Brands must, furthermore, seek to fully understand who has access to the narrative structures to approach a brand and what these consumers do on the pathways – do they share their knowledge of the brand, growing a community group, or do they work to actively dismantle the paths? If this is the case, brands might need to invest in narrative infrastructure. This investment is more likely at the edges of authenticity near the fuzzy boundaries of the mapped cultural land-scape, and less likely if the brand plans to join a cluster of brands.

While brands are ultimately businesses that need to make ends meet in order to survive, the ultimate goal for brands should go beyond simply growing their organisation, making money, or taking up space. The aim for brands should be to become a landmark in the consumers' cultural landscape; one that they can see from most locations and that they can use to navigate their journey in aligning their self-identity and self-projection. The measure of a brand's success in the cultural landscape is not solely in its visibility or size but in the depth of its connection with consumers; even if those consumers never purchase the brand or engage with it directly. It is in the brand's ability to act as a landmark for consumers, guiding them through the complexities of identity formation and navigation of the sociopolitical contexts of the cultural landscape. As brands and consumers co-create this landscape, the narratives they construct together will determine the longevity and relevance of the brand's place within it. This symbiosis, when nurtured with authenticity and a balance of power, can elevate a brand from a mere marker to a landmark.

Works Cited

84 Lumber, 2022. 84 Lumber named to 2022 INC. 5000 list of America's fastest growing companies. August 2022. Available at: https://84lumbercomv3.84-iase-v3.p.azurewebsites.net/about/press-room/84-press-releases/inc-5000-2022/, [Accessed on 19 December 2023].

Aadland, E., Cattani, G., Falchetti, D. and Ferriani, S., 2020. Reflecting glory or deflecting stigma? The interplay between status and social proximity in peer evaluations. *Plos One*, *15*(9), pp. 1–29.

Aaker, D., 2003. The power of the branded differentiator. *MIT Sloan Management Review*, *45*(1), pp. 83–87.

Aaker, A. and Alexander, L., 1993. *Brand Equity and Advertising: An Overview*. Hillsdale, NJ: Lawrence Erlbaum Associates.

Aaker, D. A. and Joachimsthaler, E., 2000. *Brand Leadership*. New York: The Free Press.

Aaker, J. L., 1997. Dimensions of brand personality. *Journal of Marketing Research*, *34*(3), pp. 347–356.

Aamoth, D., 2011. A brief history of Skype. 10 May 2011. *Time*. Available at: https://techland.time.com/2011/05/10/a-brief-history-of-skype/, [Accessed on 13 February 2024].

Abercrombie, N. and Longhurst, B., 2003. *Audiences: A Sociological Theory of Performance and Imagination*. London: SAGE Publications.

Aboim, S., 2020. Gender in a box? The paradoxes of recognition beyond the gender binary. *Politics and Governance*, *8*(3), pp. 231–241.

Ace Metrix, 2020. Nike's 'For Once, Don't Do It' rallies strong support, but not without controversy. Available at: www.acemetrix.com/insights/blog/nike-for-once-dont-do-it/, [Accessed on 08 December 2023].

ACLU, 2023. The ACLU is tracking '508' anti-LGBTQ bills in the U.S. Available at: www.aclu.org/legislative-attacks-on-lgbtq-rights, [Accessed on 14 December 2023].

Advertising Association, 2022. Written evidence submitted by the advertising association to the DCMS Select Committee's Influencer Culture inquiry. Available at: https://committees.parliament.uk/writtenevidence/35359/html/, [Accessed on 25 September 2023].

Agarwal, J. and Malhotra, N. K., 2019. Reflections on the state-of-the-art in 'ethics & morality in customer-brand relationships': Directions for future research. *Journal of Business Research*, 95, pp. 392–400.

Aggerholm, H.K., Andersen, S.E. and Thomsen, C., 2011. Conceptualising employer branding in sustainable organisations. *Corporate Communications: An International Journal*, 16(2), pp. 105–123.

Ahrendts, A., 2013. Burberry's CEO on turning an aging British icon into a global luxury brand. *Harvard Business Review*. Available at: https://hbr.org/2013/01/burberrys-ceo-on-turning-an-aging-british-icon-into-a-global-luxury-brand, [Accessed on 15 February 2024].

Ahuvia, A., Rauschnabel, P. A. and Rindfleisch, A., 2020. Is brand love materialistic? *Journal of Product & Brand Management*, 30(3), pp. 467–480.

Akeroyd, J., 2022. Strategic report, 2021–22. *Burberry*. Available at: www.burberryplc.com/content/dam/burberry/corporate/oar/2022/pdfs/Burberry_2021-22_Strategic_Report.pdf, [Accessed on 15 February 2024].

Akgün, A. E., Koçoğlu, İ. and İmamoğlu, S. Z., 2013. An emerging consumer experience: Emotional branding. *Procedia-Social and Behavioral Sciences*, 99, pp. 503–508.

Alaimo, C. and Kallinikos, J., 2018, December. Objects, metrics and practices: An inquiry into the programmatic advertising ecosystem. In *Working Conference on Information Systems and Organizations*, pp. 110–123.

Alanne, J., 2017. *Online video advertising in building brand equity*. Masters Thesis. Alto University School of Business. Available at: www.academia.edu/73511336/Online_video_advertising_in_building_brand_equity, [Accessed on 28 January 2024].

Albert, N., Merunka, D. and Valette-Florence, P., 2008. When consumers love their brands: Exploring the concept and its dimensions. *Journal of Business Research*, 61(10), pp. 1062–1075.

Alexander, J. C., 1995. *Fin de siècle Social Theory: Relativism, Reduction, and the Problem of Reason*. New York: Verso.

Alhaddad, A.A., 2015. The effect of advertising awareness on brand equity in social media. *International Journal of e-Education, e-Business, e-Management and e-Learning*, 5(2), pp. 73–84.

Alhouti, S., Johnson, C.M. and Holloway, B.B., 2016. Corporate social responsibility authenticity: Investigating its antecedents and outcomes. *Journal of Business Research*, 69(3), pp. 1242–1249.

Alreck, P., Settle, R. and Belch, M., 1982. Who responds to 'Gendered' ads, and how? Masculine brands versus feminine brands. *Journal of Advertising Research*, 22, pp. 25–32.

American Foundation for Suicide Prevention, 2018. Statement by the American Foundation for Suicide Prevention on Kate Spade. 05 June 2018. Press Release. Available at: www.prnewswire.com/news-releases/ statement-by-the-american-foundation-for-suicide-prevention-on-kate-spade-300660190.html/, [Accessed on 26 December 2023].

American Psychiatric Association, 2022. Gender Dysphoria. Available at: www.psychiatry.org/file%20library/psychiatrists/practice/dsm/apa_dsm-5-gender-dysphoria.pdf, [Accessed on 10 August 2023].

Anderca, C., 2022. Minecraft X Burberry. 01 November 2022. *Minecraft*. Available at: www.minecraft.net/en-us/article/minecraft-x-burberry, [Accessed on 16 February 2024].

Anderson, C., Hildreth, J. A. D., & Howland, L., 2015. Is the desire for status a fundamental human motive? A review of the empirical literature. *Psychological Bulletin, 141*, pp. 574–601.

Anderson, S., 2023. How many ads do we really see in a day? Spoiler: It's not 10,000. *The Drum*. 03 May 2023. Available at: www.thedrum.com/news/2023/05/03/how-many-ads-do-we-really-see-day-spoiler-it-s-not-10000, [Accessed on 04 December 2023].

Andjelic, A., 2020. *The Business of Aspiration: How Social, Cultural, and Environmental Capital Changes Brands*. London: Routledge.

Anheuser-Busch, 2023. That's who we are. *Anheuser-Busch*. Available at: www.anheuser-busch.com/, [Accessed on 23 November 2023].

Antrop, M., 2020. A brief history of landscape research. In Eds. Atha, M., Howard, P., Thompson, I., & Waterton, E., *The Routledge Companion to Landscape Studies*, 2nd Edition. London and New York: Routledge.

Aratani, L., 2023. Target sees drop in sales after rightwing backlash to Pride merchandise. 16 August, 2023. *The Guardian*. Available at: www.theguardian.com/us-news/2023/aug/16/target-sales-drop-second-quarter-lgbt-pride-merchandise-conservative, [Accessed on 19 December 2023].

Archer, M. S., 2010. Routine, reflexivity, and realism. *Sociological Theory, 28*, pp. 272–303.

2012. *The Reflexive Imperative in Late Modernity*. Cambridge: Cambridge University Press.

Aribarg, A. and Schwartz, E.M., 2020. Native advertising in online news: Trade-offs among clicks, brand recognition, and website trustworthiness. *Journal of Marketing Research, 57*(1), pp. 20–34.

Armstrong, M. 2018. Who's doing Europe's housework? *Statista*. Available at: www.statista.com/chart/15880/housework-europe-gender-split, [Accessed on 10 August 2023].

2020. The UK's housework gender roles. *Statista*. Available at: www
-statista-com.oxfordbrookes.idm.oclc.org/chart/20835/household-
tasks-uk-by-gender/, [Accessed on 10 August 2023].

Arnould, E.J. and Thompson, C.J., 2005. Consumer culture theory (CCT):
Twenty years of research. *Journal of Consumer Research*, 31(4),
pp. 868–882.

Aronowitz, S., 2003. *How Class Works: Power and Social Movement*. New
Haven: Yale University Press.

Ash, J., Kitchin, R. and Leszcynski, A., 2018. Digital turn, digital geographies? *Progress in Human Geography*, 42(1), pp. 25–43.

Askalidis, G. and Malthouse, E.C., 2016, September. The value of online
customer reviews. In *Proceedings of the 10th ACM Conference on
Recommender Systems*, pp. 155–158.

Asmar, A., Raats, T. and Van Audenhove, L., 2023. Streaming difference(s):
Netflix and the branding of diversity. *Critical Studies in Television*,
18(1), pp. 24–40

Assmann, A., 2012. Authenticity – The signature of western exceptionalism? In Ed. Straub, J., *Paradoxes of Authenticity: Studies on A Critical
Concept*. Bielefeld: Transcript Verlag, pp. 33–50.

Atha, M., 2020. Ephemeral landscapes. In Eds. Atha, M., Howard, P.,
Thompson, I., & Waterton, E., *The Routledge Companion to
Landscape Studies*, 2nd Edition. London and New York: Routledge.

Atha, M., Howard, P., Thompson, I. and Waterton, E., 2020. Introduction:
Ways of knowing and being with landscapes: A beginning. In Eds.
Atha, M., Howard, P., Thompson, I., & Waterton, E., *The Routledge
Companion to Landscape Studies*, 2nd Edition. London and New
York: Routledge.

Atulkar, S. and Kesari, B., 2018. Role of consumer traits and situational
factors on impulse buying: Does gender matter? *International Journal
of Retail & Distribution Management*, 46(4), pp. 386–405.

Audy Martínek, P., Caliandro, A. and Denegri-Knott, J., 2022. Digital
practices tracing: Studying consumer lurking in digital environments.
Journal of Marketing Management, pp. 1–31.

Austin, J. E., 2000. Strategic collaboration between nonprofits and
businesses. *Nonprofit and Voluntary Sector Quarterly*, 29(1),
pp. 69–97.

Avery, J., 2012. Defending the markers of masculinity: Consumer resistance to brand gender-bending. *International Journal of Research in
Marketing*, 29(4), pp. 322–336.

B-Corp Certification, 2023. About B-corp certification. *B-Corporation*.
Available at: https://bcorporation.net/en-us/certification/, [Accessed on
21 December 2023].

Bagozzi, R.P., Romani, S., Grappi, S. and Zarantonello, L., 2021. Psychological underpinnings of brands. *Annual review of psychology*, 72, pp. 585–607.

Bailey, E.R. and Iyengar, S.S., 2022. Yours truly: On the complex relationship between authenticity and honesty. *Current Opinion in Psychology, 47*.

Bairrada, C.M., Coelho, A. and Lizanets, V., 2019. The impact of brand personality on consumer behavior: The role of brand love. *Journal of Fashion Marketing and Management: An International Journal, 23*(1), pp. 30–47.

Bakhtiari, K., 2020. Why brands need to pay attention to cancel culture. *Forbes*. Avaiable at: www.forbes.com/sites/kianbakhtiari/2020/09/29/why-brands-need-to-pay-attention-to-cancel-culture, [Accessed on 21 December 2023].

Balme, C.B. 2008. *The Cambridge Introduction to Theatre Studies*. Cambridge: Cambridge University Press.

Balmer, J.M. and Gray, E.R., 2003. Corporate brands: What are they? What of them? *European Journal of Marketing, 37*, pp. 972–997.

Balmer, J. and Greyser, S., 2003. *Revealing the Corporation: Perspectives on Identity, Image, Reputation, Corporate Branding and Corporate Level Marketing*. London: Routledge.

Banks, T., 2016. Co-op restructures, rebrands and revives 1968 logo. 24 May 2016. *Design Week*. Available at: www.designweek.co.uk/issues/23-29-may-2016/co-op-restructures-rebrands-revives-1968-logo/, [Accessed on 29 February 2024].

Bardhi, F., Rohm, A.J., and Sultan, F. 2010. Tuning in and Tuning out: Media multitasking among young consumers. *Journal of Consumer Behaviour, 9*(4), pp. 316–332.

Barnard, L., 2014. *The Cost of Creepiness: How Online Behavioral Advertising Affects Consumer Purchase Intention*. Doctoral dissertation, University of North Carolina at Chapel Hill.

Barnes, R., 2016. The ecology of participation. In Eds. Witschge, T., Anderson, C., Domingo, D., & Hermida, A., *The SAGE Handbook of Digital Journalism*. New York: Sage, pp. 179–191.
2018. *Uncovering Online Commenting Culture: Trolls, Fanboys and Lurkers*. London: Palgrave Macmillan.

Barney, J.B., Ketchen Jr, D.J. and Wright, M., 2021. Resource-based theory and the value creation framework. *Journal of Management, 47*(7), pp. 1936–1955.

Barrett, B., 2022. Tim Hwang, subprime attention crisis: Advertising and the time bomb at the heart of the internet. *International Journal of Communication, 16*, pp. 292–295.

Barth, F., 2012. Boundaries and connections. *Signifying Identities*, pp. 17–36.

Bartlett, J. C., 2023. Inclusive teaching begins with authenticity. *Faculty Focus*. Available at: www.facultyfocus.com/articles/equality-inclusion-and-diversity/inclusive-teaching-begins-with-authenticity/, [Accessed on 27 January 2023].

Bartsch, F., Zeugner-Roth, K.P. and Katsikeas, C.S., 2022. Consumer authenticity seeking: Conceptualization, measurement, and contingent effects. *Journal of the Academy of Marketing Science*, pp. 1–28.

Bastos, W. and Levy, S.J., 2012. A history of the concept of branding: practice and theory. *Journal of Historical Research in Marketing*, 4(3), pp. 347–368.

Batra, R., Ahuvia, A., and Bagozzi, R.P. 2012. Brand love. *Journal of Marketing*, 76(2), pp. 1–16.

Baumeister, R. F. (1995). Self and identity. In Ed. Tesser, A., *Advanced Social Psychology*, pp. 51–99. Boston, MA: McGraw Hill.

Bayer, E., Srinivasan, S., Riedl, E.J. and Skiera, B., 2020. The impact of online display advertising and paid search advertising relative to offline advertising on firm performance and firm value. *International Journal of Research in Marketing*, 37(4), pp. 789–804.

BBC News, 2022. No Uniform Choice for Virgin Atlantic Crew on World Cup Flight. 15 November 2022. Available at: www.bbc.co.uk/news/uk-63635191, [Accessed on 26 November 2023].

Beard, A., 2021. Why Ben & Jerry's Speaks Out. 13 January 2021. *Harvard Business Review*. Available at: https://hbr.org/2021/01/why-ben-jerrys-speaks-out, [Accessed on 18 December 2023].

Becker-Olsen, K.L., Cudmore, B.A. and Hill, R.P., 2006. The impact of perceived corporate social responsibility on consumer behavior. *Journal of Business Research*, 59(1), pp. 46–53.

Beddington, E., 2024. Sometimes I long for the tradwife. Then I remember it's a reactionary fantasy. 04 February 2024. *The Guardian*. Available at: www.theguardian.com/commentisfree/2024/feb/04/sometimes-i-long-for-the-life-of-a-tradwife-then-i-remember-its-a-reactionary-fantasy, [Accessed on 05 February 2024].

Beilina, I., 2022. *The Significance of Sonic Branding to Strategically Stimulate Consumer Behavior: Content Analysis of Four Interviews from Jeanna Isham's 'Sound In Marketing' Podcast*. Masters Thesis. Baruch College. Available at: https://academicworks.cuny.edu/bb_etds/149/, [Accessed on 29 January 2024].

Belk, R.W., 1988. Possessions and the extended self. *Journal of Consumer Research*, 15(2), pp. 139–168.

Bellafante, G., 2017. The false feminism of 'Fearless Girl'. *The New York Times*. Available at: www.nytimes.com/2017/03/16/nyregion/fearless-girl-statue-manhattan.html, [Accessed on 03 October 2022].

Bellentani, F., 2016. Landscape as text. *Tartu Semiotics Library*, (16), pp. 76–88.

Bem, S.L., 1981. Gender schema theory: A cognitive account of sex typing. *Psychological Review*, 88(4): pp. 354–364.

Bem, S.L., 1993. *The Lenses of Gender: Transforming the Debate on Sexual Inequality*. New Haven: Yale University Press.

Ben & Jerry's., 2023. Our values, activism and mission. *Ben & Jerry's*. Available at: www.benjerry.co.uk/values, [Accessed on 18 December 2023].

——— 2023. Our progressive values. *Ben & Jerry's*. Available at: www.benjerry .co.uk/values/our-progressive-values, [Accessed on 18 December 2023].

Benedicktus, R.L., Brady, M.K., Darke, P.R. and Voorhees, C.M., 2010. Conveying trustworthiness to online consumers: Reactions to consensus, physical store presence, brand familiarity, and generalized suspicion. *Journal of Retailing*, 86(4), pp. 322–335.

Benevenuto, F., Rodrigues, T., Cha, M. and Almeida, V., 2009. Characterizing user behavior in online social networks. In *IMC '09: Proceedings of the 9th ACM SIGCOMM Conference on Internet Measurement*, pp. 49–62.

Benn, J., 2004. Consumer education between 'consumership 'and citizenship: Experiences from studies of young people. *International Journal of Consumer Studies*, 28(2), pp. 108–116.

Bennett, T., 2010. Culture, power, knowledge: between Foucault and Bourdieu. In *Cultural Analysis and Bourdieu's Legacy*. London: Routledge, pp. 114–128.

Bernstein, J., 2023. The Real Mystery of Bud Light: How did it become so popular in the first place? 21 July 2023. *The Atlantic*. Available at: www.theatlantic.com/ideas/archive/2023/07/rise-and-fall-bud-light-boycott/674752/, [Accessed on 27 November 2023].

Beverland, M.B. and Farrelly, F.J., 2010. The quest for authenticity in consumption: Consumers' purposive choice of authentic cues to shape experienced outcomes. *Journal of Consumer Research*, 36(5), pp. 838–856.

Bhargava, R., 2008. *Personality Not Included: Why Companies Lose Their Authenticity And How Great Brands Get it Back, Foreword by Guy Kawasaki*. Boston, MA: McGraw-Hill.

Biraghi, S. and Gambetti, R.C., 2017. Is brand value co-creation actionable? A facilitation perspective. *Management Decision*, 55(7), pp. 1476–1488.

Bishop, S., 2023. Emily Bootle's 'This Is Not Who I Am'. *The Monthly*. Available at: www.themonthly.com.au/issue/2023/february/stephanie-bishop/emily-bootle-s-not-who-i-am#mtr, [Accessed on 27 January 2023].

Bleier, A., Harmeling, C.M. and Palmatier, R.W., 2019. Creating effective online customer experiences. *Journal of Marketing*, 83(2), pp. 98–119.

Black, J.A. and Boal, K.B., 1994. Strategic resources: Traits, configurations and paths to sustainable competitive advantage. *Strategic Management Journal*, 15(S2), pp. 131–148.

Black, I and Veloutsou, C., 2017. Working consumers: Co-creation of brand identity, consumer identity and brand community identity. *Journal of Business Research*, 70, pp. 416–429.

Blockthrough, 2023. Number of adblock users worldwide in selected quarters from 2013 to 2023 (in millions). *Statista*. Available at: www.statista.com/statistics/350726/adblocking-users/, [Accessed on 18 October 2022].

Bloomberg, 2023. Corporate America Promised to hire a lot more people of color. It actually did. 26 September 2023. *Bloomberg*. Available at: www.bloomberg.com/graphics/2023-black-lives-matter-equal-opportunity-corporate-diversity/, [Accessed on 08 December 2023].

Boatcă, M., 2021. Counter-mapping as method. *Historical Social Research/Historische Sozialforschung*, 46(2), pp. 244–263.

Bode, L. 2017. Closing the gap: Gender parity in political engagement on social media. *Information, Communication & Society*, 20, pp. 587–603.

Bottoms, S.J. 2003. The efficacy/effeminacy braid: Unpacking the performance studies/theatre studies dichotomy. *Theatre Topics*, 13(2), pp. 173–187.

Bourdieu, P., 1985. The genesis of the concepts of 'Habitus' and of 'Field'. *Sociocriticism*, 2(2), pp. 11–24.

1986. 'The Forms of Capital', Trans. R. Nice. In Ed. Richardson, J., *Handbook of Theory and Research for the Sociology of Education*. New York: Greenwood Press.

1993. *The Field of Cultural Production: Essays on Art and Literature*. New York: Columbia University Press.

1996. *Distinction: A Social Critique of the Judgement of Taste*. Translated by Richard Nice. Cambridge, MA: Harvard University Press.

2021 [2016]. *Forms of Capital. General Sociology, Volume 3: Lectures at the Collège de France 1983–1984*. Translated by P. Collier. Cambridge: Polity Press.

Bowden, J. and Mirzaei, A., 2021. Consumer engagement within retail communication channels: An examination of online brand communities and digital content marketing initiatives. *European Journal of Marketing*, 55(5), pp. 1411–1439.

Bowman, S., n.d. We left Facebook groups and have seen our membership rise +130% every year we've been on Mighty Pro. *Mighty Pro*. Available at: www.mightynetworks.com/pro/case-studies/how-yoga-with-adriene-launched-their-community-on-mighty-pro, [Accessed on 21 February 2024].

Boyd, D. and Heer, J., 2006. Profiles as Conversation: Networked Identity Performance on Friendster. In *Proceedings of the 39th Annual Hawaii International Conference on System Sciences (HICSS'06)*, Vol. 3, 59c.

Boyd, D.E., Clarke, T.B. and Spekman, R.E., 2014. The emergence and impact of consumer brand empowerment in online social networks: A proposed ontology. *Journal of Brand Management*, 21, pp. 516–531.

Bramley, E., 2018. 'The people's yogi': how Adriene Mishler became a YouTube phenomenon. 25 September 2018. *The Guardian*. Available at: www.theguardian.com/lifeandstyle/2018/sep/25/yoga-adriene-mishler-youtube-interview, [Accessed on 21 February 2024].

Brand Finance, 2022. *Brand Finance Global 500 2022*. Available at: https://brandirectory.com/download-report/brand-finance-global-500-2022-preview.pdf, [Accessed on 30 September 2022].

Bray, J., Johns, N. and Kilburn, D., 2011. An exploratory study into the factors impeding ethical consumption. *Journal of Business Ethics*, 98, pp. 597–608.

Brenan, M. 2023. More than six in 10 Americans drink alcohol. *Gallup*. Available at: https://news.gallup.com/poll/509501/six-americans-drink-alcohol.aspx, [Accessed on 25 November 2023].

Brewers Association, 2023. *National Beer Sales & Production Data*. Available at: www.brewersassociation.org/statistics-and-data/national-beer-stats/. [Accessed on 06 June 2024].

Brewster, T., 2024. Musk's X fired 80% of Engineers working on trust and safety, Australian government says. 10 January 2024. *Forbes*. Available at: www.forbes.com/sites/thomasbrewster/2024/01/10/elon-musk-fired-80-per-cent-of-twitter-x-engineers-working-on-trust-and-safety/, [Accessed on 29 January 2024].

Brosdahl, D.J., and Carpenter, J.M. 2011. Shopping orientations of US males: A generational cohort comparison. *Journal of Retailing and Consumer Services*, 18 (6): pp. 548–554.

Brown, S., Kozinets, R. & Sherry Jr, J., 2003. Teaching old brands new tricks: Retro branding and the revival of brand meaning. *Journal of Marketing*, 67(7), pp.19–33.

Bupa, 2022. Gen Z seek ethical workplaces as environ-mental health burden bites. 13 January 2022. *Bupa*. Available at: www.bupa.com/news/press-releases/2022/gen-z-seek-ethical-workplaces-as-environ-mental-health-burden-bites, [Accessed on 18 December 2023].

Burberry, 2024. Burberry Heritage. *Burberry*. Available at: https://uk.burberry.com/c/burberry-heritage/, [Accessed on 14 February 2024].

Burch, S. 2015. Reading the city: Cultural mapping as pedagogical inquiry. In Eds. Duxbury, N., Garrett-Petts, W. F., & MacLennan, D., *Cultural Mapping as Cultural Inquiry*. London: Routledge.

Business Wire, 2023. Millennials Will Lead Global Economic Spending in 2023, New Study Reveals. *Business Wire*. Available at: www .businesswire.com/news/home/20230324005221/en/Millennials-Will-Lead-Global-Ecommerce-Spending-in-2023-New-Study-Reveals, [Accessed on 06 October 2023].

Busteed. M., 2007. 'Fostered to trouble the next generation': Contesting ownership of the Martyrs Commemoration Ritual in Manchester 1888–1921. In Eds. Moore, N., & Whelan, Y., *Heritage, Memory and the Politics of Identity: New Perspectives on the Cultural Landscape*. Aldershot: Ashgate Publishing Limited.

Butkowski, C. P., 2020. Beyond 'commercial realism': Extending Goffman's gender display framework to networked media contexts. *Communication, Culture, and Critique, 14*(1), pp. 89–108.

Butler, J. 1988. Performative acts and gender constitution: An essay in phenomenology and feminist theory. *Theatre Journal, 40* (4), pp. 519–531.

2008. *Gender Trouble: Feminism and the Subversion of Identity*. New York and London: Routledge.

Cahill, L., Haier, R.J., Fallon, J., Alkire, M.T., Tang, C., Keator, D., Wu, J. and McGaugh, J.L., 1996. Amygdala activity at encoding correlated with long-term, free recall of emotional information. *Proceedings of the National Academy of sciences, 93*(15), pp. 8016–8021.

Calderón Gómez, D., 2021. The third digital divide and Bourdieu: Bidirectional conversion of economic, cultural, and social capital to (and from) digital capital among young people in Madrid. *New Media & Society, 23*(9), pp. 2534–2553.

Calling All Contestants, 2023. 2023 Bud Light – Easy Carry Contest. Available at: https://callingallcontestants.com/contest/2023-bud-light-easy-carry-contest/, [Accessed on 24 November 2023].

Cameron, S. 2003. Gentrification, housing redifferentiation and urban regeneration: 'Going for growth' in Newcastle upon Tyne. *Urban Studies, 40*, pp. 2367–2382.

Camilleri, M.A., 2022. Strategic attributions of corporate social responsibility and environmental management: The business case for doing well by doing good! *Sustainable Development, 30*(3), pp. 409–422.

Cammarota, A., D'Arco, M., Marino, V. and Resciniti, R., 2023. Brand activism: A literature review and future research agenda. *International Journal of Consumer Studies, 47*(5), pp. 1669–1691.

Cantor, M., 2023. Parades but no public posts: which brands are supporting pride in the wake of backlash? 07 June 2023. *The Guardian*. Available at: www.theguardian.com/world/2023/jun/07/pride-month-boycotts-target-bud-light-brands-companies, [Accessed on 14 December 2023].

Carlsson, B. and Gustavsson, R., 2001, December. The rise and fall of Napster – An evolutionary approach. In *International Computer Science Conference on Active Media Technology*, pp. 347–354.

Carneiro, J., 2020. What makes craft beer so popular with Millennials. *DSM*. Available at: www.dsm.com/food-beverage/en_US/insights/insights/beverage/craft-beer-millennials-consumer-insights.html#, [Accessed on 23 November 2023].

Carpenter, G.S., Glazer, R. and Nakamoto, K., 1994. Meaningful brands from meaningless differentiation: The dependence on irrelevant attributes. *Journal of Marketing Research, 31*(3), pp. 339–350.

Carroll, A.B., 2021. Corporate social responsibility: Perspectives on the CSR construct's development and future. *Business & Society, 60*(6), pp. 1258–1278.

Carroll, B. and Ahuvia, A., 2006. Some antecedents and outcomes of Brand love. *Marketing Letters, 17*(2), pp. 79–89.

Ceci, L., 2022. BeReal – Statistics and Facts. *Statista*. Available at: www.statista .com/topics/10096/bereal/#topicOverview, [Accessed on 12 October 2023].

Ceron, E. 2023. Despite Backlash, Companies Benefit from being Pro-LGBTQ. 06 October 2023. *Bloomberg*. Available at: www .bloomberg.com/news/articles/2023-10-06/lgbtq-spending-power-outweighs-hate-campaign-risk-for-businesses#xj4y7vzkg, [Accessed on 27 November 2023].

César Machado, J., Fonseca, B. and Martins, C. 2021. Brand logo and brand gender: Examining the effects of natural logo designs and color on brand gender perceptions and affect. *Journal of Brand Management, 28* (2), pp. 152–170.

Champlin, S., Sterbenk, Y., Windels, K. and Poteet, M., 2019. How brand-cause fit shapes real world advertising messages: a qualitative exploration of 'femvertising'. *International Journal of Advertising, 38*(8), pp. 1240–1263.

Chang, H., Kwak, H., Puzakova, M., Park, J. and Smit, E.G., 2015. It's no longer mine: The role of brand ownership and advertising in cross-border brand acquisitions. *International Journal of Advertising, 34*(4), pp. 593–620.

Change Please, 2022. UK Impact Report 2021–22. Available at: https:// cdn.shopify.com/s/files/1/0281/7825/1836/files/ChangePlease_ AnnualReport_2021-22.pdf?v=1684335932, [Accessed on 25 December 2023].

2023a. About Us. Available at: https://changeplease.org/pages/about-us-1, [Accessed on26 December 2023].

2023b. UK Impact Report 2022–23. Available at: https://cdn.shopify.com /s/files/1/0281/7825/1836/files/ChangePlease_ImpactReport_2022_2023 .pdf?v=1702477257, [Accessed on 25 December 2023].

Chen, J., 2022. What is your startup's North Star metric? 11 November 2022. *Forbes*. Available at: www.forbes.com/sites/forbesbusinesscouncil/202 2/11/11/what-is-your-startups-north-star-metric/?sh=1c70bd466423, [Accessed on 04 February 2024].

Chen, J., Yang, X. and Smith, R.E., 2016. The effects of creativity on advertising wear-in and wear-out. *Journal of the Academy of Marketing Science*, 44, pp. 334–349.

Chen, T., Ou Yang, S. and Leo, C., 2017. The beginning of value co-creation: Understanding dynamics, efforts and betterment. *Journal of Service Theory and Practice*, 27(6), pp. 1145–1166.

Chenarides, L., Çakır, M. and Richards, T.J., 2024. Dynamic model of entry: Dollar stores. *American Journal of Agricultural Economics*, 106(2), pp. 852–882.

Chenarides, L., Cho, C., Nayga Jr, R.M. and Thomsen, M.R., 2021. Dollar stores and food deserts. *Applied Geography*, 134.

Chetty, R., Jackson, M.O., Kuchler, T., Stroebel, J., Hendren, N., Fluegge, R.B., Gong, S., Gonzalez, F., Grondin, A., Jacob, M. and Johnston, D., 2022. Social capital I: Measurement and associations with economic mobility. *Nature*, 608(7921), pp. 108–121.

Chiang, H.H., Chang, A., Han, T.S. and Mcconville, D., 2013. Corporate branding, brand psychological ownership and brand citizenship behaviour: Multilevel analysis and managerial implications. *Journal of General Management*, 39(1), pp. 55–80.

Chinchanachokchai, S., Duff, B.R. and Sar, S. 2015. The effect of multitasking on time perception, enjoyment, and ad evaluation. *Computers in Human Behavior*, 45, pp. 185–191.

Cho, S., 2019. December. Creative design thinking process: Fashion is cyclical then, now, and future. *International Textile and Apparel Association Annual Conference Proceedings*, 76(1).

Chowdhry, A., 2017. Microsoft Monday: negative Skype reviews, increasing broadband in rural areas, new Outlook features. 17 July 2017. *Forbes*. Available at: www.forbes.com/sites/amitchowdhry/2017/07/17/ microsoft-monday-negative-skype-reviews-increasing-broadband-in-rural-areas-new-outlook-features/, [Accessed on 13 February 2024].

Christodoulides, G., De Chernatony, L., Furrer, O., Shiu, E. and Abimbola, T., 2006. Conceptualising and measuring the equity of online brands. *Journal of Marketing Management*, 22(7–8), pp. 799–825.

Chu, S.C., and Sung, Y. 2011. Brand personality dimensions in China. *Journal of Marketing Communications*, 17(3), pp. 163–181.

Cinelli, M.D. and LeBoeuf, R.A., 2020. Keeping it real: How perceived brand authenticity affects product perceptions. *Journal of Consumer Psychology*, 30(1), pp. 40–59.

CivicScience, 2022. Share of BeReal users in the United States who believe the app is an authentic social media as of July 2022. *Statista*. Available at: www.statista.com/statistics/1339109/us-bereal-users-bereal-authenticity, [Accessed on 12 October 2023].

CMO Survey, 2022. Return to normalcy? Leading marketing in a post-Covid era. 13 September 2022. Available at: https://cmosurvey.org/return-to-normalcy-leading-marketing-in-a-post-covid-era/, [Accessed on 19 December 2023].

———. 2023. Managing AI, digital strategies, and DE&I in marketing. Available at: https://cmosurvey.org/wp-content/uploads/2024/03/The_CMO_Survey-Highlights_and_Insights_Report-Fall_2023-20240328-142725.pdf, [Accessed on 13 June 2024].

Coca-Cola Co. (NYSE:KO), 2021. Analysis of Property, Plant and Equipment. *Stock Analysis On Net*. Available at: www.stock-analysis-on.net/NYSE/Company/Coca-Cola-Co/Analysis/Property-Plant-and-Equipment, [Accessed on 30 September 2022].

Coca-Cola, 2014. How a groundbreaking campaign got its start 'Down under'. 25 September 2014. *Coca-Cola*. Available at: www.coca-colacompany.com/media-center/how-a-campaign-got-its-start-down-under, [Accessed on 28 February 2024].

Coleman, J., 2023. Global Trends Shaping Marketing. *We Are Social*. 5 January 2023. Available at: https://wearesocial.com/uk/blog/2023/01/global-trends-shaping-marketing-in-2023/, [Accessed on 25 September 2023].

Coley, A., and Burgess, B. 2003. Gender differences in cognitive and affective impulse buying. *Journal of Fashion Marketing and Management*, 7(3), pp. 282–295.

Commerce.senate.gov., 2023. *Sens. Cruz, Blackburn open and call for probe of Bud Light potentially marketing to underage individuals through partnership with Dylan Mulvaney*. 17 May 2023. Press Release. Available at: www.commerce.senate.gov/2023/5/sens-cruz-blackburn-open-and-call-for-probe-of-bud-light-potentially-marketing-to-underage-individuals-through-partnership-with-dylan-mulvaney, [Accessed on 26 November 2023].

Conmy, S., n.d. What is a stakeholder? *Corporate Governance Institute*. Available at: www.thecorporategovernanceinstitute.com/insights/lexicon/what-is-a-stakeholder/, [Accessed on 18 January 2024].

Co-op, 2018. Co-op profits rise sharply on continued investment in brand, business and people. 06 April 2018. Available at: www.co-operative.coop/media/news-releases/annual-results-2017, [Accessed on 29 February 2024].

Cooper, D., 1994. Productive, relational and everywhere? Conceptualising power and resistance within Foucauldian feminism. *Sociology, 28*(2), pp. 435–454.

Cosgrove, D. and Jackson, P., 1987. New directions in cultural geography. *Area, 19*(2), pp. 95–101.

Cossío Aparicio, C., 2021. *Millennials and the New Emotional Branding.* Thesis. Comillas Universidad Pontífica.

Cote, C., 2021. Making the business case for sustainability. 13 April 2021. *Harvard Business School Business Insights.* Available at: https://online .hbs.edu/blog/post/business-case-for-sustainability, [Accessed on 18 December 2023].

Cova, B. and Paranque, B., 2016. Value slippage in brand transformation: A conceptualization. *Journal of Product & Brand Management, 25*(1), pp. 3–10.

Crespo-Pereira, V., Membiela-Pollán, M. and Sánchez-Amboage, E., 2022. Nostalgia, retro-marketing, and neuromarketing: An exploratory review. *Journal of Creative Industries and Cultural Studies,* (7), pp. 107–126.

Csikszentmihalyi, M., 1993. Why we need things. In Eds. Lubar, S. & Kingery, D., *History from Things: Essays on Material Culture,* 1st Edition. Washington and London: Smithsonian Institution Press, pp. 20–29.

Cunningham, S.J., and Macrae, C.N. 2011. The colour of gender stereotyping. *British Journal of Psychology, 102*(3), pp. 598–614.

D'Antonio, V., 2019. From Tupperware to Scentsy: The gendered culture of women and direct sales. *Sociology Compass, 13*(5).

Dahlman, S., 2023. Affective boundaries: The power effects of objects of emotion in collaborative encounters. *Organization, 31*(6). Available at: https://doi.org/10.1177/13505084231151764.

D'andrade, R., 2001. A cognitivist's view of the units debate in cultural anthropology. *Cross-Cultural Research, 35*(2), pp. 242–257.

Dam, T.C., 2020. Influence of brand trust, perceived value on brand preference and purchase intention. *The Journal of Asian Finance, Economics and Business (JAFEB), 7*(10), pp. 939–947.

Datawords, 2020. Why we all need more brand activism in 2021 – And how to make it work. *Datawords Multicultural Technologies.* Available at: www.datawords.com/insights/why-we-all-need-more-brand-activism-in-2021-and-how-to-make-it-work/, [Accessed on 18 December 2023].

Davies, A. and Elliott, R., 2006. The evolution of the empowered consumer. *European Journal of Marketing, 40*(9/10), pp. 1106–1121.

Davis, S.M., 2000. The power of the brand. *Strategy & Leadership, 28*(4), pp. 4–9.

Davison, C., 2012. *Presentation of Digital Self in Everyday Life: Towards a Theory of Digital Identity.* Doctoral dissertation, RMIT University.

Dawar, N., 2004. What are brands good for? 15 October 2004. *MITS Loan Management Review*. Available at: https://sloanreview.mit.edu/article/what-are-brands-good-for/, [Accessed on 18 December 2023].

De Alwis, A.C. and Ramanathan, H.N. 2019. Impact of Sex Roles on Brand Gender Contamination of Purchase of Decision-Making: Case in Sri Lanka. In *4th Interdisciplinary Conference in Management*, Sabaragamuwa University of Sri Lanka, 29th – 30th October 2019.

De Bock, T., Pandelaere, M. and Van Kenhove, P., 2013. When colors backfire: The impact of color cues on moral judgment. *Journal of Consumer Psychology*, 23(3), pp. 341–348.

Dedeke, A., 2015. A cognitive–intuitionist model of moral judgment. *Journal of Business Ethics*, 126, pp. 437–457.

Dejowski, E. F., 1992. Public endorsement of restrictions on three aspects of free expression by homosexuals: Socio-demographic and trends analysis 1973–1988. *Journal of Homosexuality*, 23(4), pp. 1–18.

DeLane, J., 2018. 4 reasons why consumers view brands as relationships. *Digital Branding Institute*. Available at: https://digitalbranding institute.com/4-reasons-why-consumers-view-brands-as-relationships/, [Accessed on 12 February 2024].

Delgado-Ballester, E. and Luis Munuera-Alemán, J., 2005. Does brand trust matter to brand equity? *Journal of Product & Brand Management*, 14(3), pp. 187–196.

Delgado-Ballester, E., Munuera-Aleman, J.L. and Yague-Guillen, M.J., 2003. Development and validation of a brand trust scale. *International Journal of Market Research*, 45(1), pp. 35–54.

Deloitte, 2023. Deloitte 2023 global human capital trends report: new fundamentals for a boundaryless world. *Deloitte*. Available at: www2.deloitte.com/xe/en/insights/focus/human-capital-trends.html, [Accessed on 22 December 2023].

Dembek, K., Lüdeke-Freund, F., Rosati, F. and Froese, T., 2023. Untangling business model outcomes, impacts and value. *Business Strategy and the Environment*, 32(4), pp. 2296–2311.

Dennis, C., Brakus, J.J., Ferrer, G.G., McIntyre, C., Alamanos, E. and King, T., 2018. A cross-national study of evolutionary origins of gender shopping styles: She gatherer, he hunter? *Journal of International Marketing*, 26(4): pp. 38–53.

Desai, S., 2021. How Burberry executed one of the most successful brand identity transformations of all time … and how your business can too. 13 August 2021. *Linked In*. Available at: www.linkedin.com/pulse/how-burberry-executed-one-most-successful-brand-identity-desai/, [Accessed on 15 February 2024].

Despotakis, S., Ravi, R. and Srinivasan, K., 2021. The beneficial effects of ad blockers. *Management Science*, 67(4), pp. 2096–2125.

Dholakia, R., 1999. Going shopping: Key determinants of shopping behaviors and motivations. *International Journal of Retail & Distribution Management*, 27(4), pp. 154–165.

Diorio, S., 2019. The financial power of brand preference. *Forbes*. 22 January 2019. Available at: www.forbes.com/sites/forbesinsights/2019/01/22/the-financial-power-of-brand-preference/, [Accessed on 22 January 2024].

Dixon, S., 2022. Distribution of Twitter users worldwide as of January 2022, by gender. *Statista*. Available at: www.statista.com/statistics/828092/distribution-of-users-on-twitter-worldwide-gender/, [Accessed on 06 October 2022].

Dobrin, D., 2020. The hashtag in digital activism: A cultural revolution. *Journal of Cultural Analysis and Social Change*, 5(1), pp. 1–14.

Dodge, M. and Kitchin, R., 2001. *Mapping Cyberspace*. London: Routledge.

Dong, C. and Rim, H., 2022. Judge a nonprofit by the partners it keeps: How does cross-sector partnership disclosure influence public evaluations of the nonprofit? *VOLUNTAS: International Journal of Voluntary and Nonprofit Organizations*, 33(5), pp. 952–969.

Dore, I., 2010. Foucault on power. *UMKC Law Review*, 78(3), pp. 737–748.

Dreher, J., 2003. The symbol and the theory of the life-world: The transcendences of the life-world and their overcoming by signs and symbols. *Human Studies*, 26(2), pp. 141–163.

Drescher, T.D., 1992. The transformation and evolution of trademarks-from signals to symbols to myth. *The Trademark Reporter*, 82, p. 301.

Driscoll, B., 2013. Twitter, literary prizes and the circulation of capital. *By the Book*, pp. 103–119.

Drug Store News, 2014. Sales of the leading men's toiletries/grooming/aftershave brands in the United States in 2014 (in million U.S. dollars). *Statista*. Available at: www.statista.com/statistics/287707/mens-grooming-brands-sales-in-the-us/, [Accessed on 16 February 2024].

Duffy, B.E., 2017. *(Not) Getting Paid to Do What You Love*. New Haven: Yale University Press.

Duffy, C. and Fung, B., 2023. Two brands suspend advertising on X after their ads appeared next to pro-Nazi content. 17 August, 2023. *CNN Business*. Available at: https://edition.cnn.com/2023/08/16/tech/x-ads-pro-nazi-account-brand-safety/index.html, [Accessed on 29 January 2024].

Duffy, K., 2023. Gen Zers are bookworms but say they're shunning e-books because of eye strain, digital detoxing and their love for libraries. 13 March 2023. *World Economic Forum*. Avaiable at: www.weforum.org/agenda/2023/03/gen-zers-are-bookworms-but-say-theyre-shunning-e-books-because-of-eye-strain-digital-detoxing-and-their-love-for-libraries/, [Accessed on 25 August 2023].

Duncan, J. and Duncan, N., 1988. (Re) reading the landscape. *Environment and Planning D: Society and Space*, 6(2), pp.117–126.

Duxbury, N., Garrett-Petts, W.F. and MacLennan, D., 2015. Cultural mapping as cultural inquiry: Introduction to an emerging field of practice. In *Cultural Mapping as Cultural Inquiry*. New York: Routledge, pp. 1–42.

Dwivedi, A. and McDonald, R.E., 2020. Examining the efficacy of brand social media communication: A consumer perspective. *Journal of Marketing Theory and Practice*, 28(4), pp. 373–386.

Easton, S., Lees, L., Hubbard, P. and Tate, N., 2020. Measuring and mapping displacement: The problem of quantification in the battle against gentrification. *Urban studies*, 57(2), pp. 286–306.

Eckhardt, G.M. and Bengtsson, A., 2015. Brand meaning rigidity in China. *Journal of Macromarketing*, 35(2), pp. 218–228.

Eckhardt, G.M., Belk, R. and Devinney, T.M., 2010. Why don't consumers consume ethically? *Journal of Consumer Behaviour*, 9(6), pp. 426–436.

Edelman, 2023. 2023 Edelman Trust Barometer: Navigating a Polarized World. *Edelman*. Available at: www.edelman.com/trust/2023/trust-barometer, [Accessed on 23 November 2023].

Edelman, D., 2010. Branding in the digital age: You're spending your money in all the wrong places. *Harvard Business Review*, 88(12), pp. 62–69.

Edmans, A., 2023. How great companies deliver both purpose and profit. *Journal of Chinese Economic and Business Studies*, pp. 1–5.

Eisenchlas, S.A., 2013. Gender roles and expectations: Any changes online? *Sage Open*, 3(4).

Eisend, M., and Stokburger-Sauer, N.E. 2013. Measurement characteristics of Aaker's brand personality dimensions: Lessons to be learned from human personality research. *Psychology & Marketing*, 30 (11): pp. 950–958.

Elias, N., and Colvin, R. 2020. A third option: Understanding and assessing non-binary gender policies in the United States. *Administrative Theory & Praxis*, 42 (2): pp. 191–211.

Elliott, R. and Wattanasuwan, K., 1998. Brands as symbolic resources for the construction of identity. *International Journal of Advertising*, 17(2), pp. 131–144.

Ellis, L., Abild, M., Buker, H., Park, J.R., and He, P. 2012. Gendered shopping: A seven country comparison. *Mankind Quart*, 52, pp. 336–357.

Ellis, S., 2017. What is a North Star Metric? 05 June 2017. *Growth Hackers*. Available at: https://blog.growthhackers.com/what-is-a-north-star-metric-b31a8512923f, [Accessed on 04 February 2024].

Elwell, J.S., 2014. The transmediated self: Life between the digital and the analog. *Convergence*, 20(2), pp. 233–249.

Epley, N., Waytz, A., and Cacioppo, J., 2007. On seeing human: A three-factor theory of anthropomorphism. *Psychological Review*, 114(4), pp. 864–886.

Esterl, M., 2014. 'Share a Coke' credited with a pop in sales. 25 September 2014. *The Wall Street Journal*. Available at: www.wsj.com/articles/share-a-coke-credited-with-a-pop-in-sales-1411661519, [Accessed on 28 February 2024].

Ewens, H., 2022. Trends used to come back round every 20 years. Not anymore. 14 December 2022. *Vice*. Available at: www.vice.com/en/article/bvmkm8/how-the-20-year-trend-cycle-collapsed, [Accessed on 05 February 2024].

Eyada, B., 2020. Brand activism, the relation and impact on consumer perception: A case study on Nike advertising. *International Journal of Marketing Studies*, 12(4), pp. 30–42.

Ezel, C., 2023. About Us. *Change Please*. Available at: https://changeplease.org/pages/about-us-1, [Accessed on 21 December 2023].

Fachreza, M., Masnita, Y. and Kurniawati, K., 2023. The effect of online marketing (web based & online ads) on brand equity national switching companies through MGC (marketer generated content). *Jurnal Ekonomi*, 12(2), pp. 552–558.

Featherstone, M., 1990. Perspectives on consumer culture. *Sociology*, 24(1), pp. 5–22.

Feinberg, J.G., 2020. Understanding anti-performance: The performative division of experience and the standpoint of the non-performer. *Performance Philosophy*, 5(2), pp. 332–348.

Feinberg, R., 1979. Schneider's symbolic cultural theory: An appraisal. *Current Anthropology*, 20(3), pp. 541–560.

Feiner, L., 2023. Apple ramped up lobbying spending in 2022, outpacing tech peers. 23 January 2023. *CNBC*. Available at: www.cnbc.com/2023/01/23/apple-ramped-up-lobbying-spending-in-2022-outpacing-tech-peers.html, [Accessed on 13 December 2023].

Felix, R., Gonzalez, E.M., Castano, R., Carrete, L. and Gretz, R.T., 2022. When the green in green packaging backfires: Gender effects and perceived masculinity of environmentally friendly products. *International Journal of Consumer Studies*, 46(3), pp. 925–943.

Ferenius, J. and Kotras, V., 2021. *The Authentic Activist: Examining the antecedents of the perceived authenticity of brand activism*. Masters Paper. Lund University.

Ferrell, O.C. and Ferrell, L., 2021. New directions for marketing ethics and social responsibility research. *Journal of Marketing Theory and Practice*, 29(1), pp. 13–22.

Fetscherin, M., 2019. The five types of brand hate: How they affect consumer behavior. *Journal of Business Research*, 101, pp. 116–127.

Finch, J., 2003. Burberry's image goes from toff to tough. 25 November 2003. *The Guardian*. Available at: www.theguardian.com/business/2003/nov/25/3, [Accessed on 15 February 2024].

Fischer, S., 5 Tech giants own over half the global ad market. *Axios*. Available at: www.axios.com/2022/06/14/tech-ad-market-global, [Accessed on 18 October 2023].

Flood, B. and Kornick, L., 2023. Bud Light says pact with trans activist Dylan Mulvaney helps 'authentically connect with audiences'. *Fox News*. 03 April 2023. Available at: www.foxnews.com/media/bud-light-pact-trans-activist-dylan-mulvaney-helps-authentically-connect-with-audiences, [Accessed on 25 November 2023].

Forbes, 2022. The World's Most Valuable Brands. *Forbes*. Available at: www.forbes.com/the-worlds-most-valuable-brands/#14ddbb91119c, [Accessed on 30 September 2022].

Ford Media Center, 2021. Ford Mustang Is Best-Selling Sports Car for Second Year In A Row, Retains Sports Coupe Title for Sixth Straight Year. *Ford Media Center*. Available at: https://media.ford.com/content/fordmedia/feu/en/news/2021/04/15/ford-mustang-is-best-selling-sports-car-for-second-year-in-a-row.html, [Accessed on 02 October 2022].

Forouhar, N., Forouhar, A. and Hasankhani, M., 2022. Commercial gentrification and neighbourhood change: A dynamic view on local residents' quality of life in Tehran. *Land Use Policy*, 112.

Foucault, M., 1978. *The History of Sexuality, vol. 1, An Introduction.* Translated by Robert Hurley. New York: Pantheon Books, p. 86.

2002. *The Archaeology of Knowledge*. Translated by A.M. Sheridan Smith. London: Routledge.

1980. *Power/Knowledge: Selected Interviews and Other Writings, 1972–1977*. Edited by C. Gordon. Translated by C. Gordon, L. Marshall., J. Mepham, & K. Soper. Pantheon Books: New York.

Fournier, S. and Alvarez, C., 2019. How brands acquire cultural meaning. *Journal of Consumer Psychology*, 29(3), pp. 519–534.

Fowelstone, M.G., 2013. *The Lore of the Brand: An Investigation into How Organisations Can Build Consumer Engagement and Brand Affinity through a Shared Narrative*. Doctoral dissertation, Edinburgh Napier University.

Fowelstone, M., Williams Jr, R. and Omar, M., 2015. *How Narrative Is Magically Created by the Lore of the Brand: The Consumer Brand Affinity Fan*. Academy of Marketing Conference Paper, July 2015.

Framke, C., 2017. The story behind 84 Lumber's Super bowl ad about Trump's border wall. 06 February 2017. *Vox*. Available at: www.vox.com/culture/2017/2/5/14518244/84-lumber-super-bowl-commercial, [Accessed on 19 December 2023].

Franzak, F., Makarem, S. and Jae, H., 2014. Design benefits, emotional responses, and brand engagement. *Journal of Product & Brand Management,* 23(1), pp. 16–23.

Fraser, N., 1981. Foucault on modern power: Empirical insights and normative confusions. *Praxis International,* 1(3), pp. 272–287.

Frieden, L.R. 2013. *The Role of Consumer Gender Identity and Brand Concept Consistency in Evaluating Cross-Gender Brand Extensions.* MA in Mass Communications. University of South Florida. Available at: https://digitalcommons.usf.edu/etd/4488/, [Accessed on 20 August 2023].

Friedman, V., 2018. What Kate Spade stood for. *New York Times.* 06 June 2018. Available at: www.nytimes.com/2018/06/05/style/kate-spade-death.html/, [Accessed on 25 December 2023].

Fritz, K., Schoenmueller, V. and Bruhn, M., 2016. Authenticity in branding – Exploring antecedents and consequences of brand authenticity. *European Journal of Marketing,* 51(2), pp. 324–348.

Fromm, J., 2022. As Gen Z's buying power grows, businesses must adapt their marketing. 20 July 2022. *Forbes.* Available at: www.forbes.com/sites/jefffromm/2022/07/20/as-gen-zs-buying-power-grows-businesses-must-adapt-their-marketing/?sh=506afa9c2533, [Accessed on 09 December 2023].

Frow, P. and Payne, A., 2007. Towards the 'perfect' customer experience. *Journal of Brand Management,* 15(2), pp. 89–101.

Fuchs, C. and Schreier, M., 2011. Customer empowerment in new product development. *Journal of Product Innovation Management,* 28(1), pp. 17–32.

Füller, J., 2016. The power of community brands: How user-generated brands emerge. In Ed. Harhoff, D., & Lakhani, K.R., *Revolutionizing Innovation: Users, Communities, and Open Innovation.* Cambridge, MA: MIT Press, pp. 353–376.

Gabrina, I. and Gayatri, G., 2023. Attitude toward Femvertising: Antecedents and consequences. *Asian Journal of Engineering, Social and Health,* 2(5), pp. 301–312.

Galarza, L. and Stoltzfus-Brown, L., 2021. 84 Lumber's constrained polysemy: Limiting interpretive play and the power of audience agency in inspirational immigrant narratives. *International Journal of Communication,* 15, pp. 41–60.

Galvin, J., 2020. *The definition of branding and its impact on modern societyresearch.* MSc. University of Wisconsin-Platteville. Available at: https://minds.wisconsin.edu/bitstream/handle/1793/80480/Galvin %2C%20Joshua.pdf?sequence=1&isAllowed=y, [Accessed on 18 October 2023].

Gao, A., 2021. Catching the earworm: Understanding streaming music popularity using machine learning models. In *E3S Web of Conferences*, Vol. 253(3).

Ganeshalingam, A., 2023. *Brand activism*. [Guest Lecture]. PUBL7006: Marketing. Oxford Brookes University. 25 October 2023.

Garaus, M. and Wolfsteiner, E., 2023. Media multitasking, advertising appeal, and gender effects. *Review of Managerial Science, 17*(2), pp. 539–567.

Garbarino, E. and Strahilevitz, M. 2004. Gender differences in the perceived risk of buying online and the effects of receiving a site recommendation. *Journal of Business Research, 57*(7): pp. 768–775.

Garcia, R.C., 2023. Global trends shaping marketing. *We Are Social. 5* January 2023. Available at: https://wearesocial.com/uk/blog/2023/01/global-trends-shaping-marketing-in-2023/, [Accessed on 25 September 2023].

Garg, N. and Saluja, G., 2022. A tale of two 'Ideologies': Differences in consumer response to brand activism. *Journal of the Association for Consumer Research, 7*(3), pp. 325–339.

Gaucher, D., Friesen, J. and Kay, A.C., 2011. Evidence that gendered wording in job advertisements exists and sustains gender inequality. *Journal of Personality and Social Psychology, 101*(1), pp. 109–128.

Gaunt, R., 2006. Biological essentialism, gender ideologies, and role attitudes: What determines parents' involvement in child care. *Sex Roles, 55*, pp. 523–533.

Gay, A., 2022. The greatest thing about owning a Ford Mustang is the community around it. *GQ*. 22 April 2022. Available at: www.gq-magazine.co.uk/cars/article/ford-mustang-community, [Accessed on 02 October 2022].

Geertz, C., 1973. *The Interpretation of Cultures: Selected Essays*. New York: Basic Books.

Gerrard, Y., 2023. BeReal is now in freefall. Why are new social media apps doomed to fail? *The Guardian*. Available at: www.theguardian.com/commentisfree/2023/may/04/bereal-instagram-social-media-apps-fail, [Accessed on 12 October 2023].

Geuens, M., Weijters, B. and De Wulf, K. 2009. A new measure of brand personality. *International Journal of Research in Marketing, 26*(2): pp. 97–107.

Gielens, K. and Steenkamp, J. B. E., 2019. Branding in the era of digital (dis)intermediation. *International Journal of Research in Marketing, 36*(3), pp. 367–384.

Gilmore, J.H. and Pine, J., 2007. *Authenticity: What Consumers Really Want*. Boston, MA: Harvard Business School Press.

Gitnux, 2023. Gitnux Marketdata Report 2023: The most surprising brand authenticity statistics in 2023. *Gitnux*. Available at: https://blog.gitnux.com/brand-authenticity-statistics/, [Accessed on 06 October 2023].

Glavas, A., 2016. Corporate social responsibility and organizational psychology: An integrative review. *Frontiers in Psychology*, 7.

GOBankingRates, 2021. All-time most expensive Super Bowl ads as of January 2021 (in million U.S. dollars). *Statista Inc*. Available at: www.statista.com/statistics/1282348/most-expensive-super-bowl-ads/, [Accessed on 4 June 2024].

Gobe, M., 2010. *Emotional Branding: The New Paradigm for Connecting Brands to People*. London and New York: Simon and Schuster.

2010. *Brandjam: Humanizing Brands through Emotional Design*. London and New York: Simon and Schuster.

Goffman, E., 1990. *The Presentation of Self in Everyday Life*. London: Penguin Books.

Golden, G., 2023. Forget Authenticity at Work and Embrace Growth Instead. *Psychology Today*. Available at: www.psychologytoday.com/gb/blog/curating-your-life/202301/forget-authenticity-at-work-and-embrace-growth-instead, [Accessed on 27 January, 2023].

Goldfarb, A., & Tucker, C. 2011. Online display advertising: Targeting and obtrusiveness. *Marketing Science*, 30(3), pp. 389–404.

Golossenko, A., Pillai, K.G. and Aroean, L., 2020. Seeing brands as humans: Development and validation of a brand anthropomorphism scale. *International Journal of Research in Marketing*, 37(4), pp. 737–755.

Gómez-Suárez, M., Martínez-Ruiz, M.P. and Martínez-Caraballo, N., 2017. Consumer-brand relationships under the marketing 3.0 paradigm: A literature review. *Frontiers in Psychology*, 8.

Gond, J.P., El Akremi, A., Swaen, V. and Babu, N., 2017. The psychological microfoundations of corporate social responsibility: A person-centric systematic review. *Journal of Organizational Behavior*, 38(2), pp. 225–246.

Ghosh, A., 2021. When brands should shut up – A study on brand activism. 02 Sepember 2021. *Brandingmag*. Available at: www.brandingmag.com/2021/09/02/when-brands-should-shut-up-a-study-on-brand-activism/, [Accessed on 19 December 2023].

González-Mansilla, O.L., Serra-Cantallops, A. and Berenguer-Contrí, G., 2023. Effect of value co-creation on customer satisfaction: The mediating role of brand equity. *Journal of Hospitality Marketing & Management*, 32(2), pp. 242–263.

Grau, S.L. and Zotos, Y.C., 2018. Gender stereotypes in advertising: A review of current research. *Current Research on Gender Issues in Advertising*, pp. 3–12.

Grayson, K. and Martinec, R., 2004. Consumer perceptions of iconicity and indexicality and their influence on assessments of authentic market offerings. *Journal of Consumer Research, 31*(2), pp. 296–312.

Griffiths, A., 2018. Brands and corporate power. *Journal of Corporate Law Studies, 18*(1), pp. 75–112.

Grillo, C.M., 2018. Revisiting Fromm and Bourdieu: Contributions to habitus and realism. *Journal for the Theory of Social Behaviour, 48*(4), pp. 416–432.

Grimes, T., 2013. What the Share a Coke campaign can teach other brands. 24 July 2013. *The Guardian*. Available at: www.theguardian.com/media-network/media-network-blog/2013/jul/24/share-coke-teach-brands, [Accessed on 28 February 2024].

Grimmer, L. and Mortimer, G., 2018. Kate Spade, the archetypal New Yorker, sold whimsical, affordable luxury to women. *The Conversation*, pp. 1–3.

Grohmann, B. 2016. Communicating brand gender through type fonts. *Journal of Marketing Communications, 22*(4), pp. 403–418.

Gross, J., 2018. Use Nostalgia To Improve Your Marketing Results. *Forbes*. Available at: www.forbes.com/sites/forbesagencycouncil/2018/05/24/use-nostalgia-to-improveyour-marketing-results/, [Accessed on 20 January 2024].

Guba, E.G. and Lincoln, Y.S., 1994. 'Competing paradigms in qualitative research'. In (Eds) Denzin, N.K., & Lincoln, Y.S., *Handbook of Qualitative Research*. Thousand Oaks, CA: Sage, pp. 105–117.

Giadiano, N., Dua, T., Leonard, K., Michelson, A., Sundar, S., Ungarino, R., & Wang, A., 2022. AT&T, Walmart, Citi, and other megacorporations bankrolled a wave of state abortion bans. *Business Insider*. 24 June 2022. Available at: www.businessinsider.com/state-abortion-ban-sponsors-bankrolled-by-att-walmart-citi-corporations-2022-5?r=US&IR=T, [Accessed on 03 October 2022].

Guido, G. and Peluso, A. 2015. Brand anthropomorphism: Conceptualization, measurement, and impact on brand personality and loyalty. *Journal of Brand Management, 22*(1), pp.1–19.

Gupta, P., Chauhan, S., Paul, J. and Jaiswal, M.P., 2020. Social entrepreneurship research: A review and future research agenda. *Journal of business research, 113*, pp. 209–229.

Gupta, S., 2022. Gen Z has 86% less purchasing power than baby boomers did in their 20s. 12 August, 2022. *Fast Company*. Available at: www.fastcompany.com/90778446/gen-z-vs-baby-boomers-purchasing-power, [Accessed on 28 January 2024].

Gupta, S., Grant, S. and Melewar, T.C., 2008. The expanding role of intangible assets of the brand. *Management Decision, 46*(6), pp. 948–960.

Gurrieri, L. and Finn, F., 2023. Gender transformative advertising pedagogy: Promoting gender justice through marketing education. *Journal of Marketing Management*, 39(1–2), pp. 108–133.

Gusfield, J.R. and Michalowicz, J., 1984. Secular symbolism: Studies of ritual, ceremony, and the symbolic order in modern life. *Annual Review of Sociology*, 10(1), pp. 417–435.

Gustafsson, C., 2015. Sonic branding: A consumer-oriented literature review. *Journal of brand management*, 22, pp. 20–37.

Gwynne, J. ed., 2022. *The Cultural Politics of Femvertising: Selling Empowerment*. London: Palgrave Macmillan.

Gyrd-Jones, R.I. and Kornum, N., 2013. Managing the co-created brand: Value and cultural complementarity in online and offline multi-stakeholder ecosystems. *Journal of business research*, 66(9), pp. 1484–1493.

Haarhoff, G. and Kleyn, N., 2012. Open source brands and their online brand personality. *Journal of Brand Management*, 20, pp. 104–114.

Häglund, E. and Björklund, J., 2022. AI-driven contextual advertising: A technology report and implication analysis. *arXiv:2205.00911*. Available at: https://doi.org/10.48550/arXiv.2205.00911.

Haigh, A., 2022. How much value is there in intangible assets. 29 November 2022. *BrandFinance*. Available at: https://brandfinance.com/insights/how-much-value-is-there-in-intangible-assets, [Accessed on 22 January 2024].

Haigh, E., 2022. 'I bet pilots would rather have a pay rise!' Travellers slam Virgin Atlantic's 'inclusivity drive' that will allow a male staff to wear skirts as they call on airline to concentrate on lowering fares a and making flights run on time. *Mail Online*. 28 September 2022. Available at: www.dailymail.co.uk/news/article-11257795/Virgin-Atlantic-pilots-crew-choose-male-female-uniforms-express-true-identity.html, [Accessed on 25 November 2023].

Hainneville, V., Guèvremont, A. and Robinot, É., 2023. Femvertising or femwashing? Women's perceptions of authenticity. *Journal of Consumer Behaviour*, 22(4), pp. 933–941.

Halwani, L., 2019. Making sense of heritage luxury brands: Consumer perceptions across different age groups. *Qualitative Market Research: An International Journal*, 22(3), pp. 301–324.

Handler, R., 1986. Authenticity. *Anthropology Today*, 2(1), pp. 2–4.

happi Magazine, 2022. Sales growth of the leading deodorant brands in the United States in 2022 (change to prior sales year). *Statista*. Available at: www.statista.com/statistics/739589/us-sales-growth-of-deodorant-brands/, [Accessed on 16 February 2024].

2023. Leading body wash brands in the United States in 2022, based on sales (in million U.S. dollars). *Statista*. Available at: www.statista .com/statistics/1445775/leading-body-wash-brands-in-the-us-based-on-sales/, [Accessed on 16 February 2024].

Harley, J.B., 1989. Deconstructing the map. *Cartographica 26*, pp. 1–20.

Harrington, B. 2018. The Bad Behaviours of the Richest: What I Learned from Wealth Managers. *The Guardian*. 19 October 2018. Available at: www.theguardian.com/us-news/2018/oct/19/billionaires-wealth-richest-income-inequality, [Accessed on 23 December 2022].

Harrison W. and Hood-Williams, J. 2002. *Beyond Sex and Gender*. London: SAGE Publications.

Hasri, M.N., Silva, N., Susanto, Y.B. and Winarno, P.M., 2022, April. The Attitude toward The Programmatic Advertising on Click-Through Intention. In *ICEBE 2021: Proceedings of the 4th International Conference of Economics, Business, and Entrepreneurship, ICEBE 2021*, 7 October 2021, Lampung, Indonesia (p. 182). European Alliance for Innovation.

Hastie, A. and Saunders, R., 2023. (Em)placing the popular in cultural geography. *Social & Cultural Geography*. [Online] Available at: https://doi.org/10.1080/14649365.2023.2289987, [Accessed on 07 March 2024].

Helal, G., Ozuem, W. and Lancaster, G., 2018. Social media brand perceptions of millennials. *International Journal of Retail & Distribution Management*, 46(10), pp. 977–998.

Helkkula, A., Kelleher, C. and Pihlström, M., 2012. Characterizing value as an experience: Implications for service researchers and managers. *Journal of Service Research*, 15(1), pp. 59–75.

Hemsley-Brown, J., 2023. Antecedents and consequences of brand attachment: A literature review and research agenda. *International Journal of Consumer Studies*, 47(2), pp. 611–628.

Henderson, B., 2023. Not Just Bud Light: Culture War Hits Other Anheuser-Busch Beers. 31 May 2023. *The Wall Street Journal*. Available at: www .wsj.com/livecoverage/stock-market-today-dow-jones-05-31-2023/card/not-just-bud-light-culture-war-hit-other-anheuser-busch-beers-wLJBJjHsXyJDb06tvujy, [Accessed on 26 November 2023].

Henderson, P. W., Giese, J. L., and Cote, J. A. 2004. Impression management using typeface design. *Journal of Marketing, 68*, pp. 60–83.

Henwood, F. and Wyatt, S., 2019. Technology and in/equality, questioning the information society. *Digital Culture & Society*, 5(1), pp. 183–194.

Hepburn, P., Louis, R. and Desmond, M., 2024. Beyond gentrification: housing loss, poverty, and the geography of displacement. *Social Forces*, 102(3), pp. 880–901.

Herdt, G. (Ed.), 2020. *Third Sex, Third Gender: Beyond Sexual Dimorphism in Culture and History*. New Jersey: Princeton University Press.

Herincx, G., 2016. After 52 Years, Ford Mustang Muscles into the British car market. *CNN*, 27 April 2016. Available at: https://edition.cnn.com/style/article/ford-mustang-muscles-into-british-car-market/index.html, [Accessed on 02 October 2022].

Heřmanová, M., 2022. 'I'm always telling you my honest opinion': Influencers and gendered authenticity strategies on Instagram. *Cultures of Authenticity*, pp. 231–245.

Hess, A., and Melnyk, V. 2016. Pink or blue? The impact of gender cues on brand perceptions. *European Journal of Marketing*, *50*(9/10), pp. 1550–1574.

Hill, L., 2017. 84 Limber responds to controversy (and confusion) over its Super Bowl commercial. 06 February 2017. *Los Angeles Times*. Available at: www.latimes.com/entertainment/la-et-entertainment-news-updates-84-lumber-courts-controversy-and-1486409814-htmlstory.html, [Accessed on 19 December 2023].

Hodge, E., and Hallgrimsdottir, H., 2019. Networks of hate: The alt-right, 'troll culture', and the cultural geography of social movement spaces online. *Journal of Borderlands Studies*, *35*(4), pp. 563–580.

Hoek, J. and P. Gendall. 2010. Colors, brands, and trademarks: The marketing (and legal) problem of establishing distinctiveness. *Journal of Advertising Research*, *50*(3), pp. 316–322.

Hoffmann, S., 1975. Notes on the elusiveness of modern power. *International Journal*, *30*(2), pp. 183–206.

Holden, R., 2017. The New Starbucks CEO seems to stumble out of the gate. 26 May 2017. *Forbes*. Available at: www.forbes.com/sites/ronaldholden/2017/05/26/the-new-starbucks-ceo-seems-to-stumble-out-of-the-gate/?sh=4e5e16e150ac, [Accessed on 04 February 2024].

Hollenback, K.L., 2016. Ritual and religion. In Ed. Schiffer, M. B., *Behavioral Archaeology*. London: Routledge, pp. 156–163.

Holt, D. B. 2004. *How Brands Become Icons: The Principles of Cultural Branding*. Boston: Harvard Business School Press.

Hood, B., 2012. *The Self-Illusion: How the Social Brain Creates Identity*. New York: Oxford University Press.

Horoszko, N., Moskowitz, D. and Moskowitz, H., 2018. *Understanding the Marketing Exceptionality of Prestige Perfumes*. London: Routledge.

Houraghan, S., 2023. Successful brand strategy example (Old Spice repositioning). 21 November 2023. *Brand Master Academy*. Available at: https://brandmasteracademy.com/brand-strategy-example/, [Accessed on 15 February 2024].

Huaman-Ramirez, R. and Merunka, D., 2019. Brand experience effects on brand attachment: The role of brand trust, age, and income. *European Business Review*, 31(5), pp. 610–645.

Huang, T.L. 2019. Psychological mechanisms of brand love and information technology identity in virtual retail environments. *Journal of Retailing and Consumer Services*, 47, pp. 251–264.

Huang, X., 2019. Understanding Bourdieu-cultural capital and habitus. *Review of European Studies*, 11(3), pp. 45–49.

Hughes, R.E., n.d. Authenticity in marketing: how your brand can start benefitting today. *NYT Licensing* from *The New York Times*. Available at: https://nytlicensing.com/latest/marketing/why-do-brands-need-authenticity-marketing/, [Accessed on 26 February 2024].

Hume, D., 2009. *A Treatise of Human Nature: Being an Attempt to Introduce the Experimental Method of Reasoning into Moral Subjects*. Waiheke Island: Floating Press.

Hunter, F., 2017. *Community Power Structure: A Study of Decision Makers*. North Carolina: UNC Press Books.

Hydock, C., Paharia, N. and Blair, S., 2020. Should your brand pick a side? How market share determines the impact of corporate political advocacy. *Journal of Marketing Research*, 57(6), pp. 1135–1151.

Hypebeast, 2019. Old Spice and Danner Boots: team up for an unexpected footwear collaboration. 31 May 2019. *Hypebeast*. Available at: https://hypebeast.com/2019/5/old-spice-danner-boots-hiking-boots-collaboration, [Accessed on 16 February 2024].

2022. Old Spice and Arby's create epic collab to defeat the meat sweats. *HypeBeast*. Available at: https://hypebeast.com/2022/6/old-spice-arbys-meat-sweats-defense-collaboration, [Accessed on 16 February 2024].

IAG, 2023. British Airways Plc's worldwide revenue from FY 2010 to FY 2022 (in million GBP). *Statista*. Available at: www.statista.com/statistics/264296/british-airways-worldwide-revenues-since-2006/, [Accessed on 23 November 2023].

Ianenko, M., Stepanov, M. and Mironova, L., 2020. Brand identity development. *E3S Web of Conferences*, Vol. 164.

IAS, 2024. The State of Brand Safety: Exploring consumer perception of appropriate online content and misinformation. January 2024. *IAS*. Available at: https://integralads.com/insider/state-of-brand-safety-research, [Accessed on 29 January 2024].

Ignatow, G. and Robinson, L., 2017. Pierre Bourdieu: Theorizing the digital. *Information, Communication & Society*, 20, pp. 650–966.

IFRS, 2023. IAS 38 Intangible Assets. *IFRS*. Available at: www.ifrs.org/issued-standards/list-of-standards/ias-38-intangible-assets/, [Accessed on 22 January 2024].

Interbrand, 2023. Brand value of Burberry worldwide from 2010 to 2023 (in million U.S. dollars). *Statista.* Available at: www.statista.com/statistics/985253/burberry-brand-value-worldwide/, [Accessed on 14 February 2024].

International Society of Women Airline Pilots, 2021. Major airlines with the highest share of female pilots in the world in 2021. *Statista.* Available at: www.statista.com/statistics/1177719/female-pilots-airlines-worldwide/, [Accessed on 06 November 2023].

Insoll, T. (Ed.), 2011. *The Oxford Handbook of the Archaeology of Ritual and Religion.* Oxford: Oxford University Press.

Interbrand, 2021. Best Global Brands 2021: Coca-Cola. Available at: https://interbrand.com/best-global-brands/coca-cola/, [Accessed on 30 September 2022].

      2023. Brand value of Tiffany & Co. worldwide from 2010 to 2023 (in million U.S. dollars). *Statista.* Available at: www.statista.com/statistics/985289/tiffany-and-co-brand-value-worldwide/, [Accessed on 22 February 2024].

IPSOS, 2023. Making belonging joyful: inclusive representation in advertising to grow brands. Available at: www.ipsos.com/en-uk/making-belonging-joyful-inclusive-representation-advertising-grow-brands, [Accessed on 17 October 2023].

IPSOS, 2023. Percentage of consumers tending to buy brands that reflected their personal values in selected markets worldwide as of October 2023. *Statista.* www.statista.com/statistics/350685/buying-brands-that-reflect-personal-values-europe/, [Accessed on 09 December 2023].

Iqbal, A., Waris, I. and Farooqui, R., 2022. Predictors and outcomes of brand love: An evaluation of customers' love for neo-luxury brands. *Pakistan Business Review,* 24(1).

Jackson, A.Y. 2004. Performativity identified. *Qualitative Inquiry,* 10(5), pp. 673–690.

Jackson, J.B., 1971. A new kind of space. In Ed. Salter, C., *The Cultural Landscape.* California: Duxbury Press.

Jain, K. and Sharma, I., 2019. Negative outcomes of positive brand relationships. *Journal of Consumer Marketing,* 36(7), pp. 986–1002.

Janmaat, J.G. and Keating, A., 2019. Are today's youth more tolerant? Trends in tolerance among young people in Britain. *Ethnicities,* 19(1), pp. 44–65.

Japutra, A., Ekinci, Y., and Simkin, L. 2014. Exploring brand attachment, its determinants and outcomes. *Journal of Strategic Marketing,* 22(7), pp. 616–630.

Jenkins, R., 1982. Pierre Bourdieu and the reproduction of determinism. *Sociology,* 31, pp. 270–281.

Jenkins, H.; Clinton, K., Purushotma, R., Robison, A. J. and Weigel, M., 2006. Confronting the Challenges of Participatory Culture: Media Education for the 21st Century. *Building the Field of Digital media and Learning*, The John D. and Catherine T. MacArthur Foundation, Chicago, pp. 1–68. Available at: www.nwp.org/cs/public/download/ nwp_file/10932/Confronting_the_Challenges_of_Participatory_ Culture.pdf?x-r¼pcfile_d, [Accessed on 28 October 2022].

Jezer-Morton, K., 2023. Is Tradwife Content Dangerous, or Just Stupid? *The Cut*. Available at: www.thecut.com/2023/09/tradwife-content-influencers-conservative-ideology.html, [Accessed on 25 September 2023].

Johnson, M., 2021. *Books and Social Media: How the Digital Age Is Shaping the Printed Word*. Oxon: Routledge.

Johnson, R., 1993. Introduction. In *The Field of Cultural Production: Essays on Art and Literature*. New York: Columbia University Press.

Johnston, J. and Cairns, K., 2012. Eating for change. In Eds. Mukherjee, R. & Banet-Weiser, S., *Commodity Activism: Cultural Resistance in Neoliberal Times*. New York and London: New York University Press.

Jokilehto, J., 2006. Considerations on authenticity and integrity in world heritage context. *City & Time*, 2(1), pp. 7–12.

Jones, M., 2003. The concept of cultural landscape: Discourse and narratives. In Eds. Palang, H., & Fry, G., *Landscape Interfaces: Cultural Heritage in Changing Landscapes*. Dordrecht: Springer, pp. 21–51.

Jones, R., 2017. The history of branding. In *Branding: A Very Short Introduction*. Oxford: Oxford Academic.

Jones, S.C., 2003. Sexism is in the eye of the beholder: Does the Advertising Standards Board reflect' community standards'? *Research Online*, University of Wollongong, pp. 21–47.

Joseph, J., 2004. Foucault and reality. *Capital & Class*, 28(1), pp. 143–165.

Jung, C.G. 1964. *Man and His Symbols*. New York: Anchor Press.

Jung, K. 2006. *Cross-Gender Brand Extensions: Effects of Gender of Brand, Gender of Consumer and Product Type on Evaluation of Cross-Gender Extensions*. ACR North American Advances.

Justin Boots, 2023. Our Story. *Justin Boots*. Available at: www.justinboots .com/en/our-story.html, [Accessed on 23 August 2023].

Kacen, J. 2000. Girrrl power and Boyyy nature: The past, present and paradisal future of consumer gender identity. *Marketing Intelligence & Planning*, 18(3), pp. 45–355.

Kähr, A., Nyffenegger, B., Krohmer, H. and Hoyer, W.D., 2016. When hostile consumers wreak havoc on your brand: The phenomenon of consumer brand sabotage. *Journal of Marketing*, 80(3), pp. 25–41.

Kapitan, S., Kemper, J.A., Vredenburg, J. and Spry, A., 2022. Strategic B2B brand activism: Building conscientious purpose for social impact. *Industrial Marketing Management, 107*, pp. 14–28.

Karpinska-Krakowiak, M. 2021. Women are more likely to buy unknown brands than men: The effects of gender and known versus unknown brands on purchase intentions. *Journal of Retailing and Consumer Services, 58.*

Kate Spade New York, 2018. Kate Spade, the visionary founder of our brand, has passed.... X. Posted on 05 June 2018. Available at: https://twitter.com/katespadeny/status/1004060289569042432, [Accessed on 26 December 2023].

Kate Spade, 2019. Social impact report 2019. *Kate Spade.* Available at: https://assets.katespade.com/na/assets/img/landing-page/01_2019_OP_Social_Impact_Report.pdf, [Accessed on 26 December 2023].

2022. Social impact report 2022. *Kate Spade.* Available at: https://assets.katespade.com/na/images/main/landing-pages/social-impact/pdf/2022_ks_social_impact_v2.pdf, [Accessed on 26 December 2023].

2023a. Google interest over time 'Kate Spade' 2004–2023.

2023b. Our Mission. *Kate Spade.* Available at: www.katespade.com/social-impact/our-mission, [Accessed on 26 December 2023].

Kaur, J., 2016. Allure of the abroad: Tiffany & Co., its cultural influence, and consumers. *M/C Journal, 19*(5). Available at: https://doi.org/10.5204/mcj.1153, [Accessed on 12 June 2024].

Kefi, H., & Maar, D., 2018. The power of lurking: Assessing the online experience of luxury brand fan page followers. *Journal of Business Research, 117*, pp. 579–586.

Keller, K. L., 2003. Brand synthesis: The multidimensionality of brand knowledge. *Journal of Consumer Research, 29*(March), pp. 595–600.

Keller, K.L., Lehmann, D.R., 2003. How do brands create value? *Marketing Management, 12*(3), pp. 26–31.

Kelly, C., 2022. Old Spice teams up with Arby's to tackle 'meat sweats'. 29 June 2022. *Marketing Dive.* Available at: www.marketingdive.com/news/old-spice-arbys-meat-sweats/626227/, [Accessed on 16 February 2024].

Kemp, 2023. Making belonging joyful: Inclusive representation in advertising to grow brands. *IPSOS.* Available at: www.ipsos.com/en-uk/making-belonging-joyful-inclusive-representation-advertising-grow-brands, [Accessed on 17 October 2023].

Kemp, E., Cho, Y.N., Bui, M. and Kintzer, A., 2023. Music to the ears: The role of sonic branding in advertising. *International Journal of Advertising*, pp. 1–21.

Kernstock, J. and Brexendorf, T.O., 2009. Implications of Habermas's 'theory of communicative action' for corporate brand management. *Corporate Communications: An International Journal*, 14, pp. 389–403.

Key, T.M., Keel, A.L., Czaplewski, A.J. and Olson, E.M., 2021. Brand activism change agents: Strategic storytelling for impact and authenticity. *Journal of Strategic Marketing*, pp. 1–17.

Khodabandeh, A. and Lindh, C., 2021. The importance of brands, commitment, and influencers on purchase intent in the context of online relationships. *Australasian Marketing Journal*, 29(2), pp. 177–186.

Killingly, C., Lacherez, P. and Meuter, R., 2021. Singing in the brain: Investigating the cognitive basis of earworms. *Music Perception: An Interdisciplinary Journal*, 38(5), pp. 456–472.

Kilmann, R.H., Saxton, M.J. and Serpa, R., 1986. Issues in understanding and changing culture. *California Management Review*, 28(2), pp. 87–94.

Kim, Y.K. and Sullivan, P., 2019. Emotional branding speaks to consumers' heart: The case of fashion brands. *Fashion and textiles*, 6(1), pp. 1–16.

Kitchin, R., & Dodge, M., 2007. Rethinking maps. *Progress in Human Geography*, 31(3), pp. 331–344.

Klein, O., Spears, R., and Reicher, S., 2007. Social identity performance: Extending the strategic side of SIDE. *Personality and Social Psychology Review*, 11(1), pp. 28–45.

Klink, R.R. 2000. Creating brand names with meaning: The use of sound symbolism. *Marketing Letters*, 11(1), pp. 5–20.

Koc-Michalska, K., Schiffrin, A., Lopez, A., Boulianne, S., and Bimber, B. 2021. From online political posting to mansplaining: The gender gap and social media in political discussion. *Social Science Computer Review* 39 (2), pp. 197–210.

Koch, C.H., 2020. Brands as activists: The Oatly case. *Journal of Brand Management*, 27(5), pp. 593–606.

Koh, J. 2012. The history of the concept of gender identity disorder. *Seishin Shinkeigaku Zasshi*, 114 (6), pp. 673–680.

Koller, V. 2008. Not just a colour': Pink as a gender and sexuality marker in visual communication. *Visual Communication*, 7(4), pp. 395–423.

Korschun, D., 2021. Brand activism is here to stay: Here's why. *NIM Marketing Intelligence Review*, 13(2), pp. 10–17.

Kotzé, T., North, E., Stols, M., and Venter, L. 2012. Gender differences in sources of shopping enjoyment. *International Journal of Consumer Studies*, 36(4), pp. 416–424.

Kou, Y. and Powpaka, S., 2021. Pseudo-ownership advertising appeal creates brand psychological ownership: The role of self-construal and customer type. *Journal of Product & Brand Management*, 30(2), pp. 215–230.

Kovacs, B., Negro, G., Schultz, M. and Suddaby, R.R., 2018, July. The dark side of authenticity in organizational life. *Academy of Management Proceedings, 13*(1), pp. 1–42.

Koydemir, S., Şimşek, Ö.F., Kuzgun, T.B. and Schütz, A., 2020. Feeling special, feeling happy: Authenticity mediates the relationship between sense of uniqueness and happiness. *Current Psychology, 39*, pp. 1589–1599.

Kozinets, R., 2001. Utopian enterprise: Articulating the meaning of Star Trek's culture of consumption. *Journal of Consumer Research, 28* (June), pp.67–89.

Kristal, S., Baumgarth, C. and Henseler, J., 2018. 'Brand play' versus 'Brand attack': The subversion of brand meaning in non-collaborative co-creation by professional artists and consumer activists. *Journal of Product & Brand Management, 27*(3), pp. 334–347.

Kubiak, K. and Ouda, S., 2020. *Brand Activism-the Battle Between Authenticity and Consumer Scepticism.* Masters Paper. Lund University.

Kucuk, S.U., 2018. Macro-level antecedents of consumer brand hate. *Journal of Consumer Marketing, 35*(5), pp. 555–564.

Kumar, J., 2019. How psychological ownership stimulates participation in online brand communities? The moderating role of member type. *Journal of Business Research, 105*, pp. 243–257.

Kumar, V. and Kaushal, V., 2021. Perceived brand authenticity and social exclusion as drivers of psychological brand ownership. *Journal of Retailing and Consumer Services, 61*.

Kurniawan, R., 2020, May. The effect of online experience on revisit intention mediated with offline experience and brand equity. In *2nd International Seminar on Business, Economics, Social Science and Technology*, pp. 97–103.

Kusume, Y., & Gridley, N., 2013. *Brand Romance: Using the Power of High Design to Build a Lifelong Relationship with Your Audience.* Hampshire: Palgrave Macmillan.

Leitch, S. and Merlot, E., 2018. Power relations within brand management: The challenge of social media. *Journal of Brand Management, 25*(2), pp. 85–92.

Langner, T., Bruns, D., Fischer, A. and Rossiter, J.R., 2016. Falling in love with brands: A dynamic analysis of the trajectories of brand love. *Marketing Letters, 27*, pp. 15–26.

Lasser, W., Mittal, B. and Sharma, A., 1995. Measuring customer-based brand equity. *Journal of Consumer Marketing, 2*(4), pp. 11–19.

Latham, T., 2018. What Kate Spade meant for women. 05 June 2018. *The Atlantic.* Available at: www.theatlantic.com/entertainment/archive/2018/06/what-kate-spade-meant-for-young-women/562142/, [Accessed on 25 December 2023].

Lawes, R., 2019. Big semiotics: Beyond signs and symbols. *International Journal of Market Research*, 61(3), pp. 252–265.

Leach, R., 2013. *Theatre Studies: The Basics*. London: Routledge.

Leban, M., Seo, Y. and Voyer, B.G., 2020. Transformational effects of social media lurking practices on luxury consumption. *Journal of Business Research*, 116, pp. 514–521.

Lee, J.K., 2021. Emotional expressions and brand status. *Journal of Marketing Research*, 58(6), pp. 1178–1196.

Lee, A.Y. and Bruckman, A.S., 2007, November. Judging you by the company you keep: Dating on social networking sites. In *Proceedings of the 2007 ACM International Conference on Supporting Group Work*, pp. 371–378.

Le Grand, E., 2013. The 'Chav' as folk devil. In Eds. Petley J., Critcher C., Hughes J., & Rohloff A., *Moral Panics in the Contemporary World*. London: Bloomsbury Academic, pp. 215–234.

Lehman, D.W., O'Connor, K., Kovács, B. and Newman, G.E., 2019. Authenticity. *Academy of Management Annals*, 13(1), pp. 1–42.

Leitch, S. & Merlot, E. 2018. Power relations within brand management: The challenge of social media. *Journal of Brand Management*, 25, pp. 85–92.

Lemon, K.N., Rust, R.T. and Zeithaml, V.A., 2001. What drives customer equity? *Marketing management*, 10(1), pp. 20–25.

Leone, R.P., Rao, V.R., Keller, K.L., Luo, A.M., McAlister, L. and Srivastava, R., 2006. Linking brand equity to customer equity. *Journal of Service Research*, 9(2), pp. 125–138.

Levin, A., 2020. *Influencer Marketing for Brands*. New York: Apress.

Levy, S.J., 1959. Symbols for sale. *Harvard Business Review*, 37(4), pp. 117–124.

Lewis, N. and Vredenburg, J., 2023. Contemporary consumption of brand activism. In Eds. Bäckström, K., Egan-Wyer, C., Samsioe, E., *The Future of Consumption: How Technology, Sustainability and Wellbeing will Transform Retail and Customer Experience*. Cham: Palgrave Macmillan, pp. 263–280.

Lex, 2016. Burberry: not Coach Class. 5 December 2016. *Financial Times*. Available at: www.ft.com/content/97fd848a-bb03-11e6-8b45-b8b81dd5d080, [Accessed on 15 February 2024].

Lian, L., 2022, March. Changing times, shifting attitudes: Explaining Americans' attitudes toward same-sex relations from 1973 to 2018. *Sociological Forum*, 37(1), pp. 269–292.

Lieven, T., Grohmann, B., Herrmann, A., Landwehr, J.R. and Van Tilburg, M., 2015. The effect of brand design on brand gender perceptions and brand preference. *European Journal of Marketing*, 49(1/2), pp. 146–169.

Lindahl, B., 2020. When Uber met the Nordics. 02 June 2020. *Nordic Labour Journal.* Available at: www.nordiclabourjournal.org/nyheter/ news-2020/article.2020-06-02.8567702645, [Accessed on 21 February 2024].

Liu, S., 2022, June. The Development of Male Gender Roles Depiction in American Commercials – Taking Old Spice as an Example. In *2022 8th International Conference on Humanities and Social Science Research (ICHSSR 2022),* pp. 2895–2899.

Liu, J., Wang, H., Hui, C. and Lee, C., 2012. Psychological ownership: How having control matters. *Journal of Management Studies,* 49(5), pp. 869–895.

Lobschat, L., Zinnbauer, M.A., Pallas, F. and Joachimsthaler, E., 2013. Why social currency becomes a key driver of a firm's brand equity–insights from the automotive industry. *Long Range Planning,* 46(1–2), pp. 125–148.

Lopez, R., 2024. #Expert Insight: Here's what can happen when dollar stores move in. 04 January 2024. *UConn Today.* Available at: https:// today.uconn.edu/experts/expert-spotlight/9568/expert-insight-heres-what-can-happen-when-dollar-stores-move-in/#, [Accessed on 23 February 2024].

Lorber, J., 1994. *Paradoxes of Gender.* New Haven, CT: Yale University Press.

Losi, R.V., Bernardo, T.J., Sibuea, T.F. and Ananda, R., 2022. The persuasive techniques of Starbucks and Burger King advertisements on Instagram posts. *International Journal of English and Applied Linguistics (IJEAL),* 2(2), pp. 313–324.

Loureiro, S., T. Gorgus and H. Kaufmann. 2017. Antecedents and outcomes of online brand engagement. *Online Information Review,* 41(7), pp.985–1005.

Loxley, J., 2007. *Performativity.* London and New York: Routledge.

Lucky Generals, 2022. See the World Differently. Available at: www .luckygenerals.com/see-the-world-differently, [Accessed on 06 November 2023].

Luria, D.D., 1976. Wealth, capital, and power: The social meaning of home ownership. *The Journal of Interdisciplinary History,* 7(2), pp. 261–282.

Lyft, 2019. Taking a stand for immigration rights with RAICES and Lyft. 01 July 2019. Available at www.lyft.com/blog/posts/immigration-rights, [Accessed on 19 December 2023].

Lyon, T.P., Delmas, M.A., Maxwell, J.W., Bansal, P., Chiroleu-Assouline, M., Crifo, R.D., Gond, J.P., King, A., Lenox, M., Toffel, M., Vogel, D. and Wijen, F., 2018. CSR needs CPR: Corporate sustainability and politics. *California Management Review,* 60(4), pp. 5–24.

Mack, E., 2017. If Uber disappeared what would you do? One city's story. 20 June 2017. *CNET*. Available at: www.cnet.com/culture/uber-copenhagen-denmark-ride-sharing/, [Accessed on 21 February 2024].

Madianou, M., 2014. Smartphones as polymedia. *Journal of Computer-Mediated Communication*, 19(3), pp. 667–680.

Madianou, M. and Miller, D., 2013. Polymedia: towards a new theory of digital media in interpersonal communication. *International Journal of Cultural Studies*, 16(2), pp. 169–187.

Magids, S., Zorfas, A. and Leemon, D., 2015. The new science of customer emotions. November 2015. *Harvard Business Review*. Available at: https://hbr.org/2015/11/the-new-science-of-customer-emotions, [Accessed on 12 February 2024].

Mahalingam, R., 2003. Essentialism, culture, and power: Representations of social class. *Journal of Social Issues*, 59(4), pp. 733–749.

Mahbub, R. and Shoily, K.F., 2016. The place of Pierre Bourdieu's theories in (popular) cultural studies. *BRAC University Journal*, 11(01), pp. 1–9.

Maloney, J. and Weber, L., 2023. How Bud Light Handled an Uproar over a Promotion with a Transgender Advocate. 22 May 2023. *The Wall Street Journal*. Available at: www.wsj.com/articles/how-bud-light-handled-an-uproar-over-a-promotion-with-a-transgender-advocate-e457d5c6, [Accessed on 26 November 2023].

Månsson, M. and Stéen, O., Exploring brand activism practices of small businesses. A multiple case study in the craft food industry. *Human Resource Development Review*, 17, p. 37.

MarketingCharts, 2023. Most wanted qualities in brands according to millennials worldwide in 2023. *Statista*. Available at: www-statista-com./1410698/brand-qualities-desired-by-millennials-worldwide/, [Accessed on 06 October 2023].

Marketing Mag, 2012. Share a Coke campaign post-analysis. 22 June 2012. *Marketing Mag*. Available at: www.marketingmag.com.au/news/share-a-coke-campaign-post-analysis/, [Accessed on 28 February 2024].

Marketing Week, 2017. Why 'The Towers, London' remain the UK's most prominent advertising location. *Marketing Week*. Published on 21 May 2017. Available at: www.marketingweek.com/towers-london/, [Accessed on 17 October 2022].

Markovic, S., Iglesias, O. and Ind, N., 2023. Conscientious business-to-business organizations: Status quo and future research agenda. *Industrial Marketing Management*, 112, pp. A8–A11.

Marshall, A., 2022. How a tiny British publisher became the home of Nobel laureates. 13 October 2022. *New York Times*. Available at: www.nytimes.com/2022/10/13/books/fitzcarraldo-nobel-prize-ernaux.html, [Accessed on 21 February 2024].

Marshall, P.D., Moore, C. and Barbour, K., 2019. *Persona Studies: An Introduction*. John Wiley & Sons.

Martin, A.E. and Slepian, M.L., 2018. Dehumanizing gender: The debiasing effects of gendering human-abstracted entities. *Personality and Social Psychology Bulletin*, 44(12), pp. 1681–1696.

Mason, R., & Wigley, G., 2013. The 'Chav' subculture: Branded clothing as an extension of the self. *Journal of Economics and Behaviour Studies*, 5(3), pp. 173–184.

Mayer, C., 2021. The future of the corporation and the economics of purpose. *Journal of Management Studies*, 58(3), pp. 887–901.

McCalla-Leacy, J., 2023. Climate quitting – Younger workers voting with their feet on employer's ESG commitments. 24 January 2023. *KPMG*. Available at: https://kpmg.com/uk/en/home/media/press-releases/2023/01/climate-quitting-younger-workers-voting-esg.html, [Accessed on 18 December 2023].

McCants, C., 2023. Comparing the costs of generations. 01 June 2023. *Consumer Affairs*. Available at: www.consumeraffairs.com/finance/comparing-the-costs-of-generations.html, [Accessed on 08 December 2023].

McCarthy, E.D., 2009. Emotional performances as dramas of authenticity. In Eds. Vannini, P. & Williams, P., *Authenticity in Culture, Self, and Society*, pp. 257–272. London: Routledge.

McCracken, G., 1986. Culture and consumption: A theoretical account of the structure and movement of the cultural meaning of consumer goods. *Journal of Consumer Research*, 13(1), pp. 71–84.

McCracken, G., 2005. *Culture and Consumption II: Markets, Meaning, and Brand Management*. Indiana: Indiana University Press.

McDonald's, 2024. Our Mission and Values. *McDonald's*. Available at: https://corporate.mcdonalds.com/corpmcd/our-company/who-we-are/our-values.html, [Accessed on 04 February 2024].

McLean, J., 2020. *Changing Digital Geographies: Technologies, Environments and People*. Switzerland: Palgrave Macmillan.

McLuhan, M., 1962. *The Gutenberg Galaxy: The Making of Typographic Man*. Toronto: University of Toronto Press.

    2005. *Culture and Consumption II: Markets, Meaning, and Brand Management*. Indiana: Indiana University Press.

    2013. *Understanding Media: The Extensions of Man*. Edited by W. T. Gordon. Berkeley, CA: Gingko Press.

McNeill, L.S. and Douglas, K., 2011. Retailing masculinity: Gender expectations and social image of male grooming products in New Zealand. *Journal of Retailing and Consumer Services*, 18(5), pp. 448–454.

McShane, L. and Sabadoz, C., 2015. Rethinking the concept of consumer empowerment: Recognizing consumers as citizens. *International Journal of Consumer Studies*, 39(5), pp. 544–551.

Media Dynamics Inc., 2014. Adults spend almost 10 hours per day with the media, but note only 150 ads. *The Drum*. Available at: www.thedrum.com/news/2023/05/03/how-many-ads-do-we-really-see-day-spoiler-it-s-not-10000#:~:text=362%20exposures%20per%20day, [Accessed on 04 December 2023].

Medlock, G., 2012. The evolving ethic of authenticity: From humanistic to positive psychology. *The Humanistic Psychologist*, 40(1), pp. 38–57.

Meek, S., Ogilvie, M., Lambert, C. and Ryan, M.M., 2019. Contextualising social capital in online brand communities. *Journal of Brand Management*, 26(4), pp. 426–444.

Meiting, L. and Hua, W., 2021. Angular or rounded? The effect of the shape of green brand logos on consumer perception. *Journal of Cleaner Production*, 279, 123801.

Melloul, E., Black B., van den Branded, J-C., & Deryckere, M. 2022. Purpose-led brands can reshape the consumer goods industry if they can scale .... 27 October 2022. *Bain & Company*. Available at: www.bain.com/insights/purpose-led-brands-can-reshape-the-consumer-goods-industry-if-they-can-scale/, [Accessed on 08 December 2023].

Meltzer, D., 1997. Concerning signs and symbols. *British Journal of Psychotherapy*, 14(2), pp. 175–181.

Mercer, J., 2010. A mark of distinction: Branding and trade mark law in the UK from the 1860s. *Business History*, Vol. 22 No. 1, pp. 17–42.

Merrilees, B., 2016. Interactive brand experience pathways to customer-brand engagement and value co-creation. *Journal of Product & Brand Management*, 25(5), pp. 402–408.

Merrilees, B., Miller, D. and Yakimova, R., 2017. The role of staff engagement in facilitating staff-led value co-creation. *Journal of Service Management*, 28(2), pp. 250–264.

Merrilees, B., Miller, D. and Yakimova, R., 2021. Building brands through internal stakeholder engagement and co-creation. *Journal of Product & Brand Management*, 30(6), pp. 806–818.

Merz, M.A., He, Y. and Vargo, S.L., 2009. The evolving brand logic: A service-dominant logic perspective. *Journal of the Academy of Marketing Science*, 37, pp. 328–344.

Merz, M.A., Zarantonello, L. and Grappi, S., 2018. How valuable are your customers in the brand value co-creation process? The development of a Customer Co-Creation Value (CCCV) scale. *Journal of Business Research*, 82, pp. 79–89.

Meyers, H. and Gerstman, R. (Eds.), 2001. *Branding @ the Digital Age.* New York: Palgrave.

Meyersohn, N., 2023. Starbucks' CEO wants people to stop protesting its stores over Israel war in Gaza. 21 December 2023. *CNN Business.* Available at: https://edition.cnn.com/2023/12/21/business/starbucks-israel-war-union/index.html, [Accessed on 18 February 2024].

Mingione, M., Cristofaro, M. and Mondi, D., 2020. 'If I give you my emotion, what do I get?' Conceptualizing and measuring the co-created emotional value of the brand. *Journal of Business Research, 109,* pp. 310–320.

Mingione, M., Kashif, M. and Petrescu, M., 2020. Brand power relationships: A co-evolutionary conceptual framework. *Journal of Relationship Marketing, 19*(1), pp. 1–28.

Mirzaei, A., Wilkie, D.C. and Siuki, H., 2022. Woke brand activism authenticity or the lack of it. *Journal of Business Research, 139,* pp. 1–12.

Mitchell, S., Smith, K. and Holmberg, S., 2023. The dollar store invasion: Communities are in revolt, but the chains' predatory tactics also call for federal action. *Institute for Local Self-Reliance.* Available at: chrome-extension://efaidnbmnnnibpcajpcglclefindmkaj/https://cdn.ilsr.org/wp-content/uploads/2023/01/ILSR-Report-The-Dollar-Store-Invasion-2023.pdf, [Accessed on 23 February 2024].

Mohtar, M., Rudd, J.M. and Evanschitzky, H., 2019. Clarifying the brand personality construct in Malaysia. *Journal of Consumer Marketing, 36*(7), pp. 869–884.

Moi, T., 1999. *What is a Woman? And Other Essays.* Oxford: Oxford University Press.

Moliner, M.Á., Monferrer-Tirado, D. and Estrada-Guillén, M., 2018. Consequences of customer engagement and customer self-brand connection. *Journal of Services Marketing, 32,* pp. 387–399.

Moore, N., 2007. Preface. In Eds. Moore, N., & Whelan, Y., *Heritage, Memory and the Politics of Identity: New Perspectives on the Cultural Landscape.* Aldershot: Ashgate Publishing Limited.

       2007. Valorizing urban heritage? Redevelopment in a changing city. In Eds. Moore, N., & Whelan, Y., *Heritage, Memory and the Politics of Identity: New Perspectives on the Cultural Landscape.* Aldershot: Ashgate Publishing Limited.

Moore, C.M. and Birtwistle, G., 2004. The Burberry business model: Creating an international luxury fashion brand. *International Journal of Retail & Distribution Management, 32*(8), pp. 412–422.

Morgenroth, T. and Ryan, M.K., 2021. The effects of gender trouble: An integrative theoretical framework of the perpetuation and disruption of the gender/sex binary. *Perspectives on Psychological Science, 16*(6), pp. 1113–1142.

Morhart, F., Malär, L., Guèvremont, A., Girardin, F. and Grohmann, B., 2015. Brand authenticity: An integrative framework and measurement scale. *Journal of Consumer Psychology*, 25(2), pp. 200–218.

Mourits, B., 2021. In search of the most effective way of branding: The label 'literature' as a means to an end. In Eds. van den Braber, H., Dera, J., Joosten, J., & Steenmeijer, M., *Branding Books Across the Ages*. Amsterdam: Amsterdam University Press.

Mubushar, M., Rasool, S., Haider, M.I. and Cerchione, R., 2021. The impact of corporate social responsibility activities on stakeholders' value co-creation behaviour. *Corporate Social Responsibility and Environmental Management*, 28(6), pp. 1906–1920.

Mughees, M.H. and Qian, Z., 2017. January. Detecting anti ad-blockers in the wild. *Privacy Enhancing Technologies Symposium*.

Mukherjee, S. and Althuizen, N., 2020. Brand activism: Does courting controversy help or hurt a brand? *International Journal of Research in Marketing*, 37(4), pp. 772–788.

Mulder, K., 167 Community participation in deciding on local renewable energy projects. In *20th European Round Table on Sustainable Consumption and Production*, Austria, 08–10 September 2012.

Mulder, S. and Yaar, Z., 2006. *The User Is Always Right: A Practical Guide to Creating and Using Personas for the Web*. California: New Riders.

Mullany, L., 2004. 'Become the man that women desire': Gender identities and dominant discourses in email advertising language. *Language and Literature*, 13(4), pp. 291–305.

Mulvaney, D., 2023. Happy March Madness! [Instagram]. 11 February 2023. Available at: www.instagram.com/p/CqgTftujqZc/, [Accessed on 24 November 2023].

2023. Trans people like beer too. [Tiktok]. 29 June 2023. Available at: www.tiktok.com/@dylanmulvaney/video/7250155134087449898?lang=en, [Accessed on 24 November 2023].

Muniz, K.M. and Marchetti, R.Z., 2012. Brand personality dimensions in the Brazilian context. *BAR-Brazilian Administration Review*, 9, pp. 168–188.

Muniz Jr, A.M. and O'guinn, T.C., 2001. Brand community. *Journal of Consumer Research*, 27(4), pp. 412–432.

Munton, R., 2009. Rural land ownership in the United Kingdom: Changing patterns and future possibilities for land use. *Land Use Policy*, 26, pp. S54–S61.

Musicco, J., 2021, June. To affinity and beyond: Exploring the origins and history of the brand affinity construct. In *Proceedings of the Conference on Historical Analysis and Research in Marketing*, Vol. 20, pp. 49–51.

Mutch, N., & Aitken, R., 2009. Being fair and being seen to be fair: Corporate reputation and CSR partnerships, *Australasian Marketing Journal (AMJ)*, 17(2), pp. 92–98.

NAMIBUCKS, 2023. *Join NAMI Bucks County PA on Thursday, February 1, 2024 for our 3rd Annual Kate Spade Designer Bag Bingo event for mental health and suicide awareness.* 04 December 2023. Available at: https://twitter.com/NAMIBUCKS/status/1731740415622054140, [Accessed on 27 December 2023].

Nandy, S. and Sondhi, N., 2022. Brand pride in consumer–brand relationships: Towards a conceptual framework. *Global Business Review*, 23(5), pp. 1098–1117.

Napoli, J., Dickinson, S. J., Beverland, M. B. & Farrelly, F. (2014). Measuring consumer-based brand authenticity. *Journal of Business Research*, 67(6), pp. 1090–1098.

Neale, L., Robbie, R. and Martin, B., 2016. Gender identity and brand incongruence: When in doubt, pursue masculinity. *Journal of Strategic Marketing*, 24(5), pp. 347–359.

Nejati, M., Salamzadeh, Y. and Loke, C.K., 2020. Can ethical leaders drive employees' CSR engagement? *Social Responsibility Journal*, 16(5), pp. 655–669.

Nelson-Field, K., 2020. *The Attention Economy and How Media Works: Simple Truths for Marketers.* Singapore: Palgrave Macmillan.

Németh, Á., Nielse, A., Nonboe, I., Gordon-Orr, R., 2019. *'Dangerous waters' of doing social activism in advertising.* Available at: https://rucforsk.ruc.dk/ws/portalfiles/portal/64954972/Gillette_Project___Social_Activism.pdf, [Accessed on 02 January 2024].

Neuendorf, K. A., 2002. *The Content Analysis Guidebook.* Thousand Oaks: Sage.

Newman, A.A., 2010. Old Spice argues that real men smell good. 15 July 2010. *The New York Times.* Available at: www.nytimes.com/2010/07/16/business/media/16adco.html, [Accessed on 16 February 2024].

Newman, G.E. and Smith, R.K., 2016. Kinds of authenticity. *Philosophy Compass*, 11(10), pp. 609–618.

Nieborg, D.B., Poell, T. and van Dijck, J., 2022. Platforms and platformization. In Eds. Flew, T., Holt, J., & Thomas, J., *The Sage Handbook of the Digital Media Economy.* London: Sage Publications. pp. 29–49.

Nielsen BookData, 2022. *The UK Book Market in Review.* Nielsen.

Nike, 2021. Summing up the last year of NIKE, Inc.'s commitment to the black community. *Nike.* Available at: https://about.nike.com/en/newsroom/releases/nike-inc-s-black-community-funding-commitment-partners, [Accessed on 08 December 2023].

Nisbett, R.E. and Wilson, T.D., 1977. Telling more than we can know: Verbal reports on mental processes. *Psychological Review*, *84*, pp. 231–259.

Normann, R. and Ramirez, R., 1993. From value chain to value constellation: Designing interactive strategy. *Harvard Business Review*, 71(4), pp. 65–77.

Nostrand, H.L., 1989. Authentic texts and cultural authenticity: An editorial. *Modern Language Journal*, pp. 49–52.

Novet, J., 2020. Skype is still around – It's just been upstaged by Microsoft Teams. 10 October 2020. *CNBC*. Available at: www.cnbc.com/2020/10/10/skype-upstaged-by-microsoft-teams.html, [Accessed on 13 February 2024].

2023. The rise and fall of Skype. 02 July 2023. *CNBC*. Available at: www.cnbc.com/2023/07/02/the-rise-and-fall-of-skype.html, [Accessed on 13 February 2024].

Nunes, P.A. and Schokkaert, E., 2001. Warm glow and embedding in contingent valuation. Available at: https://dx.doi.org/10.2139/ssrn.286833 [Accessed on 13 Jue 2024].

Nysveen, H. and Pedersen, P.E., 2014. Influences of cocreation on brand experience. *International Journal of Market Research*, *56*(6), pp. 807–832.

O'Brien, S., 2022. Research reveals Gen Z avoids ads at all costs. *Digital Marketing Briefing*. Available at: https://digitalmarketingsolutionssummit.co.uk/briefing/research-reveals-gen-z-avoids-ads-at-all-costs/, [Accessed on 10 October 2022].

O'Connor, K., Lehman, D. and Carroll, G., 2019. The kind of authenticity customers will pay more for. 27 June 2019. *Harvard Business Review*. Available at: https://hbr.org/2019/06/the-kind-of-authenticity-customers-will-pay-more-for, [Accessed on 15 December 2023].

O'Guinn, Thomas C., Albert M. Muñiz Jr. and Erika Paulson, 2018. Brands and branding: A critique of extant brand research and the need for a sociological conception of brands. In Eds. Wherry, F., & Woodward, I., *The Oxford Handbook of Consumption*. New York: Oxford University Press.

O'Keeffe, 2007. Landscape and memory: Historiography, theory, methodology. In Eds. Moore, N., & Whelan, Y., *Heritage, Memory and the Politics of Identity: New Perspectives on the Cultural Landscape*. Aldershot: Ashgate Publishing Limited.

O'Keeffe, G.A., 2019. *The Role of Anthropomorphism and Authenticity in Value Creation: The Case of Artisanal Luxury Brands*. Doctoral dissertation, Stellenbosch University.

O'Reilly, D., 2005. Cultural brands/Branding cultures. *Journal of Marketing Management*, *21*(5–6), pp. 573–588.

Ocasio, W., 1994. Political dynamics and the circulation of power: CEO succession in US industrial corporations, 1960–1990. *Administrative science quarterly*, pp. 285–312.

ONS (Office of National Statistics), 2019. Introduction. In *What is the difference between sex and gender: Exploring the difference between sex and gender, looking at concepts that are important to the Sustainable Development Goals*. Available at: www.ons.gov.uk/economy/environmentalaccounts/articles/whatisthedifferencebetweensexandgender/2019-02-21, [Accessed on 17 November 2022].

Ogilvy, n.d. Share a Coke. *Ogilvy*. Available at: www.ogilvy.com.au/Our-Work/Coca-Cola-Share-a-Coke#, [Accessed on 28 February 2024].

Oh, H., Prado, P. H., Korelo, J. C., & Frizzo, F., 2019. The effect of brand authenticity on consumer–brand relationships. *Journal of Product & Brand Management*, pp. 231–241.

Ohlander, J. & Batalova, J., & Treas, J., 2005. Explaining educational differences on attitudes toward homosexual relations. *Social Science Research*, *34*, pp. 781–799.

Oliver, R.L., 1999. Whence consumer loyalty? *Journal of Marketing*, *63*, (4_suppl1), pp. 33–44.

On Purpose, 2023. Mission. *Kate Spade*. Available at: www.katespade.com/social-impact/on-purpose, [Accessed on 26 December 2023].

Onkila, T. and Sarna, B., 2022. A systematic literature review on employee relations with CSR: State of art and future research agenda. *Corporate Social Responsibility and Environmental Management*, *29*(2), pp. 435–447.

Osuna Ramírez, S.A., Veloutsou, C. and Morgan-Thomas, A., 2017. A systematic literature review of brand commitment: Definitions, perspectives and dimensions. *Athens Journal of Business and Economics*, *3*(3), pp. 305–332.

Otis, G. A., Weber, L., & Maloney, J., 2023. Bud Light Brewer Puts Two Executives on Leave After Uproar Over Transgender Influencer. 22 April 2023. *The Wall Street Journal*. Available at: www.wsj.com/articles/anheuser-busch-shake-up-after-transgender-influencer-was-featured-on-beer-can-a0ed8009?mod=business_featst_pos2, [Accessed on 26 November 2023].

Ouwersloot, H. and Odekerken-Schröder, G., 2008. Who's who in brand communities–and why? *European Journal of Marketing*, *42*(5/6), pp. 571–585.

Ozdemir, E. and Akcay, G., 2019. The effect of gender identity on consumers' impulse buying behavior and the moderating role of biological sex. *Business and Economics Research Journal*, *10*(5), pp. 1109–1125.

Palmieri, L. H., 1963. The impermanence of power. *Human Relations*, 16(2), pp. 199–205.

Palos-Sanchez, P., Saura, J.R. and Martin-Velicia, F., 2019. A study of the effects of programmatic advertising on users' concerns about privacy overtime. *Journal of Business Research*, 96, pp. 61–72.

Palumbo, J., 2022. The artist behind 'Fearless Girl' wants to spread her message far and wide. A lawsuit is getting in the way. *CNN Style*. 17 February 2022. Available at: https://edition.cnn.com/style/article/fearless-girl-statue-lawsuit-nfts/index.html, [Accessed on 03 October 2022].

Palusuk, N., Koles, B. and Hasan, R., 2019. 'All you need is brand love': A critical review and comprehensive conceptual framework for brand love. *Journal of Marketing Management*, 35(1–2), pp. 97–129.

Pan, Y., Zinkhan, G.M. and Sheng, S., 2007. The subjective well-being of nations: A role for marketing? *Journal of Macromarketing*, 27(4), pp. 360–369.

Paouleanou, K., 2020. *Resistance to advertising and marketing saturation in social media*. MSc Thesis. International Hellenic University.

Papacharissi, Z. (Ed.), 2010. *A Networked Self: Identity, Community, and Culture on Social Network Sites*. London: Routledge.

Park, C.W., MacInnis, D.J. and Priester, J., 2008. Brand attachment: Constructs, consequences, and causes. *Foundations and Trends® in Marketing*, 1(3), pp. 191–230.

Parris, D.L. and Guzmán, F., 2022. Evolving brand boundaries and expectations: looking back on brand equity, brand loyalty, and brand image research to move forward. *Journal of Product & Brand Management*, 32, pp. 191–234.

Pasidis, I. 2013. Why do shops cluster? Spatial competition and agglomeration in the Netherlands. 16 July 2013. *Urban Economics.NL*. Available at: www.urbaneconomics.nl/why-do-shops-cluster-spatial-competition-and-agglomeration-in-the-netherlands/, [Accessed on 11 February 2024].

Passyn, K.A., Diriker, M. and Settle, R.B., 2011. Images of online versus store shopping: have the attitudes of men and women, young and old really changed? *Journal of Business & Economics Research (JBER)*, 9(1).

Pastak, I., Kindsiko, E., Tammaru, T., Kleinhans, R. and Van Ham, M., 2019. Commercial gentrification in post-industrial neighbourhoods: A dynamic view from an entrepreneur's perspective. *Tijdschrift voor economische en sociale geografie*, 110(5), pp. 588–604.

Pauwels, K., Demirci, C., Yildirim, G. and Srinivasan, S., 2016. The impact of brand familiarity on online and offline media synergy. *International Journal of Research in Marketing*, 33(4), pp. 739–753.

Pavlovica, N. and Lendeng, J., 2023. *The consumer perspective of brand activism: A qualitative study of how consumers view brand activism and the genuineness of it.* Masters Thesis. Stockholm University.

Payne, A., Storbacka, K., Frow, P. and Knox, S., 2009. Co-creating brands: Diagnosing and designing the relationship experience. *Journal of Business Research,* 62(3), pp. 379–389.

Pearson, L., 2013. Fluid marks 2.0: Protecting a dynamic brand. *Managing Intellectual Property,* 229, p. 26.

Pechmann, C. and Stewart, D.W., 1988. Advertising repetition: A critical review of wearin and wearout. *Current Issues and Research in Advertising,* 11(1–2), pp. 285–329.

Pecot, F., Valette-Florence, P. and De Barnier, V., 2019. Brand heritage as a temporal perception: Conceptualisation, measure and consequences. *Journal of Marketing Management,* 35(17–18), pp. 1624–1643.

Pelligra, V. and Vásquez, A., 2020. Empathy and socially responsible consumption: An experiment with the vote-with-the-wallet game. *Theory and Decision,* 89(4), pp. 383–422.

Percy, L., 2003. *Branding and Advertising.* 1st Edition. Edited by Hansen, F. and Christensen, L. B. Copenhagen: Copenhagen Business School Press.

Pérez, A., 2019. Building a theoretical framework of message authenticity in CSR communication. *Corporate Communications: An International Journal,* 24(2), pp. 334–350.

Pérez, A., García de los Salmones, M.D.M. and Liu, M.T., 2020. Information specificity, social topic awareness and message authenticity in CSR communication. *Journal of Communication Management,* 24(1), pp. 31–48.

Perez, S., 2023. BeReal pushes back at report that it's losing steam, says it how has 25M daily users. *TechCrunch.* Available at: https://techcrunch .com/2023/09/29/bereal-pushes-back-at-report-that-its-losing-steam-says-it-now-has-25m-daily-users/, [Accessed on 12 October 2023].

Petroff, A., 2017. Coach buying Kate Spade in 2.4 billion deal. 08 May 2017. *CNN Business.* Available at: https://money.cnn.com/2017/05/08/ investing/coach-kate-spade-takeover/index.html, [Accessed on 25 December 2023].

Pierce, J.L., Kostova, T. and Dirks, K.T., 2001. Toward a theory of psychological ownership in organizations. *Academy of Management Review,* 26(2), pp. 298–310.

Pilgrim, A.N., 2001. Performance and the performative. *Body & Society,* 7(4), pp. 87–96.

Pilot Institute, 2023. Women Pilot Statistics: Female Representation in Aviation. *Pilot Institute.* Available at: https://pilotinstitute.com/ women-aviation-statistics/, [Accessed on 06 November 2023].

Pinna, M., 2020. Do gender identities of femininity and masculinity affect the intention to buy ethical products? *Psychology & Marketing, 37*(3), pp. 384–397.

Pinto, N., 2017. Fearless Girl Is Not Your Friend. *The Village Voice.* Available at: www.villagevoice.com/2017/04/25/fearless-girl-is-not-your-friend/, [Accessed on 03 October 2022].

Pires, G.D., Stanton, J. & Rita, P., 2006. The internet, consumer empowerment and marketing strategies. *European Journal of Marketing, 40*(9/10), pp. 936–949.

Pitta, D.A. and Katsanis, L.P., 1995. Understanding brand equity for successful brand extension. *Journal of Consumer Marketing, 12*(4), pp. 51–64.

Pollard, A., 2021. Gen Z has $360 Billion to spend, trick is getting them to buy. 17 November 2021. *Bloomberg.* Available at: www.bloomberg.com/news/articles/2021-11-17/gen-z-has-360-billion-to-spend-trick-is-getting-them-to-buy?leadSource=uverify%20wall, [Accessed on 08 December 2023].

Pollay, R.W., 1986. The distorted mirror: Reflections on the unintended consequences of advertising. *Journal of Marketing, 50*(2), pp. 18–36.

Polletta, F. and Redman, N., 2020. When do stories change our minds? Narrative persuasion about social problems. *Sociology Compass, 14*(4).

Post, C., and Byron, K., 2014. Women on boards and firm financial performance: A meta-analysis. *Academy of Management*, Vol. 58, No. 5.

Postlewaite, A., 2011. Social norms and social assets. *Annual Review of Economics, 3*(1), pp. 239–259.

Power, D. and Hauge, A., 2008. No man's brand – Brands, institutions, and fashion. *Growth and Change, 39*(1), pp. 123–143.

Power, R., 2023. How unexpected brand partnerships are redefining success. 12 November 2023. *Forbes.* Available at: www.forbes.com/sites/rhettpower/2023/11/12/how-unexpected-brand-partnerships-are-redefining-success/, [Accessed on 15 February 2024].

Pöyry, E. and Laaksonen, S.M., 2022. Opposing brand activism: Triggers and strategies of consumers' antibrand actions. *European Journal of Marketing, 56*(13), pp. 261–284.

Pradhana, F. and Sastiono, P., 2019, March. Gender differences in online shopping: Are men more shopaholic online? In *12th International Conference on Business and Management Research (ICBMR 2018)*, pp. 123–128.

Prey, R., 2020. Locating power in platformization: Music streaming playlists and curatorial power. *Social Media+ Society, 6*(2).

Puustinen, L., 2005. The age of consumer-audience conceptualising reception in media studies, marketing, and media organisations. In *European Communication Conference.* Amsterdam, Netherlands, 24–26 November 2005.

Puzakova, M., Kwak, H., and Rocereto, R., 2009. Pushing the envelope of brand and personality: Antecedents and moderators of anthropomorphized brands. In Eds. McGill, A.L. & Shavitt, S., *NA – Advances in Consumer Research*, Vol. 36, Duluth, MN: Association for Consumer Research, pp. 413–420.

Qiang, A.J., Timmins, C. and Wang, W., 2021. *Displacement and the consequences of gentrification*. Unpublished manuscript. Duke University. Available at: https://sites.duke.edu/christophertimmins/files/2021/11/displacement_paper_2021_11.Pdf, [Accessed on 22 February 2024].

Quinlan, P. 2018. Corporate Activism: three reasons staying silent is the bigger risk. 17 April 2018. *Forbes*. Available at: www.forbes.com/sites/forbestechcouncil/2018/04/17/corporate-activism-three-reasons-staying-silent-is-the-bigger-risk/, [Accessed on 18 December 2023].

Raeymaekers, T., 2019. 4. The laws of impermanence: Displacement, sovereignty, subjectivity. In Eds. Mitchell, K., Jones, R., & Fluri, J., *Handbook on Critical Geographies of Migration*. Cheltenham: Edward Elgar Publishing, pp. 58–68.

Rainey, C., 2022. What happened to Starbucks? How a progressive company lost its way. 17 March 2022. *Fast Company*. Available at: www.fastcompany.com/90732166/what-happened-to-starbucks-how-a-progressive-company-lost-its-way, [Accessed on 04 February 2024].

Rakestraw, B., 2022. The dynamics of brand ownership: how brands and customers co-create value. 19 December 2022. *Brandingmag*. Available at: www.brandingmag.com/brett-rakestraw/the-dynamics-of-brand-ownership-how-brands-and-customers-co-create-value/, [Accessed on 12 February 2024].

Ramaswamy, V. and Ozcan, K., 2016. Brand value co-creation in a digitalized world: An integrative framework and research implications. *International Journal of Research in Marketing*, 33(1), pp. 93–106.

Randhawa, K.K., 2023. *Influence of femvertising on brand image and buying behaviour: an exploration of consumers' attitudes regarding brands pursuing brand activism through femvertising*. Minor Project, Management. Khalsa College, Patiala. Available at: https://khalsacollegepatiala.org/uploads/files/Minor%20project%20Final.pdf, [Accessed on 05 November 2023].

Rao, B., Angelov, B. and Nov, O., 2006. Fusion of disruptive technologies: Lessons from the skype case. *European Management Journal*, 24(2–3), pp. 174–188.

Rao, U., 2006. Ritual in society. In Eds. Kreinath, J., Snoek, J.A.M., & Stausberg, M., *Theorizing Rituals, Volume 1: Issues, Topics, Approaches, Concepts*. Leiden: Brill, pp. 143–160.

Rappaport, R.A., 1999. *Ritual and Religion in the Making of Humanity*, (Vol. 110). Cambridge: Cambridge University Press.

Redondo, I. and Aznar, G., 2018. To use or not to use ad blockers? The roles of knowledge of ad blockers and attitude toward online advertising. *Telematics and Informatics*, 35(6), pp. 1607–1616.

Reed II, A., Forehand, M.R., Puntoni, S. and Warlop, L., 2012. Identity-based consumer behavior. *International Journal of Research in Marketing*, 29(4), pp. 310–321.

Reghunathan, A. and Joseph, J., 2017. Men will be men, women will be women: The case of cross-gender brand extensions. *Advances in Consumer Research*, 45, pp. 465–468.

Renn, J., 2006. Appresentation and simultaneity: Alfred Schutz on communication between phenomenology and pragmatics. *Human Studies*, 29(1), pp. 1–19.

Reichheld, F. and Schefter, P., 2000. E-loyalty: Your secret weapon on the web. *Harvard Business Review*, 78(4), pp. 105–13.

Reynolds, L., Koenig-Lewis, N., Doering, H. and Peattie, K., 2022. Competing for legitimacy in the place branding process: (Re)negotiating the stakes. *Tourism Management*, 91, pp. 1–12.

Rice, J., 2022. Rainbow-washing. *Northeastern University Law Review*, 15(2), pp. 285–358. Available at: https://ssrn.com/abstract=4193059.

Rikap, C., 2021. *Capitalism, Power and Innovation: Intellectual Monopoly Capitalism Uncovered*. London: Routledge.

Rios, R.E. and Riquelme, H.E., 2008. Brand equity for online companies. *Marketing Intelligence & Planning*, 26(7), pp. 719–742.

Ritcher, F., 2018. More likely to vent than to recommend? 25 June 2018. *Statista*. Available at: www.statista.com/chart/14405/sharing-of-customer-experiences/, [Accessed on 11 February 2024].

Ritson, M., 2020. If 'Black Lives Matter' to brands, where are your black board members? *Marketing Week*. 03 June 2020. Available at: www.marketingweek.com/mark-ritson-black-lives-matter-brands/, [Accessed on 08 December 2023].

Rivera, G.N., Christy, A.G., Kim, J., Vess, M., Hicks, J.A. and Schlegel, R.J., 2019. Understanding the relationship between perceived authenticity and well-being. *Review of General Psychology*, 23(1), pp. 113–126.

Robbins, D., 2005. The origins, early development and status of Bourdieu's concept of 'cultural capital'. *The British Journal of Sociology*, 56(1), pp. 13–30.

Robertson, R., 1994. Globalisation or Glocalisation? *The Journal of International Communication*, 1(1), pp. 33–52.

Robinson, L., 2009. A taste for the necessary: A Bourdieuian approach to digital inequality. *Information, Communication & Society*, 12(4), pp. 488–507.

Robinson, I., Hall, T., 2007. Memory, identity and the memoralization of conflict in the Scottish highlands. In Eds. Moore, N., & Whelan, Y., *Heritage, Memory and the Politics of Identity: New Perspectives on the Cultural Landscape*. Aldershot: Ashgate Publishing Limited.

Rodionova, Z., 2017. Uber to end its services in Denmark over new taxi regulations. 28 March 2017. *Independent*. Available at: www .independent.co.uk/news/business/news/uber-shut-down-business-denmark-taxi-law-regulation-a7654571.html, [Accessed on 21 February 2024].

Roe, M., 2020. Landscape and participation. In Eds. Atha, M., Howard, P., Thompson, I., & Waterton, E., *The Routledge Companion to Landscape Studies*, 2nd Edition. London and New York: Routledge.

Rogers C.R. (1959). A theory of therapy, personality and interpersonal relationships, as developed in the client-centered framework. In Ed. Koch S., *Psychology: A Study of a Science: Vol. 3. Formulations of the Person and the Social Context*, pp. 184–256. Boston, MA: McGraw-Hill.

Rodgers, D., 2022. Burberry and the chequered politics of working-class appropriation. 26 May 2022. *Dazed*. Available at: www .dazeddigital.com/fashion/article/56064/1/burberry-working-class-appropriation-nova-check-danniella-westbrook-chav-y2k, [Accessed on 07 February 2024].

Romani, S., Grappi, S. and Bagozzi, R.P., 2013. Explaining consumer reactions to corporate social responsibility: The role of gratitude and altruistic values. *Journal of Business Ethics*, *114*, pp. 193–206.

Romani, S., Grappi, S., Zarantonello, L. and Bagozzi, R.P., 2015. The revenge of the consumer! How brand moral violations lead to consumer anti-brand activism. *Journal of Brand Management*, *22*, pp. 658–672.

Rook, D.W., 1985. The ritual dimension of consumer behavior. *Journal of Consumer Research*, *12*(3), pp. 251–264.

Room, A., 1998. History of Branding. In Eds. Hart, S., & Murphy, J., *Brands*. London: Palgrave Macmillan.

Rose, G., 2016. Rethinking the geographies of cultural 'objects' through digital technologies: Interface, network and friction. *Progress in Human Geography*, Vol. *40*(3), pp. 334–351.

Rossiter, J. and Bellman, S., 2012. Emotional branding pays off: How brands meet share of requirements through bonding, companionship, and love. *Journal of Advertising Research*, *52*(3), pp. 291–296.

Rowntree, L.B., 1996. The cultural landscape concept in American human geography. In Eds. Earle, C., Mathewson, K., & Kenzer, M.S., *Concepts in Human Geography*, pp. 127–159. Lanham: Rowman & Littlefield.

Rowntree, L.B. and Conkey, M.W., 1980. Symbolism and the cultural landscape. *Annals of the Association of American Geographers*, 70(4), pp. 459–474.

Rubtsova, A. and Dowd, T.J., 2004. Cultural capital as a multi-level concept: The case of an advertising agency. *Legitimacy Processes in Organizations*, 22, pp. 117–146.

Rucker, D.D., Galinsky, A.D. and Dubois, D., 2012. Power and consumer behavior: How power shapes who and what consumers value. *Journal of Consumer Psychology*, 22, pp. 352–368.

Rudge, J., 2014. How a groundbreaking campaign got its start 'Down under'. 25 September 2014. *Coca-Cola*. Available at: www.coca-colacompany.com/media-center/how-a-campaign-got-its-start-down-under, [Accessed on 28 February 2024].

Rudito, Y.Y. and Anita, A., 2020. Persuasive strategies used in Burger King's Instagram posts caption. *Journal of Language and Literature*, 8(1), pp. 96–104.

Rusch, M., 2023. True Colours or Rainbow-Washing Exposed!?–Company Pride in and through Digital and Social Media Reviewed. *ILCEA. Revue de l'Institut des langues et cultures d'Europe, Amérique, Afrique, Asie et Australie*, (51).

Sachdeva, S., Iliev, R. and Medin, D.L., 2009. Sinning saints and saintly sinners: The paradox of moral self-regulation. *Psychological Science*, 20(4), pp. 523–528.

Salaky, K., 2020 McDonald's has responded to that video of a 24-year-old hamburger that didn't decompose. *Delish*. Available at: www.delish.com/food-news/a33895332/mcdonalds-response-old-hamburger-decompose/, [Accessed on 20 January 2024].

Salas, A., 2017. Empowering women in global supply chains. 28 June 2017. *Georgetown University*. Available at: https://msb.georgetown.edu/news-story/empowering-women-global-supply-chains/, [Accessed on 26 December 2023].

Saldanha, N., Mulye, R. and Rahman, K., 2023. Cancel culture and the consumer: A strategic marketing perspective. *Journal of Strategic Marketing*, 31(5), pp. 1071–1086.

Saleem, F.Z. and Iglesias, O., 2016. Mapping the domain of the fragmented field of internal branding. *Journal of Product & Brand Management*, 25(1), pp. 43–57.

Salter, C. L., 1971. Introduction: A note on focus. In Ed. Salter, C., *The Cultural Landscape*. California: Duxbury Press.

Samuel, A., White, G. R., Thomas, R. and Jones, P., 2021. Programmatic advertising: An exegesis of consumer concerns. *Computers in Human Behavior*, 116. https://doi.org/10.1016/j.chb.2020.106657

Santora, J., 2023. Highest paid TikTok influencers of 2024. 8 November 2023. *Influencer Marketing Hub.* Available at: https://influencermarketinghub.com/tiktok-highest-paid-stars/#toc-0, [Accessed on 12 February 2024].

Sarasvuo, S., Rindell, A. and Kovalchuk, M., 2022. Toward a conceptual understanding of co-creation in branding. *Journal of Business Research, 139,* pp. 543–563.

Sariçam, H., 2015. Life satisfaction: Testing a structural equation model based on authenticity and subjective happiness. *Polish Psychological Bulletin,* Vol 46(2), pp. 278–284.

Sarkar, C. and Kotler, P. 2020. *Brand Activism: From Purpose to Action.* Idea Bite Press.

Sassatelli, R., 2007. *Consumer Culture: History, Theory and Politics.* London: Sage.

Sauer, C.O., 1969. The morphology of landscape. In Ed. Leighly, J., *Land and Life: A Selection from the Writings of Carl Ortwin Sauer.* Berkeley and Los Angeles: University of California Press.

Sayer, A., 1992. *Methods in Social Science. A Realist Approach,* 2nd Edition. London: Routledge.

Schaefer, S.D., Terlutter, R. and Diehl, S., 2021. Talking about CSR matters: Employees' perception of and reaction to their company's CSR communication in four different CSR domains. In Eds. Yoon, S., Choi, Y. K., & Taylor, C. R., *Leveraged Marketing Communications.* London: Routledge, pp. 186–207.

Schiappa, E., 2022. *The Transgender Exigency: Defining Sex and Gender in the 21st Century.* London: Taylor & Francis, p. 252.

Schmidt, H.J., Ind, N., Guzman, F. and Kennedy, E., 2021. Sociopolitical activist brands. *Journal of Product & Brand Management, 31*(1), pp. 40–55.

Schmidt, K.N. and Iyer, M.K.S., 2015. Online behaviour of social media participants' and perception of trust, comparing social media brand community groups and associated organized marketing strategies. *Procedia-Social and Behavioral Sciences, 177,* pp. 432–439.

Schmidt, S. and Eisend, M., 2015. Advertising repetition: A meta-analysis on effective frequency in advertising. *Journal of Advertising, 44*(4), pp. 415–428.

Schlenker, B.R. and Wowra, S.A., 2003. Carryover effects of feeling socially transparent or impenetrable on strategic self-presentation. *Journal of Personality and Social Psychology, 85*(5), p. 871.

Schirato, T. and Roberts, M., 2018. *Bourdieu: A Critical Introduction.* Sydney: Allen & Unwin.

Scott, P.J., 2004. *The Ford Mustang and the Chevrolet Corvette: Icons in American Culture.* Fullerton: California State University.

SeeHer & Ipsos, 2022. Strive for More: Optimizing predictive creative drivers to improve gender equality in advertising. *See Her.* Available at: www.seeher.com/wp-content/uploads/2022/11/Strive-For-More-White-Paper-2022-final.pdf, [Accessed on 06 November 2023].

Sergiu, B., 2010. M. Foucault's view on power relations. *Cogito-Multidisciplinary Research Journal*, (02), pp. 55–61.

Shah, D. V., McLeod, D. M., Kim, E., Lee, S. Y., Gotlieb, M. R., Ho, S. S. and Breivik, H., 2007. Political consumerism: How communication and consumption orientations drive 'Lifestyle Politics.' *The Annals of the American Academy of Political and Social Science*, 611, pp. 217–235.

Shariq, M., 2018. Brand equity dimensions – A literature review. *International Research Journal of Management and Commerce*, 5(3), pp. 312–330.

Sharon, K., 2022. *A historical analysis of brand activism and its impact on company success.* Senior Honors Project, 148. James Madison University.

Sherry, J.F., 1987. Advertising as a cultural system. In Ed. Umiker-Sebeok, J., *Marketing and Semiotics: New Directions in the Study of Signs for Sale.* Berlin: Mouton de Gruyter, pp. 441–461.

Sheth, J.N. and Solomon, M.R., 2014. Extending the extended self in a digital world. *Journal of Marketing Theory and Practice*, 22(2), pp. 123–132.

Shimul, A.S., 2022. Brand attachment: A review and future research. *Journal of Brand Management*, 29(4), pp. 400–419.

Shin, M. and Pae, J.H., 2022. Authenticity or homogeneity? Contextualising the urban revitalisation of a post-industrial landscape through the Red Brick Landscape Preservation Project in Seoul. *Habitat International*, 124, 102574.

Shklovski, I., Mainwaring, S.D., Skúladóttir, H.H. and Borgthorsson, H., 2014, April. Leakiness and creepiness in app space: Perceptions of privacy and mobile app use. *Proceedings of the SIGCHI Conference on Human Factors in Computing Systems*, pp. 2347–2356.

Siano, A., Vollero, A. and Bertolini, A., 2022. From brand control to brand co-creation: An integrated framework of brand paradigms and emerging brand perspectives. *Journal of Business Research*, 152, pp. 372–386.

Silver, I., 1996. Role transitions, objects, and identity. *Symbolic Interaction*, 19(1), pp. 1–20.

Simonson, A. and Schmitt, B.H., 1997. *Marketing Aesthetics: The Strategic Management of Brands, Identity, and Image.* London: Simon and Schuster.

Simpson, B., Robertson, J.L. and White, K., 2020. How co-creation increases employee corporate social responsibility and organizational engagement: The moderating role of self-construal. *Journal of Business Ethics*, 166, pp. 331–350.

Simpson, H., 2023. Interview with Miriam J. Johnson (2 February).

Sinke, S., 2009. *Start With Why: How Great Leaders Inspire Everyone to Take Action*. New York and London: Penguin Group.

Sinek, S., 2011. *Start With Why: How Great Leaders Inspire Everyone to Take Action*. London: Penguin.

Singh, J., Shukla, P. and Schlegelmilch, B.B., 2022. Desire, need, and obligation: Examining commitment to luxury brands in emerging markets. *International Business Review*, 31(3).

Singh, S., 2006. Impact of color on marketing. *Management decision*, 44(6), pp. 783–789.

Singhal, D., 2011. Why this Kolaveri Di: Maddening phenomenon of earworm. *SSRN*. Available at: https://papers.ssrn.com/sol3/papers.cfm?abstract_id=1969781, [Accessed on 21 February 2024].

Skydsgaard, N., 2017. Uber to end service in Denmark after less than three years. 28 March 2017. *Reuters*. Available at: www.reuters.com/article/idUSKBN16Z10W, [Accessed on 21 February 2024].

Smith, J., 2010. Marrying the old and the new in historic urban landscapes. In Eds. Van Oers, R., & Haraguchi, S. *Managing Historic Cities*, World Heritage Papers No. 27, Paris: UNESCO, pp. 45–51.

Smith, J. W., 2020. The Era of the Public: Fast and Slow in the Future of Marketing. *Kantar*. Available at: www.kantar.com/inspiration/brands/the-era-of-the-public-fast-and-slow-in-the-future-of-marketing, [Accessed on 08 December 2023].

Smith, N. and Williams, P. (Eds.), 1986. *Gentrification of the City*. London: Unwin Hyman.

Slepian, M.L., Weisbuch, M., Rule, N.O. and Ambady, N., 2011. Tough and tender: Embodied categorization of gender. *Psychological Science*, 22(1), pp. 26–28.

Sobande, F., 2019. Woke-washing: 'intersectional' femvertising and branding 'woke' bravery. *European Journal of Marketing*, 54(11), pp. 2723–2745.

Social Blade, 2024. Yoga with Adriene. February 2024. *Social Blade*. Available at: https://socialblade.com/youtube/user/yogawithadriene, [Accessed on 21 Februrary 2024].

Södergren, J., 2021. Brand authenticity: 25 years of research. *International Journal of Consumer Studies*, 45(4), pp. 645–663.

Soederberg, S., 2010. *Corporate Power and Ownership in Contemporary Capitalism: The Politics of Resistance and Domination*. London: Routledge.

Solga, K., 2019. *Theory for Theatre Studies: Space*. London: Bloomsbury Publishing.

Sørensen, A., 2019. The basic concepts of stratification research: Class, status, and power. *Social Stratification*, pp. 287–300.

Sortlist, 2022. Attempts needed for BeReal users in selected countries in Europe to post photo content on the app as of September 2022, by gender. *Statista*. Available at: www.statista.com/statistics/1358378/bereal-selected-countries-europe-takes-needed-to-post-by-gender/, [Accessed on 12 October 2023].

Spagnuolo, E., 2020. Meet Generation Z: shaping the future of shopping. Podcast transcript. 4 August 2020. *McKinsey Podcast*. Available at: www.mckinsey.com/industries/consumer-packaged-goods/our-insights/meet-generation-z-shaping-the-future-of-shopping, [Accessed on 15 February 2024].

Spielmann, N., Dobscha, S. and Lowrey, T.M., 2021. Real men don't buy 'Mrs. Clean': Gender bias in gendered brands. *Journal of the Association for Consumer Research*, 6(2), pp. 211–222.

SproutSocial, 2019. #BrandsGetReal: what consumers want from brands in a divided society. *SproutSocial*. Available at: https://sproutsocial.com/insights/data/social-media-connection/, [Accessed on 16 February 2024].

SSGA, 2018. Drive Change: SPDR@ SSGA Gender Diversity Index ETF (SHE). *SSGA*. Available at: www.ssga.com/investment-topics/general-investing/2018/04/drive_change_gender_diversity.pdf, [Accessed on 03 October 2022].

Stach, J., 2019. Meaningful experiences: An embodied cognition perspective on brand meaning co-creation. *Journal of Brand Management*, 26(3), pp. 317–331.

Stäheli, U. and Stoltenberg, L., 2022. Digital detox tourism: Practices of analogization. *New Media & Society*, pp. 1056–1073.

Stallone, V., Rozumowski, A., Pelka, A., Reisig, D. and Pankratz, C., 2021. Now you see me: A quantitative study on the effects of ad blocker usage on users' brand perception. *Marketing and Smart Technologies*, pp. 699–708.

Starbucks, 2024. Culture and Values. *Starbucks*. Available at: www.starbucks.com/careers/working-at-starbucks/culture-and-values/, [Accessed on 04 February 2024].

Statista A, 2023. Airlines: Virgin Atlantic customers in the United Kingdom. Consumer Insight Report, *Statista*.

Statista B, 2023. Brand KPIs for beers: Bud Light in the U.S. Consumer Insight Report, *Statista*.

Statista, 2023. Digital advertising touchpoints in the U.S. as of September 2023. *Statista*. Available at: www.statista.com/forecasts/805827/digital-advertising-touchpoints-in-the-us, [Accessed on 04 December 2023].

Sterbenk, Y., Champlin, S., Windels, K. and Shelton, S., 2022. Is femvertising the new greenwashing? Examining corporate commitment to gender equality. *Journal of Business Ethics*, 177(3), pp. 491–505.

Stewart, J., 2018. 'Mustang Means Freedom': Why Ford is Saving an American Icon. *The New York Times*. 24 May 2018. Available at: www.nytimes.com/2018/05/24/business/ford-mustang-american-icon .html, [Accessed on 02 October 2022].

Stobart, P. (Ed.), 2016. Introduction. In *Brand Power*. Switzerland: Springer.

Stone, C.N., 1988. Preemptive power: Floyd Hunter's 'Community power structure' reconsidered. *American Journal of Political Science*, pp. 82–104.

Stourm, V. and Bax, E., 2017. Incorporating hidden costs of annoying ads in display auctions. *International Journal of Research in Marketing*, 34(3), pp. 622–640.

Suicide, 2023. Google interest over time 'suicide' 2004–2023.

Sundar, A. and Kellaris, J.J., 2015. Blue-washing the green halo: How colors color ethical judgments. *The Psychology of Design*, pp. 63–74.

Sung, K.H. and Kim, S., 2014. I want to be your friend: The effects of organizations' interpersonal approaches on social networking sites. *Journal of Public Relations Research*, 26(3), pp. 235–255.

Suciu, P., 2023. Bud Light's New Ad Met with Backlash on Social Media. 23 June 2023. *Forbes*. Available at: www.forbes.com/sites/ petersuciu/2023/06/23/bud-light-launched-new-ad-and-it-was-met- with-backlash-on-social-media/?sh=105e3c5736c1, [Accessed on 27 November 2023].

Swaminathan, V., Sorescu, A., Steenkamp, J.B.E., O'Guinn, T.C.G. and Schmitt, B., 2020. Branding in a hyperconnected world: Refocusing theories and rethinking boundaries. *Journal of Marketing*, 84(2), pp. 24–46.

Sweet Cherry, 2023. About us. *Sweet Cherry*. Available at: https:// sweetcherrypublishing.com/about-us/, [Accessed on 19 December 2023].

T3 Technology Hub, 2023. Market share of videoconferencing software worldwide in 2023, by program. *Statista*. Available at: www.statista .com/statistics/1331323/videoconferencing-market-share, [Accessed on 13 February 2024].

Tacikowski, P., Fust, J. and Ehrsson, H.H., 2020. Fluidity of gender identity induced by illusory body-sex change. *Scientific reports*, 10, 14358.

Tadajewski, M. & Jones, B., 2008. *The History of Marketing Thought*. London: Sage Publications Ltd.

Tantillo, J., Lorenzo-Aiss, J.D. and Mathisen, R.E., 1995. Quantifying perceived differences in type styles: An exploratory study. *Psychology & Marketing*, 12(5), pp. 447–457.

Tapestry, 2023. Number of stores of Kate Spade worldwide in 2023, by region. *Statista*. Available at: www.statista.com/statistics/665285/ number-kate-spade-stores-worldwide-by-type/, [Accessed on 25 December 2023].

Taylor, C., 1992. *Ethics of Authenticity*. Cambridge, MA: Harvard University Press.

Taylor, K., 2012. Landscape and meaning: Context for a global discourse on cultural landscape values. In Eds. Taylor, K., & Lennon, J., *Managing cultural landscapes*. London: Routledge.

Taylor, K., 2017. Starbucks is quietly changing the business as furious baristas slam the 'cult that pays $9 per hour'. 23 May 2017. *Business Insider*. Available at: www.businessinsider.com/starbucks-north-star-agenda-causes-barista-backlash-2017-5?r=US&IR=T, [Accessed on 04 February 2024].

Taylor, K. & Xu, Q., 2020. Challenging landscape eurocentrism: An Asian perspective. In Eds. Atha, M., Howard, P., Thompson, I., & Waterton, E., *The Routledge Companion to Landscape Studies*, 2nd Edition. London and New York: Routledge.

Ten Brinke, L. and Keltner, D., 2022. Theories of power: Perceived strategies for gaining and maintaining power. *Journal of Personality and Social Psychology*, 122(1), pp. 53–72.

Tewari, V. and Mittal, H., 2014. Co creation and collaboration: Branding tools. *International Journal of Knowledge and Research in Management & E-Commerce*, 4(3), pp. 11–18.

The Drum Team, 2003. Burberry stained by undesirable clientele. 27 November 2003. *The Drum*. Available at: www.thedrum.com/news/2003/11/27/burberry-stained-undesirable-clientele, [Accessed on 15 February 2024].

The Herald, 2003. Burberry shown the door as bars band the thug's uniform. 12 November 2003. *The Herald*. Available at: www.heraldscotland.com/news/12526061.burberry-shown-the-door-as-bars-ban-the-thugs-uniform/, [Accessed on 15 February 2024].

Thinkbox, 2022. Number of television advertisements seen daily per individual in the United Kingdom (UK) from 2005 to 2021. *Statista*. Available at: www.statista.com/statistics/486685/number-of-tv-ads-seen-daily-in-the-uk/, [Accessed on 04 December 2023].

Thomas, G. and Wyatt, S., 2002. Access is not the only problem: Using and controlling the Internet. *Technology and In/Equality*, pp. 33–57.

Thomas, L., 2018. Fashion designer Kate Spade found dead in New York in an apparent suicide. 06 June 2018. *CNBC*. Available at: www.cnbc.com/2018/06/05/shares-of-fashion-house-tapestry-fall-after-media-reports-of-designer-kate-spades-death.html#:~:text=Tapestry%2C%20which%20also%20owns%20Stuart,%2D800%2D273%2D8255, [Accessed on 26 December 2023].

Thrift, N., 2007. *Non-Representational Theory: Space, Politics, Affect*. London: Routledge.

Till, B.D., Baack, D. and Waterman, B., 2011. Strategic brand association maps: Developing brand insight. *Journal of Product & Brand Management*, 20(2), pp. 92–100.

Tiu Wright, L., Newman, A. and Dennis, C., 2006. Enhancing consumer empowerment. *European Journal of Marketing*, 40(9/10), pp. 925–935.

Todri, V., 2022. Frontiers: The impact of ad-blockers on online consumer behavior. *Marketing Science*, 41(1), pp. 7–18.

Topp, W., 2000. Knowledge system diagnostics: Applying Foucault's archaeological framework to organizations. *Systems Research and Behavioral Science*, 17, pp 365–374.

Trilling, L. 1972. *Sincerity and Authenticity*. Cambridge, MA: Harvard University Press.

Tripp, J., 2021. The Potential of Cyclical Fashion. *UEN Digital Press with Pressbooks: Open Educational Resources for Utah*. Available at: https://uen.pressbooks.pub/voicesofusuvol15/chapter/the-potential-of-cyclical-fashion/, [Accessed on 05 February 2024].

Trone, M., 2015. Kate Spade & social impact you can wear. 09 December 2015. *Wharton Magazine*. Available at: https://magazine.wharton .upenn.edu/digital/kate-spade-social-impact-you-can-wear/, [Accessed on 26 December 2023].

Trudeau, S. and Shobeiri, S., 2016. Does social currency matter in creation of enhanced brand experience? *Journal of Product & Brand Management*, 25, pp. 98–114.

Tuan, Y., 1980. The significance of the artifact. *Geographical Review*, 70 (4), 462–472.

Tuite, A., 2018. Jenny Kee and Flamingo Park: Independent fashion retailers as creative practitioners. *Fashion, Style & Popular Culture*, 5(2), pp. 169–183.

Ulrich, I., 2013. The effect of consumer multifactorial gender and biological sex on the evaluation of cross-gender brand extensions. *Psychology & Marketing*, 30(9), pp. 794–810.

Tuite, A., 2021. Gendered entrepreneurialism and the labour of online consumption in the independent fashion sector. *Fashion Theory*, 25(3), pp. 419–438. Available at: https://doi.org/10.1080/13627 04X.2019.1633831, [Accessed on 13 June 2024].

Turner, C. and Manning, P., 1988. Placing authenticity – On being a tourist: a reply to pearce and Moscardo. *Australia and New Zealand Journal of Sociology*, 24(1), pp. 136–139.

Tuškej, U., Golob, U. and Podnar, K., 2013. The role of consumer-brand identification in building brand relationships. *Journal of Business Research*, 66(1), pp. 53–59.

Uber, 2024. Use Uber in cities around the world. *Uber*. Available at: www .uber.com/global/en/cities/, [Accessed on 21 February 2024].

Ulrich, I. and Tissier-Desbordes, E., 2018. 'A feminine brand? Never!' Brands as gender threats for 'resistant' masculinities. *Qualitative Market Research: An International Journal*, 21(3), pp. 274–295.

UNIQLO, 2023. Our Story. *Uniqlo*. Available at: www.uniqlo.com/uk/en/ info/about-uniqlo.html, [Accessed on 24 August 2023].

Urban, G., Sultan, F. and Qualls, W. 2000. Placing trust at the center of your internet strategy. *Sloan Management Review*, 42(1), pp. 39–48.

Urban Outfitters, 2023. About Us. *Urban Outfitters*. Available at: www.urbn .com/our-brands/urban-outfitters/about-us, [Accessed on 23 August 2023].

Urde, M., Greyser, S.A. and Balmer, J.M., 2007. Corporate brands with a heritage. *Journal of Brand Management*, 15, pp. 4–19.

US Department of Health and Human Services, 2022. Deaths by suicide per 100,000 resident population in the U.S. from 1950 to 2019. *Statista*. Available at: www.statista.com/statistics/187465/death-rate-from-suicide-in-the-us-since-1950/, [Accessed on 26 December 2023].

Vailshery, L.S., 2022. U.S. desktop internet browser market share 2015–2022. *Statista*. Available at: www.statista.com/statistics/272697/market-share-desktop-internet-browser-usa/, [Accessed on 10 October 2022].

Vallaster, C. and Von Wallpach, S., 2013. An online discursive inquiry into the social dynamics of multi-stakeholder brand meaning co-creation. *Journal of Business Research*, 66(9), pp. 1505–1515.

Valenzuela, S. and Gil de Zúñiga, H., 2018. Ties, likes, and tweets: Using strong and weak ties to explain differences in protest participation across Facebook and Twitter use. *Political Communication*, 35, pp. 117–134.

van Deursen, A.J.A.M. and Helsper, E.J., 2015. The third-level digital divide: Who benefits most from being online? *Communication and Information Technologies Annual: Studies in Media and Communications*, 10, pp. 29–52.

Van Dijk, J., 2020. *The Digital Divide*. John Wiley & Sons.

2009. Users like you? Theorizing agency in user-generated content. *Media, Culture & Society*, 31 (1), pp. 41–58.

2005. *The Deepening Divide: Inequality in the Information Society*. London: Sage.

2021. Seeing the forest for the trees: Visualizing platformization and its governance. *New Media & Society*, 23(9), pp. 2801–2819.

Van Laer, T., De Ruyter, K., Visconti, L.M. and Wetzels, M., 2014. The extended transportation-imagery model: A meta-analysis of the antecedents and consequences of consumers' narrative transportation. *Journal of Consumer Research*, 40(5), pp. 797–817.

Van Leeuwen, T., 2001. What is authenticity? *Discourse Studies*, 3(4), pp. 392–397.

Varghese, N. and Kumar, N., 2022. Feminism in advertising: Irony or revolution? A critical review of femvertising. *Feminist Media Studies*, 22(2), pp. 441–459.

Veg, N. and Nyeck, S., 2007. Brand gender and cross-gender extensions. *Dans: Thought Leaders International Conference on Brand Management (CD-Rom)*. University of Birmingham.

Veg-Sala, N. and Roux, E., 2018. Cross-gender extension potential of luxury brands: A semiotic analysis. *Journal of Brand Management*, 25, pp. 436–448.

Veloutsou, C., 2009. Brands as relationship facilitators in consumer markets. *Marketing Theory*, 9(1), pp. 127–130.

Verhoeven, M., 2011. The many dimensions of ritual. In Ed. Insoll, T., *The Oxford Handbook of the Archaeology of Ritual and Religion*, pp. 115–132.

Verlegh, P.W., 2023. Perspectives: A research-based guide for brand activism. *International Journal of Advertising*, pp. 1–15.

Veselinova, E. and Samonikov, M.G., 2020. Defining the Concept of Brand Equity with Radical Transparency. In *Global Branding: Breakthroughs in Research and Practice*, pp. 1–17.

Virgin Atlantic, 2023. Our Story. *Virgin Atlantic*. Available at: https://corporate.virginatlantic.com/gb/en/our-story.html, [Accessed on 03 November 2023].

2023. Our People. *Virgin Atlantic*. Available at: https://corporate.virginatlantic.com/gb/en/business-for-good/our-people.html, [Accessed on 06 November 2023].

2022. Our Be Yourself Manifesto. *Virgin Atlantic*. Available at: https://corporate.virginatlantic.com/content/dam/corporate/Be%20Your self%20Manifesto%202022.pdf, [Accessed on 06 November 2023].

2023. Annual revenue of Virgin Atlantic Airways Limited from 2013 to 2022 (in million GBP). *Statista*. Available at: www.statista.com/statistics/1010512/virgin-atlantic-airways-ltd-revenue/, [Accessed on 03 November 2023].

n.d. SCARLET @ Virgin Atlantic. Available at: https://careersuk.virgin-atlantic.com/diversity-equity-and-inclusion, [Accessed on 13 June 2024].

Visconti, L.M., Peñaloza, L. and Toulouse, N. (Eds.), 2020. *Marketing Management: A Cultural Perspective*, 2nd Edition. London: Routledge, Taylor & Francis Group.

Vredenburg, J., Kapitan, S., Spry, A. and Kemper, J.A., 2020. Brands taking a stand: Authentic brand activism or woke washing? *Journal of Public Policy & Marketing*, 39(4), pp. 444–460.

Vukasović, T., 2022. Customer-based brand equity: Conceptual model. *Management*, *19*, pp. 303–310.

Wainwright, J., & Bryan, J., 2009. Cartography, territory, property: Postcolonial reflections on indigenous counter-mapping in Nicaragua and Belize. *Cultural Geographies*, *16* (2), pp. 153–178.

Wang, L. and Graddy, E., 2008. Social capital, volunteering, and charitable giving. Voluntas. *International Journal of Voluntary and Nonprofit Organizations*, *19*, pp. 23–42.

Wang, C.L., Sarkar, J.G. and Sarkar, A., 2019. Hallowed be thy brand: Measuring perceived brand sacredness. *European Journal of Marketing*, *53*(4), pp. 733–757.

Wang, Y., Xu, S. and Wang, Y., 2020. The consequences of employees' perceived corporate social responsibility: A meta-analysis. *Business Ethics: A European Review*, *29*(3), pp. 471–496.

Ward, E., Yang, S., Romaniuk, J. and Beal, V., 2020. Building a unique brand identity: Measuring the relative ownership potential of brand identity element types. *Journal of Brand Management*, *27*, pp. 393–407.

Waseem, D., Biggemann, S. and Garry, T., 2021. An exploration of the drivers of employee motivation to facilitate value co-creation. *Journal of Services Marketing*, *35*(4), pp. 442–452.

We Are Social, 2023a. Digital 2023 April Global Snapshot Report. Available at: https://wearesocial.com/uk/blog/2023/04/the-global-state-of-digital-in-april-2023/, [Accessed on 01 September 2023].

We Are Social, 2023b. Think Forward 2023: Margin Chasers. Available at: https://thinkforward.wearesocial.com/margin_chasers.html, [Accessed on 25 September 2023].

Webb, J., Schirato, T. and Danaher, G., 2002. *Understanding Bourdieu*. Australia: Allen & Unwin.

Weber, L. 2009. *Sticks & Stones: How Digital Reputations Are Created Over Time and Lost in a Click*. Hoboken: John Wiley & Sons, Inc.

Wendt, D., 1968. Semantic differentials of typefaces as a method of congeniality research. *Visible Language*, *2*(1), pp. 3–25.

West, C. and Zhong, C.B., 2015. Moral cleansing. *Current Opinion in Psychology*, *6*, pp. 221–225.

Weston, S., 2022. *The Changing Face of Burberry: Britishness, Heritage, Labour and Consumption*. London: Bloomsbury Publishing.

Wheeler, S.C. and Bechler, C.J., 2021. Objects and self-identity. *Current Opinion in Psychology*, *39*, pp. 6–11.

Whitehouse, H. 2021 *The Ritual Animal: Imitation and Cohesion in the Evolution of Social Complexity*. Oxford: Oxford University Press.

Widder, N., 2004. Foucault and power revisited. *European Journal of Political Theory*, *3*(4), pp. 411–432.

Wieden & Kennedy, 2010. Old Spice: Smell like a man, man. *Wieden & Kennedy*. Available at: www.wk.com/work/old-spice-smell-like-a-man-man/, [Accessed on 16 February 2024].

Wiener-Bronner, D., 2023. Bud Light wanted to market to all. Instead it's alienating everyone. 01 May 2023. *CNN Business*. Available at: https://edition.cnn.com/2023/05/01/business/bud-light-marketing/index.html, [Accessed on 22 November 2023].

Witte, J.C. and Mannon, S.E., 2010. *The Internet and Social Inequalities*. London: Routledge.

Woodward, K. 2002. *Understanding Identity*. London: Hodder Education.

Workman, H., 2014. *Formation of safe spaces in gendered online communities Reddit and 'the front page of the internet'*. Doctoral dissertation, Texas Christian University.

Wortham, J., 2023. A silvery, shimmering summer of Beyoncé. 27 September 2023. *New York Times*. Available at: www.nytimes.com/2023/09/27/magazine/beyonce-renaissance-tour.html, [Accessed on 22 February 2024].

Xie, C., Bagozzi, R.P. and Grønhaug, K., 2015. The role of moral emotions and individual differences in consumer responses to corporate green and non-green actions. *Journal of the academy of Marketing Science*, 43, pp. 333–356.

YouGov, 2023. Most popular airlines in the United Kingdom (UK) in Q1 2023. *Statista*. Available at: www.statista.com/statistics/951250/most-popular-airlines-uk, [Accessed on 03 November 2023].

Young, M., 2020. The Reigning queen of pandemic yoga. 25 November 2020. *New York Times*. Available at: www.nytimes.com/2020/11/25/magazine/yoga-adriene-mishler.html, [Accessed on 21 February 2024].

Yuen, T.W., Nieroda, M., He, H. and Park, Y., 2019. Can being similar in product category a liability for cross-gender brand extension. *Proceedings of the European Marketing Academy*, 48(8432).

Yüksek, D.A., 2018. Evaluating the importance of social capital for the conversion of the forms of capital: A critical approach to the Bourdieusian model. *Gaziantep University Journal of Social Sciences*, 17(3), pp. 1090–1106.

Zaichkowsky, J.L., 2010. Strategies for distinctive brands. *Journal of Brand Management*, 17, pp. 548–560.

Zhang, Y. and Du, S., 2023. Moral cleansing or moral licensing? A study of unethical pro-organizational behavior's differentiating Effects. *Asia Pacific Journal of Management*, 40(3), pp. 1075–1092.

Zinnbauer, M. and Honer, T., 2011. How brands can create social currency – A framework for managing brands in a network era. *Marketing Review St. Gallen*, 28(5), pp. 50–55.

Zuk, M., Bierbaum, A.H., Chapple, K., Gorska, K., Loukaitou-Sideris, A., Ong, P. and Thomas, T., 2015, August. Gentrification, displacement and the role of public investment: A literature review. *Journal of Planning Literature*, 33(1), pp. 31–44.

Zwick, D., Bonsu, S.K. and Darmody, A., 2008. Putting consumers to work: Co-creation and new marketing govern-mentality. *Journal of Consumer Culture*, 8(2), pp. 163–196.

Index

84 Lumber, 124–125

Abahizi Dushyigikirane, 132
activism, 4–5, 101, 114, 116–123,
    125–127, 129, 134, 136–139,
    152, 190
ad-block, 48–50
Adidas, 121, 141, 191
Adobe, 152
advertisements, 5, 18, 31, 36, 39–40,
    46, 48–49, 80–83, 85, 110,
    125, 130, 143–144, 152, 164,
    175, 181
    brands, 46–47, 73
    channel, 40
    engaging, 188
    marketing, 102
    memoraable, 175
    message, 125
    offline, 110
    photographic, 80
    portrayal, 80
    reactions, 102
    TV, 110
    volume, 126
advertisers, 70
advertising, 12, 48, 57, 61, 77, 80–81,
    145, 150, 152, 190, 194
    digital market, 39
    emotional, 130
    ESG. See environmental,
        social and corporate
        governance (ESG)
    gendered, 81
    highlights, 153
    industry, 49, 81
    messages, 150
    programmatic, 49
    saturation, 40
    style, 81

targeted, 147
unique, 104
affiliation, 27
affinity, 33, 37, 46, 70–72, 77
agglomeration, 168, 177, 189, 192
Alvarez, Jay, 103
Amazon, 37, 116–117
Anheuser-Busch, 5, 81–82, 85–91
anthropomorphism, 100
AO3, 37
app, 24–25, 106, 108, 148, 175
Apple Inc, 39
appresentation, 41, 46
approach, 170, 177, 195
    collaborative, 139
    cultural, 50
    humanistic, 99
    informational, 162
    information-based, 161
    pragmatic, 116
    psychological, 44
    pyramidal, 146
    social constructionist, 45
    strategic, 161
    top-down, 146
Arby's, 181
architecture, 7, 54, 77
asset, 2, 10, 29–30, 43–44, 61, 146,
    149, 165
AT&T, 34–35
Audi, 153
audience, 13–14, 30, 46–47, 52,
    75, 77, 88, 90–91, 102–103,
    105, 107, 129, 138, 143,
    158, 188
Australia, 114, 135, 192
authentic, 3, 5, 29, 77, 89, 93,
    95–103, 105–107, 118–120,
    122, 124, 127, 129–130, 134,
    137–139, 142, 189, 191

authenticity, 3, 84–85, 88–89, 93–100,
   103–108, 118–120, 122, 124,
   126, 130, 134, 136–140,
   142, 152, 168, 180–181, 189,
   195–196
author, 38, 46, 120, 155, 162
authority, 45–47, 50, 71, 143
   top-down, 61
AuthorSHARE, 120
axe body spray, 71, 179

Babolat La Decima, 98
Baby Boomers, 86, 89, 114, 152, 180
backlash, 72, 82, 87–92, 117,
   124–126, 158–159, 165, 167
Barbie, 67
Barbour, 162
behind the-scenes, 3
Belk's, 153
Ben & Jerry's, 17, 122
BeReal, 106–108
Beverly Hills, 12, 32
Beyoncé, 29
Black Lives Matter, 113, 126
bloggers, 30
book, 8, 14, 33–34, 44, 46, 53, 56,
   66–67, 71–72, 90, 101, 120, 122,
   184, 189
boundaries, 81, 103–104, 160,
   181–182, 189, 195. *See also*
   textual, boundaries
Bourdieu, Pierre, 2, 50, 56, 58–60
boycott, 89, 115, 119, 124–125, 130,
   159, 165, 190
branding, 7, 12, 27–28, 30, 32, 35, 37,
   44–45, 50, 61, 69, 93, 99, 101,
   108, 117, 130, 139, 160–162,
   174, 177, 192, 194
   activism, 4–5, 17, 29, 112–118,
      121–122, 124–126, 129,
      131–140, 180, 182, 190
   advocacy, 27, 54
   affinity, 63, 70, 191
   ambassadors, 150, 195
   authenticity, 100, 105, 118
   equity, 27, 38, 47–48, 50, 52, 58,
      63, 146, 154
   everyman, 16
   heritage, 181
   icon, 31

identity, 67, 101, 105, 151, 178,
   194. *See also* identity
   narrative, 134, 144, 155
   personality, 66, 74, 77, 99–100, 135
   recognition, 38, 67
   sabotage, 167, 171
British Airways, 82
Brompton, 18
Bud Light. *See* Anheuser-Busch
Burberry, 5, 159, 174, 176–179,
   181–183
Burger King, 144
business, 19–20, 25, 47, 89, 105, 114,
   117, 132, 139, 195
   model, 111, 116–117, 135, 139
buycott, 90, 190

Cambridge University Press, 34, 56
cancel culture, 17, 162, 165, 171
capital, 2, 9–10, 12, 19–20, 22, 25,
   43–44, 50, 52–61, 99, 147, 151,
   153–154, 157, 164–165, 167,
   169–170, 173, 186, 188, 190–191
   accrual, 141
   collectively owned, 54
   conception of, 57
   conceptualizes, 58
   consumers, 55
   cultural, 10–12, 17, 28, 43–44, 50,
      53–54, 56–59, 61, 96, 136, 143,
      160, 181–183
   cultural, embodied, 56
   cultural, objectified, 56
   developing, 188
   distribution, 61
   dynamics of, 57
   economic, 28, 43–44, 53–56, 58–59,
      61, 136, 164, 173, 183, 187–188
   embodied, 56
   exchange, 2, 5, 13, 15–16, 23, 39,
      59, 159, 173
   exercise of, 59
   institutional, 188
   institutionalised, 56
   movement of, 157
   possession of, 61
   power dynamics, 60
   social, 53–56, 59, 61, 151, 164,
      183, 187
   transfer of, 188

capital (cont.)
  transformation of, 59
  utilisation of, 146
  valuable, 53
  value, 57
capitalism, 4, 127, 190
Cartier, 67, 71
Change Please, 5, 115, 130, 135–139
China, 114, 175, 193
class, 50–51, 53–54, 60, 146, 153, 177
Coca-Cola, 9, 30, 56, 67, 192–193
Colgate, 137–138
commercial value, 13
communities, 1, 3, 9–10, 12, 14–18,
    20–25, 27, 33, 36–39, 41, 54–55,
    73, 98, 103, 116, 136, 138, 143,
    147–149, 153, 155, 157–161,
    164, 166–167, 169–170,
    173–174, 185–187, 191
  ad-blocking, 48
  brand, 4–5, 36–38, 40–41, 45,
    73–74, 78, 166, 147, 173,
    179–180, 187–188, 194
  brand, online, 185
  brand, space, 169
  brand, suburb, 23
  brands, grouping of, 168
  consumer, 2, 149, 153, 165–167,
    171, 174, 176, 180, 186, 191
  developing, 4, 13, 28, 138, 186, 190
  development of, 21
  development projects, 147
  drag queen, 98
  digital, 21–22, 37, 41, 142
  exclusive, 24
  free, 24
  free, app, 24
  group, 195
  grows, 166
  growth of, 21
  identity, 171
  like-minded, 33, 36
  LGBTQ, 82, 90
  local, 16, 158
  marginalised, 125
  members, 166
  micro, 105, 159
  niche, 102, 108
  non-geographically bound, 73
  noticeboards, 152

  offline, 54
  online, 54
  online brand, 38
  physical, 167
  reader/author, 38
  safe, 73
  safe, spaces, 25
  social dynamics, 146
  space, 148, 154, 168, 187
  Special Educational Needs and
    Disabilites, 122
  suburb, 23, 25
  virtual, 74
  walled, 37
  wider, 147
company, 45, 83–85, 88–90, 111–112,
    116–118, 121–122, 124, 132,
    142, 148–149, 176, 193
competition, 13, 56, 110, 113, 154,
    168, 179
competitors, 10, 145, 150, 168,
    183, 192
conform, 3, 96, 98
conformity, 95–98
Conservation International, 182
consumer
  base, 52, 91, 123
  culture, 7, 13–14, 32–34, 36–37
  culture, modern, 32
  demand, 104
  -driven, 45
  goods, 12
  groups, 41, 174, 183, 190
  landscape, 27, 73, 137, 145, 167
  loyalty, 130, 140
  relationships, 61, 161
consumption, 3, 12, 20, 23, 34, 41,
    53, 57–58, 63, 72, 77, 112,
    135–136, 139, 152, 162, 165,
    180, 192
content, 3–4, 14, 24–25, 27, 30, 32,
    38, 40–41, 46, 48–49, 74, 80, 86,
    105–106, 133, 152, 169, 182, 190
  creator, 30, 46, 86, 106, 142
  video, 24
context, 2, 5, 28, 34, 44, 52, 60, 91,
    101, 105–106, 108, 146, 154,
    175, 185, 188, 191, 194
  bound, 6
  cultural, 9, 44, 94

dependent, 17
economic, 1, 3, 5, 44
media, 44
political, 185
social, 138
socio-economic, 185
socio-political, 1, 3, 5, 154, 164, 174, 183, 196
Converse, 163, 191
co-operative, 194
corporate, 45, 120, 138, 142, 145, 150, 194
ethos, 127
governance, 141
practice, 118, 120
social responsibility, 4, 85, 111–114, 129–130, 133, 139
strategies, 118, 122
counter-culture, 23
creator, 49, 87, 107, 166. *See also* content, creator
co, 4, 165, 171
CSR. *See* corporate, social responsibility
culture, 7–10, 12–13, 20, 23, 32, 47, 51, 53, 57–59, 64–66, 75, 94, 101–102, 104, 110, 118, 155, 157, 159, 162, 186, 188. *See also* consumer, culture
activists, 152
anchors, 20
aspects, 34, 55, 57, 116
associations, 69
bodies, 16
building blocks, 51
change, 107
code, 97
connetion, 65
consciousness, 31
construct, 75, 94
demarcations, 21
digital, 16
embodiment, 65
expectations, 97
field, 50, 57
forms, 18, 25
goods, 58
group, 20
icon, 31
identity, 192

institutions, 50, 75
interpretation, 65
issues, 102
landmarks, 10, 69, 112
landscape, 2–21, 23–25, 28–29, 32, 34–36, 38–41, 43–60, 63–65, 69–78, 81, 85, 88, 91–94, 96–101, 103–105, 107–108, 110–116, 118–119, 121, 126–127, 129–132, 134, 136, 138–139, 141–148, 150–155, 157–161, 163–168, 170–171, 173–180, 182–191, 193–196
location, 15
mapping, 15–18, 20, 38, 147
markers, 14, 47, 144
meaning, 12, 51, 65
meaningfulness, 142
model, 104
norms, 76, 96
organisations, 16
panorama, 27, 33
patriarchal, 178
pop, 8, 144, 192
production, 52
recollection, 10
resources, 15, 50
savviness, 151
shift, 101
space, 16, 131, 151, 154, 165, 184
structure, 67
studies, 20
understanding, 11, 151
value, 73, 95, 135, 178
culturescape, 8
currency, 31, 36, 180
monetary, 36
social, 31, 36
customer, 38, 69, 82–85, 88, 92, 111, 117, 120, 143–144, 149, 151, 173, 178
behaviour, 38
segmentation, 65
cyberspace, 22

D'Amelio, Charli, 162
Danner, 181
demographic, 80, 88, 108, 111
Depop, 106
differentiation, 41, 119, 145, 151, 154

digital, 8, 14, 40, 83, 147, 167
  access, 24, 55
  age, 107–108, 162, 168
  artists, 181
  cities, 23, 25, 173
  consumers, 40–41
  corporations, 55
  detoxing, 14
  divide, 21
  ecosystem, 171
  formats, 55
  frontiers, 182
  hubs, 1, 21
  landscapes, 6, 22–23, 169, 178, 191
  literacy training, 137
  locations, 23, 37, 168
  map, 22
  marketing, 110, 136
  marketplace, 171
  media, 21, 23
  music, 55
  places, 48
  platforms, 38, 41, 108, 113
  power dynamic, 170
  realms, 1, 14, 21, 25, 55, 183
  representations, 182
  role, 63
  sense, 48
  settings, 14, 21, 36, 55, 74, 161, 180
  shopfronts, 188
  spaces, 2, 5, 7, 21–23, 29, 31, 36,
    40–41, 49, 55, 103, 142, 165,
    168–171, 182, 195
  sphere, 1, 169
  suburbs, 1, 7, 21–22, 24–25,
    168–170, 184, 188, 195
  ties, 37
  wilds, 170
  worlds, 21, 164, 182, 185
digitalization, 55
discourse, 14, 17, 45–46, 50, 52,
  59–60, 78
Disney, 9
diverse, 84, 113
  sexualities, 82
  voices, 81
diversity, 11, 82, 84, 91, 122
Dollar General. *See* dollar stores
dollar stores, 186–187
Dove, 67, 71

Ebay, 106, 175
economic, 53, 132, 178, 186, 188
  analysis, 58
  approach, 44
  concerns, 57
  entity, 110
  forms, 25
  gains, 132, 135
  impact, 85
  independence, 52
  influence, 188
  justice, 122
  necessity, 53
  privilege, 59
  resources, 50
  responsibility, 123
economy, 29, 41, 93, 98, 105, 110,
  126, 151
  cultural, 106
Ello, 49
empower, 132
empowerment, 35, 132–134, 139, 143,
  160–162
engage, 5, 10, 14, 20–21, 23, 29, 33,
  36–37, 41, 47, 63, 74, 77, 96–97,
  101–102, 104–106, 108, 115,
  119–122, 134, 138–139, 142,
  148, 152, 154, 160, 162, 165,
  168, 171, 174, 183, 196
  listeners, 40
engagement, 34, 37, 40, 78, 85, 108,
  110, 119, 127, 139
  community, 139
  consumer, 37, 41
  emotional, 130
  platform, 48
  public, 133
  social, 33
  societal, 127
environment, 7, 17, 32, 41, 45, 48, 69,
  77, 110, 179, 184
  credit, 151
  digital, 38
  impact statement, 4
  media, 44
  natural, 182
  protection, 122
  social, and corporate governance,
    82, 84
  sustainability, 85

environmentally friendly, 68
ESG. *See* environmental, social and
    corporate governance (ESG)
ethical, 68, 114, 123
  behaviour, 119, 123
  branded, 68
  conscious, 127
  consumerism, 126
  consumers, 68, 136
  consumption, 136
  ideal, 99
  intent, 68
  sensitive, 68
Etsy, 106
EU. *See* Europe
Europe, 28, 39, 107, 116
Every Cherry, 122
expressions, 76, 136, 168
  external, 3, 95–96
  gender, 75
  internal, 3
  power, 162
  self, 97
Ezel, Cemal, 135

Facebook, 22–23, 37, 46, 74, 86, 192
Fair Acres Press, 68
Family Dollar. *See* dollar stores
fashion, 30, 86, 104, 131, 139, 159,
    176–178, 190
FedEx, 67
female, 35, 47, 64, 66, 70, 72, 74, 83
  autonomy, 69
  codes, 67
  consumers, 179
  divide, 65
  empowerment, 132
  gender, 67, 73
  icons, 131
  identifying, 68–74, 81, 179
  ratio, 74
feminine, 3, 63, 65–72, 75, 77
  codes, 69–70
Ferrari, 191
fiction, 43, 106–107, 162
  crime, 101
  literary, 101
finance, 19, 45–46
  approaches, 44
  capability, 72

crisis, 100
districts, 19
literacy, 137
Firefly Press, 67
Floral Street, 68
fluidity, 190, 194
Folio Society, 70
follower, 30, 86, 103, 162
Forbes, 30, 49, 90
Ford Mustang, 32–33
Foucault, 2, 16, 45, 59–60, 95
Fox, 124
France, 135

Gantz, Beth, 102
GDPR, 170
GEM, 85
Gen X, 86, 88–89, 180
Gen Z, 4, 14, 40, 91, 114–115, 121,
    152, 180
gender, 3, 38, 64–68, 74–75, 77,
    80–82, 84, 98
  associations, 67
  -based content analysis, 80
  brand, 72
  connoations, 69
  contamination, 72
  cross-gender, 72
  displays, 71
  dynamics, 190
  dysmorphia, 64
  expression, 75
  -fluid, 81
  gap, 74
  identities, 64–66, 69, 71, 75, 82, 84,
    189–190
  identity disorder, 64
  indicators, 70
  inequality, 69
  intonations, 68
  markers, 70
  misgender, 89–90
  nature, 3
  neutral, 84, 190
  norms, 72
  pay gap, 120
  personality, 69
  polarisation, 66, 77
  presentation, 72
  reality, 75

gender (cont.)
  roles, 64, 72–73, 80, 102
  stereotyping, 80
  third, 64
Gender Advertisements, 80
Gender Equality Measure, 85
gendered, 3, 64–66, 71, 73, 77, 190
  advertising, 81
  aspects, 5, 63, 78
  attitudes, 72
  brand identity, 70
  elements, 3, 77–78
  fashion, 190
  language, 73
  lens, 190
  nature, 63, 66–67
  performance, 78
  self-identity, 76
gentrification, 153, 186
geographies, 6–7, 21, 105
  boundaries, 36
  concepts, 1
  cultural, 1, 8, 61
  digital, 1
  ephemeral, 8
  landscape, 20
  physical, 1, 8
  space, 22
  unreliable, 116
Gilead Sciences, 152
Gillette, 68
Giorgio Armani, 53
global village, 21–22, 36, 143
glocalisation, 158, 170
Goodreads, 37
Google, 70, 93, 116, 133, 192
  Chrome, 39
government, 21, 143
  Danish, 149
  regulations, 167
Grub Street, 67
Gucci, 36

H&M, 10
Häagen-Dazs, 193–194
habitus, 50–53, 58, 60, 188
Harley Davidson, 71
Harrods, 59, 153
hashtag, 14, 46, 87
Haynes, 72

Hermès, 141
hierarchy, 10, 52–53, 61, 161, 173,
  175, 177
  power structure, 159
HSBC, 137
Hunter Boots, 159

IBM, 56
icons, 9, 28, 32, 43, 106, 131, 139, 152,
  176, 182. *See also* culture, icon
  pop, 32
identity, 185, 189–190, 193–194, 196.
  See also communities, identity;
  culture, identity; identity
  brand, 184, 193–195
  fluid, 193
  self-, 184, 185, 188–190, 193,
  195–196
image, 2–3, 32, 46, 69, 80, 83, 86, 91,
  124, 177, 183
  brand, 4–5, 27, 29, 34, 144, 150,
  177, 187–188, 190
  brand, old and stuffy, 179
  control, 165
  public, 140
inclusive, 83–84, 89, 190, 193
  policy, 84
inclusivity, 85, 91, 122
  training, 84
industry, 5, 30, 82, 84–85, 114
  airline, 82
  automotive, 54
  average, 88, 92
  tech, 54
influencer, 30, 88–89, 91, 93,
  101–103, 108, 143
  culture, 162
Instagram, 46, 86–90, 102, 106, 117
institution, 6, 31, 44, 51, 56
  social, 66
  sole, 114
interaction, 155, 164, 171
  consumer, 183
  consumer-brand, 150, 154
internet, 21, 23, 27, 36, 39, 55,
  102, 192
  access, 36
  -based, 175
  browsers, 39
  protocol, 175

interpretations, 15, 18, 20, 25, 34–35, 51, 72, 94, 108, 111, 125, 155, 171
  brand, 34
  consumer, 35
intersex, 64
Ipsos, 83, 89
  SeeHer, 85
Italy, 48, 114

Jaguar, 159
Japan, 178
Juicy Couture, 159
Justin Boots, 9–10, 33–34

Kate Spade, 5, 131–134, 137–139
  death, 132, 134
  Foundation, 134, 137
  mental health, 134
  Mind, Body, Soul, 133
  On Purpose, 132
  social impact, 138
  Social Impact Council, 133
  stock, 132
knowledge, 16–17, 22, 45–47, 53, 112, 160, 165–166, 188, 195
  brand, 150, 163
  core, 195
  mental, cues, 44
  power complex, 174
  power dynamic, 176, 195
  power relationship, 4
  spatial, 15
Kogan Page, 67
K-Swiss, 98

L'Occitane, 153
The Landmark, 29
landmarks, 2–4, 9–11, 15–16, 18–19, 22–23, 28, 38, 40–41, 44, 47–48, 56, 58, 61, 63, 65, 71–75, 78, 80, 92, 99–101, 105, 114, 116, 118–119, 127, 132, 139, 142, 145, 147–148, 154–155, 157, 163, 167–168, 171, 178–179, 183–185, 191–192, 195–196.
  See also culture, landmarks
  brands, 13, 15, 19–20, 23, 25, 29, 73, 85, 91, 94, 97–99, 119, 129, 134, 154, 160, 170, 187
  brighter, 164

build, 16
clusters, 11
develop, 93
fixed, 94
imagined, 25
navigational, 158, 192
position, 91
shared, 16
space, 107
store, 29
leverage, 17, 61, 127
LGBT community, 91
LGBTQ, 82, 84, 117, 125
LGBTQIA, 88, 90, 92
Liberty, 159
logo, 34, 67–69, 71, 86, 116, 151, 159, 190, 194–195
  coding, 67, 70
  graphic, 69
  organic, 68
  real estate, 193
London, 10–12, 19, 28, 30, 33, 46, 48, 137, 177, 182
loyalty, 12, 20, 22, 77, 85–86, 89, 100, 123, 130
  brand, 22, 38, 162
lurkers, 40–41, 142–143
luxury, 131, 136, 164, 180
  accessories, 28
  agglomeration, 177
  brand, 58–59, 131, 153, 164, 178, 182
  fashion, 177
  goods, 28
  high-end, brands, 52
  item, 58, 94
  market, 72, 131
  village, 167
Lyft, 68, 122–123

male, 64, 66, 74, 82
  consumers, 179
  divide, 65
  dominance, 66
  and female, 65
  friends, 194
  -identifying, 72, 74, 179
  ratio, 74
map, 1, 7–9, 15–17, 19–20, 22, 25, 48, 60, 101, 108, 180

map-making, 16
mapping, 7, 15, 17, 25, 103
    counter, 17
    physical, 16
marketing, 5, 12, 20, 22, 46, 63, 70–71,
        80–81, 91, 93, 114, 118, 130, 133,
        143, 151, 177, 179, 181, 184, 194
    activist, 118
    awards, 192
    brand, 82
    campaigns, 85, 120, 175, 192
    classes, 35
    consultant, 96
    contemporary, 99
    mechanism, 35
    media, 81, 144
    messages, 144
    -micro, 158
    social, 136
    team, 90
    techniques, 145
    terms, 83
    tools, 36, 68
    traditional, paradigms, 126
    transferral, 25
masculine, 63, 65–72, 75
mass market, 53
Mattel, 67
McDonald's, 144, 158
media, 1, 37, 43–44, 76, 80, 86,
        110, 186
    buzz, 49
    format, 14
    landscape, 50
    mass, 80
    multiple, 44
    personalities, 28
    platforms, 44
    popular, 28
    power, 43
medium, 37
memories, 6, 10, 19, 25, 76, 144
mental, 191
    awareness, 51
    health, 132–134, 138–139
    representation, 150
    well-being, 133
Meta, 37, 55, 116
metaverse. *See* Facebook;
    Instagram; Meta

microsites, 29
Microsoft, 116, 175–176
    Teams, 176, 183
Millennials, 4, 88, 104, 114–115, 180
Minecraft, 182
Mishler, Adriene, 24–25
mobile devices, 27, 36, 48–49
moral, 114–115, 129, 176
    action, 115
    alignment, 126
    authority, 115
    balance, 115
    brand, 115
    cleansing, 115
    commitment, 21
    compass, 123
    concerns, 129
    conviction, 127
    identity, 115
    judgement, 116
Moss, Kate, 177
Mozilla, 39
Mr Muscle, 70
Mulvaney, Dylan, 82, 86–92
Mumsnet, 37
Mustafa, Isaiah, 179, 181

name brand, 180
Neiman Marcus, 131
New York, 29–30, 96
    City, 28–29, 131
New York Times, 32
NFT, 35, 55
NHS, 137
Nike, 58, 67, 90, 113, 121, 126, 191
NIMBY. *See* not in my back yard
non-binary, 64, 81, 85
non-collaborative, 165
    co-creation, 165
    process, 144
non-profit, 138
norms, 95–96, 98, 159
    social, 72, 76–77, 98, 194
    societal, 78
North America, 131
not in my back yard, 147, 149, 187

offline, 14, 73, 87, 90, 110, 145
    equity, 36
    power dynamics, 21

reading, 14
space, 46
Old Navy, 36
Old Spice, 5, 174, 176, 178–179, 181–183
  Danner, 181
  Fresher Collection, 181
  The Man Your Man Could Smell Like, 179
  Meat Sweat Defense, 181
  Red Zone Body Wash, 179
  revitalisation, 183
online, 14, 36, 48, 55, 63, 73, 89–90, 107, 110, 120, 145, 168
  campaign, 179
  discussions, 125
  forum, 22, 36
  identity, 22
  product, 55
  settings, 38
  spaces, 41
  spending, 49
  textual expressions, 168
organisation, 6, 8, 21, 27, 35, 46, 66, 81, 84, 90, 104–105, 111, 113–114, 117, 121–122, 132, 134, 137–139, 142–143, 145–146, 149, 151, 154, 157, 159, 161, 165, 174–175, 181, 188, 196
  grassroots, 139
  local, 138
  markets, 145
ownership, 1, 4–5, 9–10, 14, 55–56, 58, 114, 141–142, 145–146, 149, 151, 154–155, 158–159, 171, 173–174, 176–177, 191, 194
  brand, 142, 173
  claim, 16
  co-ownership, 191–192, 194
  legal, 141–142
  loss, 4, 194
  markers, 141
  part-, 29
  partial, 191
  psychological, 141–142
  rights, 141
  sense, 4, 141–143, 162, 191–192
  shared, 193
  territorial, 119

Pac man, 144
paradigm, shift, 108, 140
parent company, 85, 88, 132. *See also* company
Paris, 12, 19
partnership, 5, 87, 89–92, 132, 137–139
  activism, 138
  brand, 88
  corporations, 137
  local, 138
  paid, 89
Patagonia, 17
Penguin Random House, 67
performance, 3, 13–14, 74–76, 94, 101, 108, 141, 143, 171
  consumer, 3
  gender, 3, 65, 98
  identity, 6, 77
  studies, 75
perspective, 2, 9, 44–45, 50, 61, 185
  brand, 50, 186–187, 193–194
  consumer, 44, 95, 108
  individual, 188
  multifaceted, 61
  role, 185
  speaker, 45
physical, 8, 24, 30, 32, 59, 75, 103–104, 144, 147, 167, 195
  architecture, 77
  assets, 2, 30
  boundaries, 41
  brands, 191
  city, 22
  consumer, 137
  dimensions, 9
  distances, 178
  indicators, 29
  item, 14
  landscapes, 1, 6, 9, 153, 169, 177–178, 185, 187, 191
  locations, 28, 159, 178
  manifestation, 19
  nature, 20
  possession, 4
  presence, 185
  realms, 1, 25, 183
  role, 63
  shopfronts, 188
  shops, 136

physical (cont.)
  size, 185
  space, 5–7, 16, 20, 31, 103–104,
    154, 165, 167, 171, 186–187,
    189, 195
  substance, 146
  suburbs, 22
  worlds, 2, 21, 143, 153, 164,
    185–186
Pixi, 68
platforms, 16, 22, 24, 37–39, 49, 55,
    60, 73–74, 78, 80–81, 88, 102,
    105–106, 108, 115, 140, 143,
    150, 152, 163, 168–171, 173,
    175, 193
  constraints, 170
  dark, 170
  intermediary, 169
  key, 4
  major, 171
  news, 37
  public, 127
  ridesharing, 122
  storytelling, 102
  traditional, 106
  voice calling, 175
Polygon, 67
power, 1–7, 9–12, 14, 16–17, 29,
    33–34, 44, 46, 52, 57–61, 71,
    73, 78, 112, 115, 117, 119, 123,
    125, 136–138, 143, 145–148,
    152–155, 157–166, 168–171,
    173–174, 176–178, 180,
    185–186, 189, 191, 195–196
  accumlated, 157
  balance, 154, 173
  brand, 11, 173, 183
  changes, 184
  consumer, 166
  consumptive, 180
  distribution, 177
  dynamics, 2, 5–6, 15–17, 21, 44,
    57–61, 112, 117, 127, 145,
    147–149, 157, 159–162, 165,
    169–171, 176, 182, 184–185,
    190, 193, 195
  ebb and flows, 5, 16, 50, 60, 174
  embed, 14
  exchange, 59
  flows, 169–171, 183

immense, 10
institutionalised, 157–158
magnetic, 11
manifest, 61
market, 119
movement, 162
moves, 9
purchasing, 73, 115, 117, 127,
    151, 154
relations, 60, 159–160
remove, 193
renegotiate, 25
shifts, 5, 9, 183, 193, 195
spending, 104
structures, 155, 159–160, 171
tetrad, 170
presence, 22, 99, 103, 138, 143
  brand, 151
pride, brand, 71
Pride, 117, 125
  flag, 116
  merchandise, 125
  Seattle, 117
Primark, 36
Proctor & Gamble, 178
products, products, 4, 6, 8, 11–13, 17,
    23, 27, 29, 31, 36–37, 39, 46–47,
    50–51, 54–57, 63, 66, 68–71, 73,
    75–78, 96, 98–100, 104, 106,
    111–112, 114, 118, 122–124,
    129–130, 135–136, 139,
    141, 143, 145–146, 148–149,
    151–152, 154, 161–163, 165,
    168, 170, 185, 190, 192–193
  area, 10
  authentic, 105
  branded, 4, 68–69, 105, 142, 152,
    159, 162, 164
  by-, 121–122
  charitable, 122
  consumer, flow, 161
  core, 175, 195
  environmentally-friendly, 68
  expensive, 52
  high-end, 95
  hygiene, 179
  men's grooming, 179
  new, 82
  perceived warmth, 68
  personalise, 163

personalised branded, 193
promoting, 119
purchasing, 75, 104
reuse, 130
shaving, 178
tangible, 11–12
valuable, 117
Profile Books, 67
public, 4, 82, 113–114, 116,
    126–127, 130, 138, 150–151,
    176, 180
  approval, 117
  eye, 159
  manner, 119
  nature, 116
  relations, 82
  sentiment, 89
  space, 14, 162
  stance, 116, 126
  stand, 129
publisher, 46, 67, 69, 72
  independent, 43
Pushkin Press, 67

reader, 17, 20, 38, 44, 72, 162
rebranding, 106, 194
Reddit, 22, 37
  subreddit, 37
reputation, 71, 138
  brand, 126
  stellar, 138
review, 14, 37, 41, 46, 95, 143, 150
rigidity, 155, 194
Rios of Mercedes, 95–96
ritual, 13–14, 25, 135
  consumer's, 139
  performative, 14
Rolex, 67
roots, 85, 93, 107, 114, 131, 134,
    145–148, 151, 153–154, 164,
    170, 186, 188, 190–191
  brand, 2, 4, 13, 23, 105, 116,
    119, 130, 144, 147, 153, 157,
    159–160, 164–165, 167–169,
    173, 186–187, 191

safe space, 3, 73–74, 134, 190
Sandstone Press, 67
schematic dichotomy, 66
Sephora, 153

services, 4, 29, 36, 53, 56, 63, 77,
    104, 117, 123, 130, 145–146,
    148–149, 151, 154, 161–165,
    168, 170, 187, 195
  app-based, 24
  issues, 124
  religious, 88
  tracking, 48
sex, 3, 64–66, 77, 81, 179
  biological, 65
  bodily, 64
  differences, 66
  performed, 65
sexed body, 65
sexual orientation, 84
Shanghai, 19
signs, 30–31, 35, 41, 98, 152, 168
  and symbols, 28, 30–32, 34–36,
    41, 184
Silver Lake, 175
Skype, 5, 174–176, 178–179, 182–183
  redesign, 175
Snapchat, 175
social
  benefits, 34
  cohesion, 14, 21
  connection, 54
  dynamics, 122, 146
  enterprise, 135, 137–138
  formations, 6, 52
  influence, 72
  issues, 81, 116, 121, 123, 125–126
  metrics, 132
  networks, 54
  platforms, 23–24, 32–33, 40, 46,
    49, 107, 175
  privilege, 59
  value, 33, 121, 135
social media, 14, 31, 38, 46, 55, 90,
    96, 102, 110, 133, 143, 163, 193
  consumers, 161
  entrepreneurship, 73
  networks, 54
  platforms, 22, 55
  posts, 84
societal, 108, 126
  change, 126
  context, 44–45
  issues, 113, 115
  narratives, 127

societal (cont.)
    norms, 2–3
    outcomes, 140
    progress, 139
    standards, 98
    structure, 50, 67
    values, 139
society, 6, 9, 31, 34, 44–45, 50, 56,
    65–66, 80–81, 111, 113–114,
    116, 121, 129, 139, 141, 143,
    152, 165, 171, 189–190
    -focused approach, 2
    informed, 45
    perspective, 44
    sectors, 169
socio-cultural, 68
socio-economic, 35, 185
    issues, 190
socio-political, 124, 131, 135–136,
    146, 150, 154, 161, 163, 171, 173
    influence, 188
    issues, 119, 125, 129–130, 135, 139
    landscape, 34
    overlays, 147, 170, 178
    problems, 137
software, 148, 176
South Africa, 114
South Korea, 114
Special Educational Needs and
    Disabilities, 122
SPOKE London, 191
SSGA. *See* State Street Global Advisors
stakeholder, 111, 115, 117–118,
    120–121, 143, 160, 162, 165, 168
    internal, 192
    network, 168
Starbucks, 158–159
    Workers United Union, 159
State Street Global Advisors, 35
status, 27, 30, 58, 60–61, 102, 136,
    151, 166, 183
    quo, 17, 23, 75
    symbol, 33
stereotypes, 33
strategy, 61, 84, 114, 121, 153
    campaign, 104
    marketing, 18, 104, 127, 183
    social media, 46
Super Bowl, 87, 124–125
Supreme, 182

sustainability, 75, 86, 133, 163
Sweet Cherry Publishing, 69, 122
symbol, 2, 12, 20, 25, 28, 31, 34–36,
    44, 98, 160
    cultural, 171
symbolism, 10, 28, 30, 52–54,
    58, 118
    capital, 56, 188
    dimensions, 25
    forms, 25, 31
    load, 31
    nature, 30
    recognition, 58
    representation, 13, 184
    resources, 185
    significance, 9
    systems, 17
    value, 58, 61, 190

Tapestry, 132
Target, 125, 153
technology, 7, 21, 50, 55, 82, 95, 175
    digital, 60, 173
    innovative, 104
television, 83, 110, 143–144, 179
    viewer, 110
textual
    analysis, 19
    boundaries, 18, 167
    interactions, 168
Tiffany & Co, 28–29, 59, 153
TikTok, 37, 46, 86–88, 101–102, 162
topography, 1, 9–10, 12, 25, 54, 58,
    60, 161, 164, 167–168, 170, 173,
    183, 185
    cultural, 171
    elements, 21, 23
    individualised, 21
    interpretation, 9
    physical, 168
    trademark, 28, 145, 193, 195
    issues, 35
tradwives, 102
transgender, 64, 81, 86–88
Tweet, 32, 152
Twitter, 37, 74, 86, 89, 152, 159

Uber, 123, 148–149
    Denmark, 149
    infrastructure, 148

UK, 33, 47, 82–84, 90, 110, 114, 116, 135, 175, 177, 193–194
    Advertising Standards Agency, 46
    Office of National Statistics, 64
UNESCO, 8, 16
Uniqlo, 10
Urban Outfitters, 10–11
USA, 19, 31, 33–34, 39, 84, 86, 110, 113–114, 116, 123, 125, 133, 135, 149, 159, 175, 179, 193

Vacheron Constantine, 71
Victoria's Secret, 69–71
Victorina Press, 68
video, 24, 82, 84–90, 96, 106, 113
    call, 175
    campaign, 84–85
    conference, 176
    exclusive, 24
    free, 24
    portal, 110
    reaction, 87
    unboxing, 14
videogame, 185

Vinted, 106
Virgin Atlantic, 5, 81–85, 88–91
Visbal, 35
Von Dutch, 159

Wattpad, 37, 162
website, 41, 48, 50, 55, 69, 124, 193
Whatsap, 37
WILDFANG, 190
WOM. *See* word of mouth
word of mouth, 27, 73, 124, 143
World Of Books, 120
Wrangler, 33–34

X. *See* Twitter

yes in my back yard, 147
Yeti, 191
YIMBY. *See* yes in my back yard
YouTube, 24–25, 86–87
Yves Saint Laurent, 68

Zara, 10
Ziffit, 120
Zoom, 176, 183

Printed in the United States
by Baker & Taylor Publisher Services